The Founding Fathers

Pencil sketch by Benjamin H. Latrobe, drawn from life in Philadelphia, c. 1799

Washington. U.S. of America. July 4. 1803.

nt to undertake for the discovery of the course
most convenient water communication from
being small, it is to be expected that you
from the Indian inhabitants. should you
cific ocean, you may find it imprudent
 be forced to seek a passage round by sea.
he Western coast. but you will be without
; as a sufficient supply cannot be carried
 in that case can only be in the credit
authorise you to draw on the Secretaries
 Navy of the U.S.. according as you may find
le, for the purpose of obtaining money or
and I solemnly pledge the faith of the
all be paid punctually at the date they
Consuls, agents, merchants & citizens of any

The Founding Fathers

THOMAS JEFFERSON

A Biography in His Own Words

VOLUME 1

By
THE EDITORS OF NEWSWEEK BOOKS

With an Introduction by
JOSEPH L. GARDNER

JOAN PATERSON KERR
Picture Editor

NEWSWEEK
New York

We dedicate this series of books to the memory of
Frederick S. Beebe
friend, mentor, and "Founding Father" of Newsweek Books

Thomas Jefferson, A Biography in His Own Words,
has been produced by Newsweek Books:

Joseph L. Gardner, Editor

Janet Czarnetzki, Art Director

Judith Bentley, Copy Editor

Susan Storer, Picture Researcher

S. Arthur Dembner, President

This book is based on Volumes 1-19 of *The Papers of Thomas Jefferson,*
edited by Julian P. Boyd and others, published by Princeton University Press,
and copyright Princeton University Press.
The texts of documents published in this edition have been obtained
from photocopies in the files of *The Papers of Thomas Jefferson,*
made from original manuscripts located in various public repositories.
Specific sources are acknowledged on page 409.

ISBN: Clothbound Edition 0-88225-051-5; ISBN: Deluxe Edition 0-88225-052-3
Library of Congress Catalog Card Number 72-92143
Copyright © 1974 by Newsweek, Inc.
All rights reserved. Printed and bound in the United States of America.
Endpapers: Jefferson to Meriwether Lewis, July 4, 1803; MISSOURI HISTORICAL SOCIETY

Contents

VOLUME 1

	Introduction	6
	Chronology of Jefferson and His Times	12
1	Formative Years	15
2	Eloquent Revolutionary	34
3	Virginia Reformer	72
4	Wartime Governor	92
	A PICTURE PORTFOLIO: America's Renaissance Man	111
5	Public Service and Private Misery	130
6	Seasoning of a Diplomat	149
7	A Rising Race of Republicans	185

VOLUME 2

8	First Secretary of State	209
9	Retirement and Recall	250
10	Second Vice President	273
	A PICTURE PORTFOLIO: Foremost Republican	303
11	Third President	322
12	From Promise to Performance	349
13	Thomas Jefferson Survives	379
	Selected Bibliography	408
	Acknowledgments	409
	Index	410

Introduction

by Joseph L. Gardner
Editor, Newsweek Books

The American Colonies were at a crossroads in May, 1776. George Washington, in the field for a year, had at last forced the British to evacuate Boston, but a colonial expedition to Canada had ended in a rout. In Congress, John Adams was calling for the Colonies to establish their own governments; "Every Post and every Day rolls in upon Us Independence like a Torrent," he wrote in excitement. Acting upon the unanimous instruction of the Virginia Convention, Richard Henry Lee introduced a resolution of independence on June 7. Although debate was postponed until July 1, a committee was appointed to draft an appropriate declaration should Lee's resolution be carried. The chairman and actual draftsman of the declaration was to be thirty-three-year-old Thomas Jefferson, who had just resumed his seat as a delegate. Absent since December but a regular attendant the previous year, he had sat silent through most earlier congressional sessions; nonetheless, the tall, lanky, red-haired Virginian—his envious colleague Adams conceded—"had the reputation of a masterly Pen."

Working at a small portable writing desk of his own design, in his second-floor lodgings in a private home, Jefferson produced over the next seventeen days the ringing statement with which his name will forever be linked—indeed, it was one of the three accomplishments of his life he asked to have memorialized on his tombstone. The Declaration of Independence, Jefferson later claimed, was drafted without recourse to book, pamphlet, or previous writing of any kind. Instead, this rarely gifted man drew upon the vast reservoir of his brilliant, uniquely trained intellect to produce a timely and timeless "expression of the American mind."

An early biographer described the Jefferson of this period as a man "who could calculate an eclipse, survey an estate, tie an artery, plan an edifice, try a cause, break a horse, dance a minuet, and play the violin." Despite the incongruity of such a statement, a later scholar, Julian P. Boyd, has stated that this gives only a partial picture. Of his contemporaries, only Benjamin Franklin approached him in the extent and variety of his interests. "To catalogue the areas of his explorations," writes Boyd, "is to list most of the principal categories of knowledge—law, government, history, mathematics, architecture, medicine, agriculture, languages and literature, education, music, philosophy, religion, and almost every branch of the natural sciences from astronomy through meteorology to zoology." The attempt to capture such a life has been the tantalizing task and elusive goal of numerous biographers since Jefferson's death a century and a half ago.

Jefferson himself shied away from such an undertaking, producing only a fragmentary *Autobiography* in 1821; the work ended with his taking office as Secretary of State in March, 1790. "To become my own biographer is the last thing in the world I would undertake," he had stated in his seventy-second year. "No. If there has been anything in my course worth the public attention, they are better judges of it than I can be myself, and to them it is my duty to leave it." He thus bequeathed to posterity the obligation to reconstruct his life; fortunately, he also left the means to do so.

"The letters of a person, especially of one whose business has been chiefly transacted by letters," Jefferson observed toward the end of his remarkably long and active career, "form the only full and genuine journal of his life." In the case of the third President such a "genuine journal" runs to 60,000 items—a correspondence with thousands of people stretching over a period of seven decades. "I wonder how Mr. Jefferson made out to answer everybody who wrote to him...?" an awed contemporary asked. Even in retirement, Jefferson complained that "My greatest oppression is a correspondence afflictingly laborious." To Adams he confided in 1817 that from sunrise to two o'clock and often from dinner to dark, "I am drudging at the writing table." Answering letters, even from people he did not know, was "the burthen of my life, a very grievous one indeed, and one I must get rid of." But, of course, he continued to write.

Jefferson took extraordinary pains to be precise and felicitous in his writing, Boyd has concluded. It was therefore not merely his insatiable curiosity about technical improvements that led him to experiment with such methods of preserving his letters as the letterpress and the polygraph—only with such aids could his hours at the desk be spent creatively and not be consumed in the drudgery of copying. But with his selfless perception of the role he was playing in history and with his clear vision of future generations' interest in that role, Jefferson faithfully preserved an unrivaled and invaluable record of his life. From 1783 until 1826 he kept an "epistolary ledger" of his correspondence, a neat, precise listing in parallel columns of virtually every letter he wrote or received. This extraordinary 656-page document reveals Jefferson's love of system and order; for those who would study his life, Boyd claims, it is "an authoritative device for establishing the dates of undated or mutilated letters, for ascertaining the author's whereabouts, and for unlocking some of the mysteries of postal communication during his time." All his other papers—law cases, bank accounts, plantation records, state documents, drafts for *Notes on Virginia*—were also once systematically arranged.

A few months before his death on July 4, 1826—the fiftieth anniversary of the Declaration of Independence—Jefferson signed a will that named his beloved grandson, Thomas Jefferson Randolph, the executor of his estate and recipient of his papers. It was the principal legacy that the nearly bankrupt ex-President could convey, and for a quarter century Randolph was the faithful guardian of this treasure.

Although Jefferson had left no specific request that his papers be published, Randolph undertook to select and edit the documents he had received from his grandfather and in 1829 published a four-volume work, *Memoirs, Correspondence, and Miscellanies from the Papers of Thomas Jefferson.* Within a year the 6,000 printing was sold out; subsequent editions were printed in London, Boston, and Paris. "Have you seen Mr. Jefferson's *Works?..."* the jurist Joseph Story wrote a colleague. "It is the most precious melange of all sorts of scandals you ever read. It will elevate your opinion of his talents, but lower him in point of principle and morals not a little." The *Memoirs*—containing uncensored quotes from letters and a journal called the *Anas*—fanned political flames, and Jefferson was soon being "quoted on any side of almost any question." Many expressed shock over the candor revealed in Jefferson's writings about his contemporaries and criticized his grandson for not being more judicious in his selection. But Randolph had been acting in good faith, fully aware of the obligation imposed by the family legacy. "Short of wanton mutilation and distortion," a modern historian has stated, "no editor of the papers could have steered Jefferson's reputation into a safe harbor."

Perhaps realizing the inadequacy of his edition, Randolph next gave St. George Tucker access to the papers, and in 1837 Tucker published *The Life of Thomas Jefferson,* a sympathetic account that was criticized as "ice trying to represent fire!" Meanwhile, the federal government had acquired papers of both George Washington and James Madison. A national responsibility for safeguarding the record of the past was only beginning to receive widespread acceptance. Indeed, not until 1848 did Congress authorize the purchase of the Jefferson papers from Randolph—and then in an appropriations bill that ironically put the same price tag of $20,000 on the papers of Jefferson's archrival, Alexander Hamilton.

In due course Randolph deposited his grandfather's papers at the Department of State in Washington, D. C. There, it might be assumed, they were safe for posterity. Instead, the carefully assembled and systematically arranged collection was subjected to a bizarre "trial-by-editing" that prevented even a partial restoration of its unity for half a century.

The congressional appropriation of 1848 had also provided funds for editing and publishing the papers, and this task was assigned to Professor Henry Augustine Washington of the College of William and Mary. Preoccupied with his academic duties, Professor Washington prevailed upon Congress to ship its priceless new acquisition to Williamsburg, where he felt he could work more comfortably and efficiently. He next proposed sending certain Jefferson documents directly to the printer to save the expense of making new transcriptions, and he did not hesitate to trace over faded lines to make them more legible. His assignment completed and a ten-volume edition of *Writings* ready for printing by early 1854, Washington had 130 volumes of Jefferson's papers selected, arranged, indexed, and bound for return to the government. This left in his hands "a mass of refuse matter nearly twice as large as that which has been selected for preservation...." Three boxes of papers deemed too personal for publication were returned to the Department of State, while the "mass of refuse matter" was separately turned over to Congress.

Sixteen more years, during which the nation was sundered by civil war, passed before Congress fully evaluated its collection and finally got around to returning to the family the private papers exempted from the sale of 1848. Five years after that, in 1875, Thomas Jefferson Randolph died and the remaining papers were gradually dispersed among his heirs. These eventually came to such repositories as the University of Virginia, the Massachusetts Historical Society, and the Library of Congress—though one portion was tragically lost in a fire. Apparently St. George Tucker and Henry Augustine Washington had retained some Jefferson papers after completing their editorial endeavors, and a descendant of both acquired 2,500 documents early in the twentieth century; the largest portion of this lot went to the Missouri Historical Society. Incredibly, the federal government did not actually gather under one roof all the papers it owned until 1905, more than half a century after the original acquisition. Two years later a misplaced box of 2,000 items was found in a Library office.

By that date two more editions of Jefferson papers had been published: a ten-volume work by Paul Leicester Ford (1892–99) and a twenty-volume one by A. A. Lipscomb and A. E. Bergh (1903–4). Although competently edited, the Ford edition was too restrictive in length and reflected the editor's main preoccupation with Jefferson's political career. The Lipscomb-Bergh edition, following too closely Randolph's and Washington's works of the preceding century, a critic has noted, "reflected the inexact scholarly standards of that day." The inaccuracies, distortions, and omissions of all previous editions of Jefferson papers were increasingly recognized by twentieth-century scholars, but not until the bicentennial of the statesman's birth approached in 1943 was a solution proposed to this problem. In a report to the Bicentennial Commission, Julian P. Boyd, then librarian of Princeton University, proposed a new, comprehensive edition of Jefferson's writings.

In March, 1943, Boyd was directed by the Commission to make a study that would analyze the scope, probable cost, and length of time required for the preparation of the new edition. When his report was completed that September, Princeton proposed to sponsor the edition, with the aid of a gift of $200,000 from The New York Times Company. Despite wartime austerity, Datus C. Smith, Jr., Director of the Princeton University Press, made a courageous and farsighted commitment to publish the work. In the spring of 1944 Boyd established his editorial offices at Princeton University Library and began the time-consuming chore of gathering from all over the world photoduplicates of all known Jefferson documents. Eventually a staggering 60,000 documents in facsimile—from 425 different sources in thirty-eight states, the District of Columbia, and several foreign countries—were assembled at Princeton. The range of subjects covered in the documents astonished even the editors. "There are," wrote Associate Editor L. H. Butterfield, "mathematical calculations, designs for machines and furniture and landscape details; recipes for macaroni and other dishes; itineraries; agricultural and meteorological data; tables of useful information; book lists, and notes and memoranda on an incredible variety of subjects, from the use of Archimedes' screw at Kew to snuff, Sophocles, and specific gravity."

There was no implication in his original report, Boyd later claimed, that "a new dimension of documentary editing had been projected or that new techniques for carrying the work forward had been discovered." His modestly stated but heroically ambitious aim was to prepare "a sort of comprehensive documentary biography, not narrated, not fully analyzed, not integrated, but set forth as the whole written corpus of one individual in its totality." Once this was accomplished for Jefferson, it would never have to be undertaken again. It was to be the final, definitive record of the man and his times "in all its discoverable fullness," addressed to an unforseeable audience in the future.

Boyd's first major decision was to publish not only letters by Jefferson but also letters to him, "for the simple reason that Jefferson's own letters can scarcely achieve the fullest degree of meaning unless it is known what points in his correspondents' letters he chose to comment upon and what he chose to ignore." Although perhaps a third of the estimated 19,000 letters written by Jefferson had been previously published, less than a fifteenth of the much larger number of letters written to him had ever appeared in print. The new edition would embrace not only letters but also messages, speeches, reports, legislative bills, state papers, memoranda, travel journals, resolutions, petitions, minutes of proceedings—all "documents that were written by Jefferson or had a direct relationship with him." The highest degree of textual fidelity (consistent with modern understanding) was to be maintained; each document was to be fully annotated; all would be cross-referenced and indexed.

Publication in 1950 of the first volume of Boyd's *The Papers of Thomas Jefferson* brought paeans of praise from the scholarly world—"This is the most monumental editorial task ever undertaken in this country," wrote Louis B. Wright in the *Yale Review*; Adrienne Koch said in *The New Republic* that the first volume "gives evidence of the astonishing breadth and exacting scholarship that will characterize the entire work." Boyd and his staff, wrote Daniel Boorstin, "seem to have developed successfully a new genre of historical writing." As each volume appeared—there were nineteen by 1974—new light was shed on the historical Jefferson and renewed appreciation was expressed for Boyd's pioneering scholarship. In frank and appreciative imitation, definitive editions of the papers of the other Founding Fathers were launched—Benjamin Franklin (American Philosophical Society and Yale, 1954), John Adams (Massachusetts Historical Society and Harvard, 1954), Alexander Hamilton (Columbia University, 1955), James Madison (University of Chicago and University of Virginia, 1956), and George Washington (Mount Vernon Ladies Association of the Union and University of Virginia, 1966).

"There is properly no history, only biography," Ralph Waldo Emerson stated in a famous aphorism. And thus the Editors of Newsweek Books have sought to present in the series concluded with this work a sweeping panorama of American history through the lives of six ever-illustrious founders of the Republic. A century and a quarter elapsed between the birth of Benjamin Franklin and the death of James Madison—almost as much time as has passed since the departure from the historical stage of that last Father and the present day. There was a vast difference between the rude colonial world into which Franklin was born in 1706 and the lusty young nation facing its great test of Union that Madison left in 1836. In between, as described by the men who lived them, are some of the memorable moments of early American history—the six biographies forming a virtual library of the Revolutionary period.

The runaway apprentice printer Ben Franklin arrives in Philadelphia to make his fortune; grown up and serving his country as a diplomat abroad, the same man, fifty-two years later, leaves England for home—in the sad realization that the end to empire is at hand. George Washington takes command of the "mixed multitude...under very little discipline" that he is to shape into the Continental Army. John Adams exalts to his "dearest friend" and wife, Abigail, in the Declaration of Independence he has just signed—an event to be celebrated "from this Time forward forever more." The illegitimate merchant's clerk in the West Indies, Alexander Hamilton, dreams of military glory and finds it at the side of his hero, Washington, at Yorktown. The diminutive thinker James Madison helps shape one of mankind's most noble statements, the United States Constitution, during a sultry Philadelphia summer—and later as an unhappy President sees his capital burned and looted by the British in the War of 1812.

And finally there is the many-faceted Jefferson, colleague, friend, or adversary of all the others, a man whose life was inextricably entwined with theirs and with the destiny of the nation he helped bring to birth. He sat with Franklin in the Second Continental Congress and later joined the venerable patriot in delicate diplomacy abroad. He was a fellow delegate to Congress and diplomatic partner of John Adams as well, and later an uneasy Vice President to the Massachusetts statesman. To Madison he was a lifelong friend, partner in the most enduring and fruitful intellectual collaboration in American history. Jefferson served Washington wisely and faithfully as Secretary of State but later came to a parting of the ways with his fellow Virginian—largely because of the bitterly contested philosophies that separated him from his Cabinet rival, Alexander Hamilton.

"Thomas Jefferson survives," Adams gasped on his deathbed. He was wrong, for his great contemporary had expired earlier that same day. But he was also right, for Jefferson does indeed triumphantly survive in the words he left his grateful and admiring descendants, the American people.

EDITORIAL NOTE

Most of the Jefferson writings reprinted in this biography have been excerpted from the longer original documents being published in their entirety by Princeton University Press. Omissions at the beginning or ending of a document are indicated by ellipses only if the extract begins or ends in the middle of a sentence; omissions within a quoted passage are also indicated by ellipses. The original spellings have been retained; editorial insertions are set within square brackets.

Chronology of Jefferson and His Times

Thomas Jefferson born April 13 (April 2 Old Style) at Shadwell in Albemarle County, Virginia	1743	
	1754	French and Indian War, 1754–63
Father dies; classical studies with the Rev. James Maury	1757	
Enrolls at College of William and Mary	1760	Reign of George III of England, 1760–1820
Leaves college, begins law and general studies with George Wythe	1762	
Travels to Annapolis, Philadelphia, New York	1766	Stamp Act repealed
Admitted to Virginia bar, manages farms	1767	Townshend Acts; nonimportation movement
Begins construction at Monticello; elected to House of Burgesses	1769	Virginia Resolves and Association
Shadwell burns; moves to Monticello	1770	Boston Massacre
Marries Martha Wayles Skelton; daughter Martha born, first of six children; only two live past childhood	1772	
Appointed to committee of correspondence	1773	
Drafts Albemarle resolutions; *Summary View of the Rights of British America* published	1774	Coercive Acts; First Continental Congress
Delegate to Second Continental Congress; drafts Declaration of Causes	1775	Lexington and Concord skirmishes
Writes Declaration of Independence; drafts constitution for Virginia; leads state reform in House of Delegates	1776	Dunmore burns Norfolk; Virginia introduces independence resolution in Congress
Report of the Committee of Revisors; elected governor	1777	Battle of Saratoga
Directs war preparations in Virginia	1780	Fall of Charleston; Battle of Camden
Retires from governorship; completes *Notes on Virginia*; refutes charges in assembly	1781	Cornwallis invades Virginia; British defeat at Yorktown; Articles of Confederation ratified
Wife dies; appointed to peace commission	1782	
Released from commission; elected to Congress	1783	Congress ratifies peace treaty
Report on plan of government for Northwest Territory; joins Franklin and Adams as minister plenipotentiary in Paris	1784	Netherlands-Austria dispute over Scheldt
Succeeds Franklin as Minister to France; draws plans for Virginia state capitol	1785	Balloon craze in Paris
Visits London, tours English gardens; romance with Maria Cosway	1786	Shays' Rebellion; Statute for Religious Freedom passed by Virginia Assembly; Annapolis Convention
Trip to southern France and northern Italy; corresponds with Madison and others on Constitution	1787	Federal Convention; Louis XVI dissolves the Assembly of Notables; Northwest Ordinance adopted
Negotiates new loans; tour of Holland and Germany; *Observations on the Whale-Fishery*	1788	Constitution ratified
Urges bill of rights; advises Lafayette on	1789	Meeting of Estates General; storming of the

12

Declaration of the Rights of Man; returns home		Bastille; Washington elected President
Accepts appointment as Secretary of State; aids funding-assumption compromise; *Report on Weights and Measures*; first conflict with Alexander Hamilton in the Cabinet	1790	Hamilton's *Report on the Public Credit*; war threatens between Spain and Britain over Nootka Sound
Argues unconstitutionality of national bank; *Report on Fisheries*; tour of New England and New York with Madison; begins *Anas*	1791	Thomas Paine's *The Rights of Man* printed in Philadelphia; Freneau starts publishing *National Gazette*; First Bank of the United States established
Increases opposition to Hamiltonian policies	1792	
Submits resignation; *Report on Commerce*	1793	Louis XVI guillotined; Citizen Genêt affair; Proclamation of Neutrality
Retires to Monticello; declines mission to Spain	1794	Whisky Rebellion; Jay Treaty signed
New construction at Monticello; correspondence with Washington ends; elected Vice President	1796	Pinckney's Treaty; Washington's Farewell Address; Adams elected President
Elected president of American Philosophical Society; becomes leader of the opposition	1797	XYZ affair; Mazzei letter published
Drafts Kentucky Resolutions; begins to emerge as Republican party leader	1798	Quasi war with France; Alien and Sedition Acts
Elected President by House after electoral tie; appoints James Madison Secretary of State; fills vacancies with Republicans; annual message urges repeal of Naturalization and Judiciary Acts; promulgates economy in government	1801	Appointment of "midnight" judges; capital moved to Washington; Spain cedes Louisiana to France; Tripolitan War begins
Initiates Lewis and Clark expedition; Louisiana Purchase	1803	*Marbury* v. *Madison*; Ohio admitted to Union; renewal of Napoleonic wars
Reelected with George Clinton, Vice President; daughter Mary dies	1804	Hamilton-Burr duel; Napoleon crowned Emperor
Treaty with Tripoli; plans Floridas purchase	1805	War of the Third Coalition
Rejects Monroe-Pinkney treaty; urges embargo	1807	Burr acquitted of treason; *Chesapeake-Leopard* affair; Embargo Act
Address to Albemarle neighbors on retirement	1809	Presidency of James Madison, 1809–1817
Correspondence with John Adams resumed	1812	War declared with Great Britain
Drafts plan for Central College; sells library to Congress	1814	Washington, D.C. burned; Treaty of Ghent; severe economic depression; Congress of Vienna
Appointed member of Board of Visitors for college	1816	Second Bank of the United States
	1817	Presidency of James Monroe, 1817–25
Successfully urges Charlottesville as site for college	1818	
Appointed Rector of state university; assumes debt in Nicholas bankruptcy	1819	Financial panic
	1820	Missouri Compromise
Writes *Autobiography*	1821	
	1823	Monroe Doctrine
Recruits faculty for University of Virginia	1824	Lafayette visits the United States
	1825	University of Virginia opens; Presidency of John Quincy Adams, 1825–29
Thomas Jefferson dies July 4 at Monticello	1826	John Adams dies July 4 at Quincy

A Declaration by the Representatives of the UNITED STATES OF AMERICA, in General Congress assembled.

When in the course of human events it becomes necessary for one people to dissolve the political bands which have connected them with another, and to assume among the powers of the earth the separate and equal station to which the laws of nature & of nature's god entitle them, a decent respect to the opinions of mankind requires that they should declare the causes which impel them to the separation.

We hold these truths to be self-evident; that all men are created equal, that they are endowed by their creator with inherent & inalienable rights; that among these are life, liberty, & the pursuit of happiness; that to secure these rights, governments are instituted among men, deriving their just powers from the consent of the governed; that whenever any form of government becomes destructive of these ends, it is the right of the people to alter or to abolish it, & to institute new government, laying it's foundation on such principles & organising it's powers in such form, as to them shall seem most likely to effect their safety & happiness. prudence indeed will dictate that governments long established should not be changed for light & transient causes: and accordingly all experience hath shewn that mankind are more disposed to suffer while evils are sufferable, than to right themselves by abolishing the forms to which they are accustomed. but when a long train of abuses & usurpations [begun at a distinguished period &] pursuing invariably the same object, evinces a design to reduce them under absolute Despotism, it is their right, it is their duty, to throw off such government, & to provide new guards for their future security. such has been the patient sufferance of these colonies; & such is now the necessity which constrains them to [expunge] their former systems of government. the history of the present king of Great Britain is a history of [unremitting] injuries and usurpations, [among which appears no solitary fact to contradict the uniform tenor of the rest, all of which have] in direct object the establishment of an absolute tyranny over these states. to prove this, let facts be submitted to a candid world, [for the truth of which we pledge a faith yet unsullied by falsehood]

Chapter 1

Formative Years

The American Revolution and the nation created by that Revolution owed their existence both to men who could have looked forward to ease and advancement under the British colonial system and to men who despaired of success or recognition under the empire. Thomas Jefferson clearly belonged to the first group. At his birth on April 13, 1743, at Shadwell, the family estate on the Rivanna River in Albemarle County, he was heir to part of the seventy-five hundred acres of Jefferson land in the Virginia Piedmont. There his father had established a family reputation for ability and public service to the Crown on the expanding frontier. But Thomas Jefferson did not use the lands and position bequeathed to him to perpetuate the traditions of the Virginia planters. Instead he directed his own talents to revolution and the abolition of legal privileges and social attitudes maintaining that way of life; he fought not only for the end of the old, but for the creation of a distinctly new society.

Jefferson's character, as formed in his first twenty years, made that choice inevitable. "An honest heart being the first blessing," he advised his nephew in 1785, "a knowing head is the second." The story of his early life is an account of the influences that gave him an honest heart, which would not allow him to violate the principles in which he believed, and of his own careful cultivation of a knowing head, which made him a champion of the original, experimental, and radical dream of creating a new nation. Jefferson's terse account of his family background, recorded in the *Autobiography* he wrote when he was seventy-seven, displays his impatience with those who were preoccupied with the past.

Autobiography, 1821

The tradition in my father's family was that their ancestor came to this country from Wales, and from near the mountain of Snowden, the highest in Gr. Br. I noted once a case from Wales in the law reports where a person

Thomas Jefferson's draft of the Declaration of Independence, written when he was thirty-three

Cartouche of the map drawn by Joshua Fry and Peter Jefferson of "inhabited part of Virginia"
ALDERMAN LIBRARY, UNIVERSITY OF VIRGINIA

of our name was either pl[aintiff] or def[endant] and one of the same name was Secretary to the Virginia company. These are the only instances in which I have met with the name in that country. I have found it in our early records, but the first particular information I have of any ancestor was my grandfather who lived at the place in Chesterfield called Ozborne's and ownd. the lands afterwards the glebe of the parish. He had 3. sons, Thomas who died young, Field who settled on the waters of Roanoke and left numerous descendants, and Peter my father, who settled on the lands I still own called Shadwell adjoining my present residence. He was born Feb. 29. 1707/8 and intermarried in 1739. with Jane Randolph of the age of 19. daur of Isham Randolph one of the seven sons of that name & family settled at Dungeness in Goochld. They trace their pedigree far back in England & Scotland, to which let every one ascribe the faith & merit he chuses.

[If Jefferson scoffed at the Randolphs' claims to distinguished lineage, he expressed deep respect for his father, a tall, self-educated man who had pioneered in settling the foothills of the Blue Ridge Mountains.]

My father's education had been quite neglected; but being of a strong mind, sound judgment and eager after information, he read much and improved himself insomuch that he was chosen with Joshua Fry professor of Mathem. in W[illiam] & M[ary] college to continue the boundary line between Virginia & N. Carolina which had been begun by Colo. [William] Byrd, and was afterwards employed with the same Mr. Fry to make the 1st. Map of Virginia which had ever been made, that of Capt [John] Smith being merely a conjectural sketch. They possessed excellent materials for so much of the country as is below the blue ridge; little being then known beyond that ridge. He was the 3d. or 4th. settler of the part of the country in which I live, which was about 1737.

Peter Jefferson took care that his son's education would not be as neglected as his own. This task was made easier in 1745 when the family moved from Shadwell to Tuckahoe fifteen miles to the east. Jane Jefferson's cousin William Randolph died that year and named Peter Jefferson as one of the executors of his estate, including Tuckahoe. For seven years Jefferson managed the house and supervised the education of the four Randolph orphans and his own children in what Thomas later described as the "English school." After the family's return to Shadwell, the boy was sent to study with William Douglas, the Scot cleric at Dover Church in Northam. There he received more lessons in English grammar and an introduction to Latin, Greek, and French. Although Thomas Jefferson later questioned the quality of instruction at Douglas's small school, there were many advantages to growing up in frontier Albemarle. His letter to John Adams in 1812 described another variety of education at Shadwell.

Outacity, chief of the Cherokee

Monticello June 11. 1812.
So much in answer to your enquiries concerning Indians, a people with whom, in the very early part of my life, I was very familiar, and acquired impressions of attachment and commiseration for them which have never been obliterated. Before the revolution they were in the habit of coming often, and in great numbers to the seat of our government, where I was very much with them. I knew much the great Outassete [Outacity], the warrior and orator of the Cherokees. He was always the guest of my father, on his journies to and from Williamsburg. I was in his camp when he made his great farewell oration to his people, the evening before his departure for England. The moon was in full splendor, and to her he seemed to address himself in his prayers for his own safety on the voyage, and that of his people during his absence. His sounding voice, distinct articulation, animated action, and the solemn silence of his people at their several fires, filled me with awe and veneration, altho' I did not understand a word he uttered.

At the age of fourteen, Jefferson abruptly assumed heavy responsibilities that ended his boyish excitement over events like the Cherokees' visits. In August, 1757, Peter Jefferson died, leaving Thomas the oldest child in a family consisting of his mother, six sisters, and an infant brother. At twenty-one Thomas would inherit the lands at Shadwell, his father's estate at Snowden going to his younger brother. Even more important were the instructions Peter Jefferson had left that his son was to receive a thorough classical education. Thomas Jefferson recalled this legacy with gratitude. "I have often heard him say," his grandson later declared, "that if he had to decide between pleasure derived from the classical education which his father had given him, and the estate left him, he would decide in favor of the former."

After three years as a student of the Reverend James Maury, "a correct classical scholar," Jefferson carefully considered the next step in his education. A few months before his seventeenth birthday, he wrote to one of his guardians, John Harvie, carefully marshaling his arguments for attending William and Mary College. The letter reveals Jefferson's growing impatience with life at Shadwell and his eagerness to find intellectual stimulation.

Shadwell, Jan. 14, 1760

Sir

I was at Colo. Peter Randolph's about a Fortnight ago, and my Schooling falling into Discourse, he said he thought it would be to my Advantage to go to the College, and was desirous I should go, as indeed I am myself for several Reasons. In the first place as long as I stay at the Mountain the Loss of one fourth of my Time is inevitable, by Company's coming here and detaining me from School. And likewise my Absence will in a great Measure put a Stop to so much Company, and by that Means lessen the Expences of the Estate in House-Keeping. And on the other Hand by going to the College I shall get a more universal Acquaintance, which may hereafter be serviceable to me; and I suppose I can pursue my Studies in the Greek and Latin as well there as here, and likewise learn something of the Mathematics. I shall be glad of your opinion, and remain Sir Yr most humble Servant,

THOMAS JEFFERSON, JR.

Map of Williamsburg and surrounding country during Jefferson's time

Harvie evidently agreed, and not long after writing this letter Jefferson left Shadwell for Williamsburg, the provincial capital. The 120-mile journey brought him not to a bustling, commercial city but to a quiet town with a population of about one thousand whites and blacks. Despite its small size, Williamsburg was Virginia's social and cultural center as well as the seat of government. William and Mary College, at the head of the Duke of Gloucester Street, had been founded in 1693 and was the second oldest college in the Colonies. At seventeen, Jefferson must certainly have been impressed by the town, but some twenty years later, in his famous volume *Notes on Virginia*, he revealed a cool sophistication in describing two Williamsburg landmarks.

Notes on Virginia, 1782

The only public buildings worthy mention are the Capitol, the Palace, the College, and the Hospital for Lunatics, all of them in Williamsburg, heretofore the seat of our government. The Capitol is a light and airy structure, with a portico in front of two orders, the lower of which, being Doric, is tolerably just in its proportions and ornaments, save only that the intercolonnations are too large. The upper is Ionic, much too small for that on which it is mounted, its ornaments not proper to the order, nor proportioned within themselves. It is crowned with a pediment, which is too high for its span. Yet on the whole, it is the most pleasing piece of architecture we have. The Palace is not handsome without: but it is spacious and commodious within, is prettily situated, and, with the grounds annexed to it, is capable of being made an elegant seat. The College and Hospital are rude, mis-shapen piles, which, but that they have roofs, would be taken for brick-kilns....

[In retrospect, Jefferson was no kinder to the education he received at William and Mary than he was to the architecture of the college town.]

The admission of the learners of Latin and Greek filled the college with children. This rendering it disagreeable and degrading to young gentlemen already prepared for entering on the sciences, they were discouraged from resorting to it, and thus the schools for Mathematics and Moral philosophy, which might have been of some service became of very little. The revenues too were exhausted in accomodating those who came only to acquire the rudiments of science.

Jefferson's plan, with measurements, of the Governor's Palace, c. 1779

Fortunately Williamsburg had more to offer Jefferson than the courses at William and Mary. Soon after being admitted to the college in March, 1760, he came under the influence of two remarkable men, William Small and George Wythe. The first to befriend Jefferson was Small, a professor of natural philosophy who encouraged his budding interest in mathematics and science. Jefferson never hesitated to acknowledge his debt to the Scot scholar, who was the only faculty member at William and Mary not a member of the clergy. He easily recognized Thomas's gifts and potential for learning.

Autobiography, 1821

It was my great good fortune, and what probably fixed the destinies of my life that Dr. Wm. Small of Scotland was then professor of Mathematics, a man profound in most of the useful branches of science, with a happy

Page from bursar's book at College of William and Mary listing fees for Jefferson's room and board

talent of communication correct and gentlemanly manners, & an enlarged & liberal mind. He, most happily for me, became soon attached to me & made me his daily companion when not engaged in the school; and from his conversation I got my first views of the expansion of science & of the system of things in which we are placed. Fortunately the Philosophical chair became vacant soon after my arrival at College, and he was appointed to fill it per interim: and he was the first who ever gave in that college regular lectures in Ethics, Rhetoric & Belles lettres.

Small not only shared his liberal mind with Jefferson in the classroom; he also shared his influential and stimulating friends in the town. Among these was George Wythe, a thirty-three-year-old member of the House of Burgesses who became a prominent jurist in Virginia. Responding to a request from a biographer many years later, Jefferson described this learned gentleman who, he said, "continued until death my most affectionate Friend."

Mid-eighteenth century engraving of the College of William and Mary

Monticello Aug. 31. [18]20.
No man ever left behind him a character more venerated than G[eorge] Wythe. His virtue was of the purest tint; his integrity flexible, and his justice exact; of warm patriotism, and, devoted as he was to liberty, and the natural and equal rights of man, he might truly be called the Cato of his country, without the avarice of the Roman; for a more disinterested person never lived. Temperance and regularity in all his habits gave him general good health, and his unaffected modesty and suavity of manners endeared him to every one.

He was of easy elocution, his language chaste, methodical in the arrangement of his matter, learned and logical in the use of it, and of great urbanity in debate. Not quick of apprehension, but with a little time profound in penetration, and sound in conclusion. In his philosophy he was firm, and neither troubling, nor perhaps trusting, any one with his religious creed, he left to the world the conclusion that that religion must be good which could produce a life of such exemplary virtue.

His stature was of the middle size, well formed and proportioned and the features of his face manly, comely and engaging. Such was George Wythe, the honor of his own, and the model of future times.

Jefferson recognized his good fortune in having found advisers like Small and Wythe who encouraged the very traits Peter Jefferson might have nurtured in his son, questioning habits of mind and self-discipline. Much later, Thomas described to his grandson how he avoided an easy, aimless life in Williamsburg.

> Washington Nov. 24. [18]08.
> When I recollect that at 14. years of age, the whole care & direction of myself was thrown on myself entirely without a relation or friend qualified to advise or guide me, and recollect the various sorts of bad company with which I associated from time to time, I am astonished I did not turn off with some of them, & become as worthless to society as they were. I had the good fortune to become acquainted very early with some characters of very high standing, and to feel the incessant wish that I could ever become what they were. Under temptations & difficulties, I would ask myself what would Dr. Small, Mr. Wythe, Peyton Randolph [his mother's cousin] do in this situation? What course in it will insure me their approbation? I am certain that this mode of deciding on my conduct, tended more to its correctness than any reasoning powers I possessed. Knowing the even & dignified line they pursued, I could never doubt for a moment which of two courses would be in character for them. Whereas seeking the same object through a process of moral reasoning, & with the jaundiced eye of youth, I should often have erred. From the circumstances of my position I was often thrown into the society of horseracers, cardplayers, foxhunters, scientific & professional men, and of dignified men; and many a time have I asked myself, in the enthusiastic moment of the death of a fox, the victory of a favorite horse, the issue of a question eloquently argued at the bar or in the great council of the nation, well, which of these kinds of reputation should I prefer? That of a horse jockey? a foxhunter? an Orator? or the honest advocate of my country's rights? Be assured my dear Jefferson, that these little returns into ourselves, this self-catechising habit, is not trifling, nor useless, but leads to the prudent selection & steady pursuit of what is right.

George Wythe as an older man

The self-catechizing habit instilled early in Jefferson by his mentors in Williamsburg can be seen in his later intellectual development. Neither Small nor Wythe was bound by religious orthodoxy, but they were both profoundly moral men in a sense the Enlightenment would soon make popular. Jefferson absorbed their lessons well. In a letter to his nephew Peter Carr in 1787, Jefferson outlined his own very pragmatic philosophy of social morality and justice, a philosophy obviously influenced by his father, early teachers, and the circle at Williamsburg.

Governor Francis Fauquier

Paris Aug. 10. 1787.
Man was destined for society. His morality therefore was to be formed to this object. He was endowed with a sense of right and wrong merely relative to this. This sense is as much a part of his nature as the sense of hearing, seeing, feeling; it is the true foundation of morality, and not the...truth, &c., as fanciful writers have imagined. The moral sense, or conscience, is as much a part of man as his leg or arm. It is given to all human beings in a stronger or weaker degree, as force of members is given them in a greater or less degree. It may be strengthened by exercise, as may any particular limb of the body. This sense is submitted indeed in some degree to the guidance of reason; but it is a small stock which is required for this: even a less one than what we call Common sense. State a moral case to a ploughman and a professor. The former will decide it as well, and often better than the latter, because he has not been led astray by artificial rules.

Wythe and Small did not confine their tutelage of Jefferson to moral values; they broadened his social experience as well by introducing him to Francis Fauquier, Virginia's able and popular governor. When Fauquier learned of Jefferson's abilities as a violinist he invited him to join himself and several other amateurs in weekly concerts at the Governor's Palace. The tall, rather shy boy from Albemarle was soon part of Williamsburg society, which he later described as "the finest school of manners and morals that ever existed in America." At Fauquier's dinner table, Jefferson said, "I have heard more good sense, more rational and philosophical conversations, than in all my life besides. They were truly Attic societies."

Jefferson's education outside the college soon outstripped the instruction he gained in its classrooms, and it is not surprising that he left William and Mary at the age of nineteen. In an autobiographical memorandum written about 1821, he noted tersely after the year 1762: "Quitted College and began study of Law." His legal studies allowed him to remain in the same congenial circles in Williamsburg, however, for he entered the law office of George Wythe. For the next five years, Jefferson pored over Wythe's books, not limiting himself to law but embarking on a vigorous program of self-education and laying the groundwork of his own schooling in statecraft.

Jefferson was better equipped than most for this task; his self-discipline was the envy of his friends. John Page recalled that his own studies had suffered "for I was too sociable, and fond of the conversation of my friends, to study as Mr. Jefferson did, who could tear himself away from his dearest friends, to fly to his studies." According to family tradition, Jefferson devoted no less than fifteen hours a day to academic work at college. A letter he wrote in his old age to Dr. Vine Utley gives a notion of the strength and physical stamina that allowed him to maintain a similar schedule throughout his life.

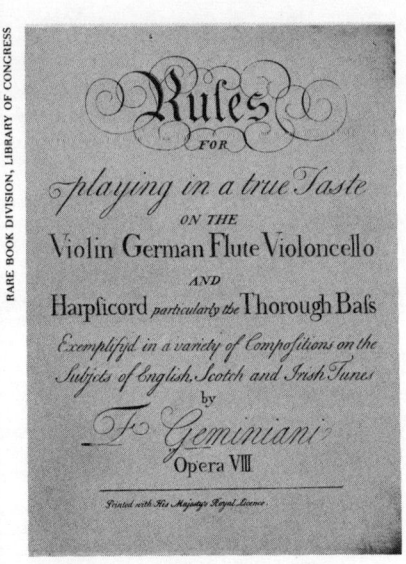

Title page of a rule book, from Jefferson's library, for playing the violin and other instruments

Monticello Mar. 21. [18]19.
Your letter of Feb. 18. came to hand on the 1st. instant; and the request of the history of my physical habits would have puzzled me not a little, had it not been for the model with which you accompanied it, of Doctor [Benjamin] Rush's answer to a similar enquiry. I live so much like other people, that I might refer to ordinary life as the history of my own. Like my friend the Doctor, I have lived temperately, eating little animal food, and that, not as an aliment so much as a condiment for the vegetables, which constitute my principal diet. I double, however, the Doctor's glass and a half of wine, and even treble it with a friend; but halve its effects by drinking the weak wines only. The ardent wines I cannot drink, nor do I use ardent spirits in any form. Malt liquors and cyder are my table drinks, and my breakfast, like that also of my friend, is of tea and coffee. I have been blest with organs of digestion which accept and concoct, without ever murmuring whatever the palate chuses to consign to them, and I have not yet lost a tooth by age. I was a hard student until I entered on the business of life, the duties of which leave no idle time to those disposed to fulfill them; and now, retired, and at the age of 76. I am again a hard student. Indeed my fondness for reading and study revolts me from the drudgery of letter writing. And a stiff wrist, the consequence of an early dislocation, makes writing both slow and painful. I am not so regular in my sleep as the Doctor says he was, devoting to it from 5. to 8. hours, according as my company or the book I am reading interests me; and I never go to bed without an hour, or half hour's previous reading of something moral, whereon to ruminate in the intervals

A *"recipe,"* consisting of six grains of calomel, which Jefferson used to treat his *"periodical headache"*

of sleep. But whether I retire to bed early or late, I rise with the sun. I use spectacles at night, but not necessarily in the day, unless in reading small print. My hearing is distinct in particular conversation, but confused when several voices cross each other, which unfits me for the society of the table. I have been more fortunate than my friend in the article of health. So free from catarrhs that I have not had one, (in the breast, I mean) on an average of 8. or 10. years through life. I ascribe this exemption partly to the habit of bathing my feet in cold water every morning for 60. years past. A fever of more than 24. hours I have not had above 2. or 3. times in my life. A periodical headache has afflicted me occasionally, once perhaps in 6. or 8. years, for 2. or 3. weeks at a time, which seems now to have left me; and, except on a late occasion of indisposition, I enjoy good health....

But in 1762, Jefferson had not quite perfected the regimen he followed in later years. His letters to John Page reveal a restless young man who rebelled at the drudgery of a law clerk's life and weighed a dozen alternative plans for his future. His life became even more unbearable when he fell in love with the pious and wealthy Rebecca Burwell. On Christmas Day he wrote Page of his disaster-filled holiday at Fairfield, not far from Shadwell, where a rainstorm had ruined a treasured silhouette of his beloved "Belinda."

Fairfeilds Dec: 25. 1762.

Dear Page

This very day, to others the day of greatest mirth and jollity, sees me overwhelmed with more and greater misfortunes than have befallen a descendant of Adam for these thousand years past I am sure; and perhaps, after excepting Job, since the creation of the world. I think his misfortunes were somewhat greater than mine: for although we may be pretty nearly on a level in other respects, yet I thank my God I have the advantage of brother Job in this, that Satan has not as yet put forth his hand to load me with bodily afflictions. You must know, dear Page, that I am now in a house surrounded with enemies, who take counsel together against my soul and when I lay me down to rest they say among themselves Come let us destroy him. I am sure if there is such a thing as a devil in this world, he must have been here last night and have had some hand in contriving what happened to me. Do you think the cursed rats (at his instigation I suppose) did not eat up my pocket-book which was in my pocket within a foot of my head? And not contented with plenty for the present they carried away my Jemmy worked silk garters and half a dozen new minuets I had just got, to serve I suppose as provision for the winter. But of this I should not have accused the devil (because you know rats will be rats, and hunger without the addition of his instigations might have urged them to do this) if something worse and from a different quarter had not happened. You know it rained last night, or if you do not know it I am sure I do. When I went to bed I laid my watch in the usual place, and going to take her up after I arose this morning I found her, in the same place it's true but! Quantum mutatus ab illo [how changed from what it was]! all afloat in water let in at a leak in the roof of the house, and as silent and still as the rats that had eat my pocket-book. Now you know if Chance had had any thing to do in this matter, there were a thousand other spots where it might have chanced to leak as well as at this one which was perpendicularly over my watch. But I'll tell you: It's my opinion that the Devil came and bored the hole over it on purpose. Well as I was saying, my poor watch had lost her speech: I should not have cared much for this, but something worse attended it: the subtle particles of the water with which the case was filled had by their penetration so overcome the cohesion of the particles of the paper of which my dear picture and watch paper were composed that in attempting to take them out to dry them Good God! mens horret referre [the mind shudders to recall it]! my cursed fingers gave them such a rent as I fear I never shall get over. This, cried I, was the last stroke Satan had in reserve for me: he knew I cared not for any thing else he could do to me, and was determined to try this last most fatal expedient.... I would have cryed bitterly, but I thought it beneath the dignity of a man.... However whatever misfortunes may attend the picture or lover, my hearty prayers shall be that all the health and happiness which heaven can send may be the portion of the original, and that so much goodness may ever meet with what may be most agreeable in this world, as I am sure it must in the next. And now although the picture be defaced there is so lively an image of her imprinted in

THE COLLEGE OF WILLIAM AND MARY

Portrait by John Wollaston of John Page, Jefferson's lifelong friend

my mind that I shall think of her too often I fear for my peace of mind, and too often I am sure to get through Old Cooke [Coke] this winter: for God knows I have not seen him since I packed him up in my trunk in Williamsburgh.

Well, Page, I do wish the Devil had old Cooke, for I am sure I never was so tired of an old dull scoundrel in my life. What! are there so few inquietudes tacked to this momentary life of ours that we must need be loading ourselves with a thousand more? Or as brother Job sais (who by the bye I think began to whine a little under his afflictions) 'Are not my days few? Cease then that I may take comfort a little before I go whence I shall not return, even to the land of darkness and the shadow of death.' But the old-fellows say we must read to gain knowledge; and gain knowledge to make us happy and be admired. Mere jargon! Is there any such thing as happiness in this world? No: And as for admiration I am sure the man who powders most, parfumes most, embroiders most, and talks most nonsense, is most admired. Though to be candid, there are some who have too much good sense to esteem such monkey-like animals as these ... and since these are the only persons whose esteem is worth a wish, I do not know but that upon the whole the advice of these old fellows may be worth following.

You cannot conceive the satisfaction it would give me to have a letter from you: Write me very circumstantially everything which happened at the wedding. Was SHE there? Because if she was I ought to have been at the devil for not being there too. If there is any news stirring in town or country, such as deaths, courtships and marriages in the circle of my acquaintance let me know it. Remember me affectionately to all the young ladies of my acquaintance, particularly the Miss Burwells and Miss Potters, and tell them that though that heavy earthly part of me, my body, be absent, the better half of me, my soul, is ever with them, and that my best wishes shall ever attend them. Tell Miss Alice Corbin that I verily believe the rats knew I was to win a pair of garters from her, or they never would have been so cruel as to carry mine away.... I would fain ask the favor of Miss Becca Burwell to give me another watch paper, of her own cutting which I should esteem much more though it were a plain round one, than the nicest in the world cut by other hands: however I am afraid she would think this pre-

BOTH: *Harper's New Monthly Magazine*, JULY, 1863

The Raleigh Tavern in Williamsburg

sumption after my suffering the other to get spoiled. If you think you can excuse me to her for this I should be glad if you would ask her....

...that I may not tire your patience by further additions I will make but this one more that I am sincerely and affectionately Dr Page your friend and servant,

T: JEFFERSON

For months Jefferson agonized over proposing to Rebecca. Page was subjected to letter after letter describing his friend's poignant indecision. Jefferson's visits to the Governor's Palace had apparently not given him the poise and assurance needed to express his feelings to the sixteen-year-old heiress. In October, 1763, he told Page of his latest embarrassment at the Apollo Room of the Raleigh Tavern.

Williamsburg, October 7, 1763.
In the most melancholy fit that ever any poor soul was, I sit down to write to you. Last night, as merry as agreeable company and dancing with Belinda in the Apollo could make me, I never could have thought the succeeding sun would have seen me so wretched as I now am! I was prepared to say a great deal: I had dressed up in my own mind, such thoughts as occurred to me, in as moving language as I knew how, and expected to have performed in a tolerably creditable manner. But, good God! When I had an opportunity of venting them, a few broken sentences, uttered in great disorder, and interrupted with pauses of uncommon length, were the too visible marks of my strange confusion! The whole confab I will tell you, word for word, if I can, when I see you, which God send may be soon.... The court is now at hand, which I must attend constantly, so that unless you come to town, there is little probability of my meeting with you any where else. For God's sake come.

Apollo Room of the Raleigh Tavern where Jefferson danced with Rebecca

This encounter was apparently one of the last between Jefferson and Miss Burwell; her engagement to another the following spring ended any hopes he had for his first love. Shortly after learning of his loss, Jefferson wrote his college friend William Fleming.

Wmsburgh. March 20. 1764.
11. o'clock at night.
With regard to the scheme which I proposed to you some time since, I am sorry to tell you it is totally frustrated

Jefferson's friend William Fleming in a portrait of a later date

by Miss R. B's marriage with Jacquelin Ambler which the people here tell me they daily expect: I say, the people here tell me so, for (can you beleive it?) I have been so abominably indolent as not to have seen her since last October, wherefore I cannot affirm that I know it from herself, though am as well satisfied that it is true as if she had told me.... You say you are determined to be married as soon as possible: and advise me to do the same. No, thank ye; I will consider of it first. Many and great are the comforts of a single state, and neither of the reasons you urge can have any influence with an inhabitant and a young inhabitant too of Wmsburgh.

Jefferson used his single state to good advantage and returned to his studies with his usual determination. Like many students of the time, he compiled several commonplace books in which he made notes of his readings and comments on his studies in law, equity, history and government, and parliamentary history and procedure. Throughout his life, Jefferson gave advice on the study of law. A letter responding to a young student in 1772 was revised in later years to answer similar requests, with the addition of new texts as they were published. From the beginning, Jefferson emphasized that the intellectual foundations must be broad, and his outline of study probably mirrors the very one he had painstakingly worked out for himself in Williamsburg.

[c. 1772]

Before you enter on the study of the law a sufficient ground-work must be laid. For this purpose an acquaintance with the Latin and French languages is absolutely necessary. The former you have; the latter must now be acquired. Mathematics and Natural philosophy are so useful in the most familiar occurrences of life, and are so peculiarly engaging & delightful as would induce every person to wish an acquaintance with them. Besides this, the faculties of the mind, like the members of the body, are strengthened & improved by exercise. Mathematical reasonings & deductions are therefore a fine preparation for investigating the abstruse speculations of the law....

This foundation being laid, you may enter regularly on the study of the Law, taking with it such of it's kindred sciences as will contribute to eminence in it's attainment. The principal of these are Physics, Ethics, Religion, Natural law, Belles lettres, Criticism, Rhetoric and Oratory. The carrying on several studies at a time is attended with advantage. Variety relieves the mind, as well as the eye, palled with too long attention to a single object. But with both, transitions from one object to another may be so frequent and transitory as to leave no impression. The mean is therefore to be steered and a competent space of time allotted to each branch of study. Again, a great inequality is observable in the vigor of the mind at different periods of the day. It's powers at these periods should therefore be attended to in marshalling the business of the day. For these reasons I should recommend the following distribution of your time.

Till VIII o'clock in the morning employ yourself in Physical studies, Ethics, Religion, natural and sectarian, and Natural law....

From VIII. to XII. read law. The general course of this reading may be formed on the following grounds. Ld. Coke has given us the first view of the whole body of law worthy now of being studied.... Coke's Institutes are a perfect Digest of the law as it stood in his day. After this, new laws were added by the legislature, and new developments of the old laws by the Judges, until they had become so voluminous as to require a new Digest. This was ably executed by Matthew Bacon, altho' unfortunately under an Alphabetical instead of Analytical arrangement of matter. The same process of new laws & new decisions on the old laws going on, called at length for the same operation again, and produced the inimitable Commentaries of Blackstone....

In reading the Reporters [reports of contemporary cases], enter in a Common-place book every case of value, condensed into the narrowest compass possible which will admit of presenting distinctly the principles of the case. This operation is doubly useful, inasmuch as it obliges the student to seek out the pith of the case, and habituates him to a condensation of thought, and to an acquisition of the most valuable of all talents, that of never using two words where one will do. It fixes the case too more indelibly in the mind.

From XII to I. read Politics...Locke on Government, Sidney on Government, Priestley's First Principles of Government, Review of Montesquieu's Spirit of Laws.... The Federalist [inserted in 1814]....

In the Afternoon read History....

Jefferson's own reading was various; his library included A Treatise of the Laws of Nature *(above) and a book on* Elements of Conchology *from which the plate below is taken.*

From Dark to Bedtime—Belles Lettres; Criticism; Rhetoric; Oratory....

NOTE. Under each of the preceding heads, the books are to be read in the order in which they are named. These by no means constitute the whole of what might be usefully read in each of these branches of science. The mass of excellent works going more into detail is great indeed. But those here noted will enable the student to select for himself such others of detail as may suit his particular views and dispositions. They will give him a respectable, an useful, & satisfactory degree of knolege in these branches, and will themselves form a valuable and sufficient library for a lawyer, who is at the same time a lover of science.

Jefferson's self-discipline was tested repeatedly, for his years in Wythe's law office coincided with the opening of the revolutionary movement in the Colonies, and Virginia's burgesses were leaders in this battle. In the spring of 1765, Jefferson stood at the door of the House of Burgesses' chamber where he heard the "splendid display of Mr. [Patrick] Henry's talents as a popular orator. They were great indeed," Jefferson recalled, "such as I have never heard from any other Man. He appeared to me to speak as Homer wrote." Jefferson never aspired to Henry's dazzling oratorical eloquence, but he genuinely admired the other's talents. Many years later he wrote this biographical sketch of Henry for William Wirt.

[Monticello, c. 1810–11]

My acqce with Mr. Henry commenced in the winter of 1759–60. On my way to college I passed the Xmas holidays at Colo. [Nathaniel West] Dandridge's in Hanover, to whom Mr. Henry was a near neighbor. During the festivity of the season I met him in society every day, & we became well acquainted, altho' I was much his junior, being then in my 17th. year, & he a married man. The spring following he came to Wmsbg to obtain a license as a lawyer, & he called on me at College. He told me he had been reading law only 6. weeks....

The next great occasion on which he signalised himself was that which may be considered as the dawn of the revoln in March 1774 [1764]. The British parliament had passed resolns. preparatory to the levying a revenue on the Colonies by a Stamp tax. The Virginia assembly, at their next session, prepared & sent to England very elaborate representns addressed in separate forms to

VIRGINIA HISTORICAL SOCIETY

A primitive painting shows Henry arguing one of his most famous cases, the Parson's Cause, in 1763.

the King, Lords, and Commons, against the right to impose such taxes. The famous Stamp act was however passed in Jan. 1765. and in the session of the Virgi assembly of May following, Mr. Henry introduced the celebrated resolns of that date. These were drawn by George Johnston, a lawyer of the Northern neck, a very able, logical and correct Speaker. Mr. Henry moved, and Johnston seconded these resolns successively. They were opposed by Randolph, Bland, Pendleton, Nicholas, Wythe & all the old members whose influence in the house had, till then, been unbroken. They did it, not from any question of our rights, but on the ground that the same sentiments had been, at their preceeding session, expressed in a more conciliatory form, to which the answers were not yet received. But torrents of sublime eloquence from Mr. Henry, backed up by the solid reasoning of Johnston, prevailed. The last however, & strongest resoln was carried but by a single vote. The debate on it was most bloody. I was then but a student, and was listening at the door of the lobby (for as yet there was no gallery) when Peyton Randolph, after the vote, came out of the house and said, as he entered the lobby 'By god, I would have given 500. guineas for a single vote.' For as this would have divided the house, the vote of Robinson, the Speaker, would have rejected the resolution....

I found Mr. Henry to be a silent & almost unmeddling member in Congress. On the original opening of that body, while general grievances were the topics, he was in his element & captivated all with his bold & splendid eloquence. But as soon as they came to specific matters, to sober reasoning and solid argumentation, he had the good sense to perceive that his declamation, however excellent in it's proper place, had no weight at all in such an assembly as that, of cool-headed, reflecting, judicious men. He ceased therefore in a great measure to take any part in the business....

A year later, the twenty-three-year-old Jefferson made his first trip outside the borders of his native province. In a three-month-long journey, undertaken for inoculation against smallpox by a Philadelphia physician, Jefferson first viewed his fellow Americans in the Middle Colonies. His journey had an unpleasant beginning, as he reported from Maryland to John Page.

Annapolis May. 25. 1766.
Surely never did small hero experience greater misadventures than I did on the first two or three days of my travelling. Twice did my horse run away with me and greatly endanger the breaking my neck on the first day. On the second I drove two hours through as copious a rain as ever I have seen, without meeting with a single house to which I could repair for shelter. On the third in going through Pamunkey, being unacquainted with the ford, I passed through water so deep as to run over the cushion as I sat on it, and to add to the danger, at that instant one wheel mounted a rock which I am confident was as high as the axle, and rendered it necessary for me to exercise all my skill in the doctrine of gravity, in order to prevent the center of gravity from being left unsupported.... I confess that on this occasion I was seised with a violent hydrophobia....

[Well versed in parliamentary proceedings and the knowledge of how a deliberative body ought to proceed, Jefferson was appalled at the way the Maryland General Assembly conducted business.]

But I will now give you some account of what I have seen in this Metropolis. The assembly happens to be sitting at this time. Their upper and lower house, as they call them, sit in different houses. I went into the lower, sitting in an old courthouse, which, judging from it's form and appearance, was built in the year one. I was surprised on approaching it to hear as great a noise and hubbub as you will usually observe at a publick meeting of the planters in Virginia. The first object which struck me after my entrance was the figure of a little old man dressed but indifferently, with a yellow queüe wig on, and mounted in the judge's chair. This the gentleman who walked with me informed me was the speaker, a man of a very fair character, but who by the bye has very little the air of a speaker. At one end of the justices' bench stood a man whom in another place I should from his dress and phis [physiognomy] have taken for Goodall the lawyer in Williamsburgh, reading a bill then before the house with a schoolboy tone and an abrupt pause at every half dozen words. This I found to be the clerk of the assembly. The mob (for such was their appearance) sat covered on the justices' and lawyers' benches, and were divided into little clubs amusing themselves in the common chit chat way. I was surprised to see them address the speaker without rising from their seats, and three, four, and five at a time without being checked. When [a motion was] made, the speaker instead of putting the question in the usual form only asked the gentlemen whether they chose that such or such a thing should be done, and was answered by a yes sir, or no sir: and tho' the voices appeared frequently to be divided, they never would go to the trouble of dividing the house, but the clerk entered the resolutions, I supposed, as he thought proper. In short every thing seems to be carried without the house in general's knowing what was proposed. The situation of this place is extremely beautiful, and very commodious for trade having a most secure port capable of receiving the largest vessels, those of 400 hh'ds [hogsheads] being able to brush against the sides of the dock. The houses are in general better than those in Williamsburgh, but the gardens more indifferent. The two towns seem much of a size. They have no publick buildings worth mentioning except a governor's house, the hull of which after being nearly finished, they have suffered to go to ruin. I would give you an account of the rejoicings here on the repeal of the stamp act but this you will probably see in print before my letter can reach you. I shall proceed tomorrow to Philadelphia where I shall make the stay necessary for inoculation, thence going on to New York. I shall return by water to Williamsburgh, about the middle of July....

Town of Annapolis, which Jefferson thought was beautifully situated

There are no records of Jefferson's impressions of Philadelphia and New York. He returned home in the summer to complete his legal apprenticeship and early the next year was admitted to the bar. His career as a lawyer continued, in his own words, "until the revolution shut up the courts of justice." By the time that Revolution came Jefferson had become a candidate for leadership of the rebels in his own province and in what was to become his own nation.

Chapter 2

Eloquent Revolutionary

Thomas Jefferson used the years before the Revolution to broaden his intellectual and cultural interests as well as to establish a successful legal practice. The man who left Virginia to join other patriots in Philadelphia at the Continental Congress in 1775 was a far more sophisticated and cultured traveler than the twenty-three-year-old visitor of 1766. The self-discipline that served him so well in George Wythe's office never disappeared, and Jefferson applied it to educating himself in such fields as literature, music, architecture, and botany.

A young attorney in provincial Virginia needed such diversions, for there was little excitement and much drudgery in the practice of law. Indeed, even after six years in the profession, Jefferson was forced to resort to such unpleasant strategies as the notice he and five fellow attorneys placed in the *Virginia Gazette* in hopes of forcing clients to pay their fees.

Virginia Gazette, May 20, 1773

On serious Consideration of the present State of our Practice in the General Court, we find it can no longer be continued on the same Terms. The Fees allowed by Law, if regularly paid, would barely compensate our incessant Labours, reimburse our Expenses, and the Losses incurred by Neglect of our private Affairs; yet even these Rewards, confessedly moderate, are withheld from us, in a great Proportion, by the unworthy Part of our Clients. Some Regulation, therefore, is become absolutely requisite to establish Terms more equal between the Client and his Counsel. To effect this, we have come to the following Resolution, for the invariable Observance of which we mutually plight our Honour to each other: "That after the 10th Day of *October* next we will not give an Opinion on any Case stated to us but on Payment of the whole Fee, nor prosecute or defend any Suit or Motion unless the Tax, and one Half the Fee, be previously advanced, excepting those Cases only where we choose to act *gratis*:" and we hope no Person whatever will think of applying to us in any other Way.

Jefferson seemed to realize that the law could not satisfy his needs for personal fulfillment and often seemed to belittle his own profession. "I was bred to the law," he once remarked, "and that gave me a view of the dark side of humanity. Then I read poetry to qualify it with a gaze upon its bright side." When he sent his friend Joseph Cabell the draft of a bill for establishing elementary schools in 1817, Jefferson commented on the literary standards of his chosen profession.

> Poplar Forest. Sep. 9. [18]17.
> I should apologize perhaps for the style of this bill. I dislike the verbose and intricate style of the English statutes.... You however can easily correct this bill to the taste of my brother lawyers, by making every other word a 'said' or 'aforesaid,' and saying every thing over 2. or 3. times, so as that nobody but we of the craft can untwist the diction, and find out what it means; and that too not so plainly but that we may conscientiously divide, one half on each side.

A musical pattern used by Jefferson to tune a harpsichord

Jefferson's new appreciation of poetry did not prevent him from pursuing his old interest in music. In 1768 he purchased a violin for five pounds and played it most of his life. Even in his hobbies he was an eminently frugal and practical man. During the Revolution he wrote to his friend Giovanni Fabbroni, an Italian musician, to complain of the "barbarism" that prevented him from enjoying music as fully as he wished and to propose an ingenious solution to his problem.

> Williamsburgh in Virginia June. 8. 1778
> If there is a gratification which I envy any people in this world, it is to your country it's music. This is the favorite passion of my soul, and fortune has cast my lot in a country where it is in a state of deplorable barbarism.... The bounds of an American fortune will not admit the indulgence of a domestic band of musicians. Yet I have thought that a passion for music might be reconciled with that œconomy which we are obliged to observe. I retain for instance among my domestic servants a gardener (Ortolano) a weaver (Tessitore di lino e lana) a cabinet maker

Engraving by twelve-year-old Horace Doolittle illustrates Jefferson's advice to nephew on carrying a gun.

Jefferson's specifications for and drawing of a partridge snare

(Stipettaio) and a stonecutter (scalpellino lavorante in piano) to which I would add a Vigneron. In a country where, like yours, music is cultivated and practised by every class of men, I suppose there might be found persons of those trades who could perform on the French horn, clarinets and hautboys, and a bassoon. So that one might have a band of two French horns, two clarinets or hautboys, and a bassoon, without enlarging their domestic expences. A certainty of employment for a half dozen years, and at the end of that time to find them a conveyance to their own country if they chose to return might induce them to come here on reasonable wages. Without meaning to give you trouble, perhaps it might be practicable for you in your ordinary intercourse with your people to find out such men, disposed to come to America. Sobriety and good nature would be desireable parts of their characters.

Balancing his interest in the arts, Jefferson developed a simultaneous passion for agriculture. Returning to Shadwell after his years in Williamsburg, he began to keep a garden book whose first entry on March 30, 1766, was merely that the "purple hyacinth begins to bloom." His concern for agriculture and botany grew naturally from his love for the outdoors—a love reinforced by his conviction that only a carefully planned program of exercise would sustain his physical strength and mental alertness. In 1785 he described this regimen to his nephew.

Paris Aug. 19. 1785.

A strong body makes the mind strong. As to the species of exercise, I advise the gun. While this gives a moderate exercise to the body, it gives boldness, enterprize, and independance to the mind. Games played with the ball and others of that nature, are too violent for the body and stamp no character on the mind. Let your gun therefore be the constant companion of your walks. Never think of taking a book with you. The object of walking is to relax the mind. You should therefore not permit yourself even to think while you walk. But divert your attention by the objects surrounding you. Walking is the best possible exercise. Habituate yourself to walk very far. The Europeans value themselves on having subdued the horse to the uses of man. But I doubt whether we have not lost more than we have gained by the use of this animal. No one has occasioned so much the degeneracy of the human body. An Indian goes on foot nearly as far in a day, for a long journey, as an enfeebled white does on his horse, and he will tire the best horses. There is no habit you will value so much as that of walking far without fatigue. I would advise you to take your exercise in the afternoon. Not because it is the best time for exercise for certainly it is not: but because it is the best time to spare from your studies; and habit will soon reconcile it to health, and render it nearly as useful as if you gave to that the more precious hours of the day. A little walk of half an hour in the morning when you first rise is adviseable also. It shakes off sleep, and produces other good effects in the animal œconomy. Rise at a fixed and an early hour, and go to bed at a fixed and early hour also. Sitting up late at night is injurious to the health, and not useful to the mind.

An estimate from Dabney Minor, a lowlands builder, of the nails and lead required for Monticello

Pleasant as life at Shadwell was, with the work of a lawyer and a planter to occupy his days and music, poetry, and good company to fill the evenings, Jefferson became enmeshed in another all-consuming project—one that would eventually encompass all the others. About a year after he had been admitted to the bar, he began to clear the summit of a hill across the river from his mother's home at Shadwell—a hill he had dubbed "Monticello," Italian for "little mountain." Here Jefferson, the self-educated architect, would build a mansion perfectly suited to Jefferson the agriculturist, the student of literature, and the musician. The beautiful Palladian structure would not be completed for more than twenty years, but by the fall of 1769 a single, one-room outbuilding had been erected. This proved a fortunate coincidence, for on February 1, 1770, Shadwell burned to the ground. Jefferson wrote to John Page of his most important personal loss—his books.

Charlottesville Feb. 21. 1770.
My late loss may perhaps have reac[hed y]ou by this time, I mean the loss of my mother's house by fire, and in it, of every pa[per I] had in the world, and almost every book. On a reasonable estimate I calculate th[e cost o]f t[he b]ooks burned to have been £200. sterling. Would to god it had been the money [; then] had it never cost me a sigh! To make the loss more sensible it fell principally on m[y books] of common law, of which I have but one left, at that time lent out. Of papers too of every kind I am utterly destitute. All of these, whether public or private, of business or of amusement have perished in

Jefferson's earliest plan for Monticello (above) was of a square wooden house divided into four rooms; above right, his sketches and notes for the slave quarters.

Virginia Gazette, FEBRUARY 22, 1770; RARE BOOK DIVISION, N.Y. PUBLIC LIBRARY

Notice in the Virginia Gazette *of the fire that destroyed Shadwell*

the flames. I had made some progress in preparing for the succeeding general court, and having, as was my custom, thrown my thoughts into the form of notes, I troubled my head no more with them. These are gone, and 'like the baseless fabric of a vision, Leave not a trace behind.' The records also and other papers, which furnished me with states of the several cases, having shared the same fate, I have no foundation whereon to set out anew.

In November, 1770, Jefferson moved to the lone building at Monticello, leaving his mother and her family at Shadwell where they made their quarters in structures that had survived the flames in the main house. After a few months in his new residence, Jefferson wrote cheerfully to James Ogilvie.

> Monticello Feb. 20 1771
> I have lately removed to the mountain from whence this is dated, and with which you are not unacquainted. I have here but one room, which, like the cobler's, serves me for parlour for kitchen and hall. I may add, for bed chamber and study too. My friends sometimes take a temperate dinner with me and then retire to look for beds elsewhere. I have hopes however of getting more elbow room this summer. But be this as may happen, whether my tenements be great or small homely or elegant they will always receive you with a hearty welcome.

A life of splendidly isolated bachelorhood at Monticello was not Jefferson's plan. Despite Rebecca Burwell's indifference, he had not turned his back on love. In the same letter in which he told John Page of Shadwell's destruction, Jefferson reminded his friend of his fondness for the company of women.

Charlottesville Feb. 21. 1770.
[I r]efl[ect of]ten with pleasure on the philosophical evenings I passed at Rosewell in my last [visit]s there. I was always fond of philosophy even in it's dryer forms, but from a ruby [lip] it comes with charms irresistible. Such a feast of sentiment must exhilarate and lengthen life at least as much as the feast of the sensualist shortens it. In a word I prize it so highly that if you will at any time collect the same Belle assemblèe on giving me three days previous notice, I shall certainly repair to my place as a member of it.

Later that year Jefferson began to visit The Forest, the estate of John Wayles near Williamsburg. Here he courted Wayles's attractive, widowed daughter, Martha Wayles Skelton. By June, 1771, he was sure enough of Martha's affection to order his London agent to purchase a pianoforte for her.

Monticello. June 1. 1771.
As it was somewhat doubtful when you left the country how far my little invoice delivered you might be complied with till we should know the fate of the association [the Virginia Nonimportation Association], I desired you to withhold purchasing the things till you should hear further from me. The day appointed for the meeting of the associates is not yet arrived, however from the universal sense of those who are likely to attend it seems reduced to a certainty that the restrictions will be taken off everything but the dutied articles. I will therefore venture to desire that branch of my invoice may be complied with in which were some shoes and other prohibited articles; since if contrary to our expectations the restrictions should be continued I can store, or otherwise dispose of them as our committees please. I must alter one article in the invoice. I wrote therein for a Clavichord. I have since seen a Forte-piano and am charmed with it. Send me this instrument then instead of the Clavichord. Let the case be of fine mahogany, solid, not vineered. The compass from Double G. to F. in alt. a plenty of spare

Frontispiece of The Compleat Tutor for the Harpsichord or Spinnet, *a book in Jefferson's library*

39

strings; and the workmanship of the whole very handsome, and worthy the acceptance of a lady for whom I intend it.

By August he had apparently made his intentions known to the Wayles family, for he concluded a letter to Martha's brother-in-law, Robert Skipwith, with this injunction.

> Monticello. Aug. 3. 1771.
> Offer prayers for me too at that shrine to which, tho' absent, I pay continual devotion. In every scheme of happiness she is placed in the fore-ground of the picture, as the principal figure. Take that away, and it is no picture for me.

On New Year's Day, 1772, Jefferson and Martha Skelton were married at The Forest. His *Autobiography* included those details Jefferson thought would be of public interest.

> *Autobiography*, 1821
> On the 1st. of January 1772. I was married to Martha Skelton widow of Bathurst Skelton, & daughter of John Wayles, then 23. years old. Mr. Wayles was a lawyer of much practice, to which he was introduced more by his great industry, punctuality & practical readiness, than to eminence in the science of his profession. He was a most agreeable companion, full of pleasantry & good humor, and welcomed in every society. He acquired a handsome fortune, died in May. 1773. leaving three daughters, and the portion which came on that event to Mrs. Jefferson, after the debts should be paid, which were very considerable, was about equal to my own patrimony, and consequently doubled the ease of our circumstances.

Virginia Gazette, JULY 15, 1773; RARE BOOK DIVISION, N.Y. PUBLIC LIBRARY

After the death of John Wayles, this advertisement for the sale of part of his estate appeared in the Gazette.

Marriage, the fascinating details of supervising the construction of Monticello, the less fascinating details of his legal practice—these occupied Jefferson's time for the first year after he brought Martha to her new home in Albemarle County. Politics, however, remained foremost. He had been elected to the House of Burgesses in 1769 but had not found the legislature a particularly congenial body.

> *Autobiography*, 1821
> In 1769. I became a member of the legislature by the

Reverse silhouette thought to be of young Martha Wayles Jefferson; no authentic likeness of her is known.

choice of the county in which I live, & continued in that until it was closed by the revolution. I made one effort in that body for the permission of the emancipation of slaves, which was rejected: and indeed, during the regal government, nothing liberal could expect success. Our minds were circumscribed within narrow limits by an habitual belief that it was our duty to be subordinate to the mother country in all matters of government, to direct all our labors in subservience to her interests, and even to observe a bigotted intolerance for all religions but hers. The difficulties with our representatives were of habit and despair, not of reflection & conviction. Experience soon proved that they could bring their minds to rights on the first summons of their attention. But the king's council, which acted as another house of legislature, held their places at will & were in most humble obedience to that will: the Governor too, who had a negative on our laws held by the same tenure, & with still greater devotedness to it: and last of all the Royal negative closed the last door to every hope of amelioration.

In his fifth year as a burgess, Jefferson began to question the mother country's authority more openly and to demonstrate more resourcefulness in circumventing conservative burgesses, councilors, and governors. When the House was convened in the spring of 1773, relations with the Crown had again become strained. Episodes such as the burning of the British customs schooner the *Gaspee* in Rhode Island threatened the comparative peace established between the mother country and the Colonies by the repeal of the Townshend duties. Jefferson recalled how he and his allies had devised a method of rallying public opinion and coordinating resistance to the Crown during that session at Williamsburg.

Autobiography, 1821

Not thinking our old & leading members up to the point of forwardness & zeal which the times required, Mr. Henry, R[ichard] H[enry] Lee, Francis L. Lee, Mr. [Dabney] Carr & myself agreed to meet in the evening in a private room of the Raleigh to consult on the state of things. There may have been a member or two more whom I do not recollect. We were all sensible that the most urgent of all measures was that of coming to an understanding with all the other colonies to consider the British claims as a common cause to all, & to produce

Jefferson's appointment as surveyor of Albemarle County, June 6, 1773

an unity of action: and for this purpose that a commee of correspondce in each colony would be the best instrument for intercommunication: and that their first measure would probably be to propose a meeting of deputies from every colony at some central place, who should be charged with the direction of the measures which should be taken by all. We therefore drew up the resolutions.... The consulting members proposed to me to move them, but I urged that it should be done by Mr. Carr, my friend & brother in law [his sister Martha's husband], then a new member to whom I wished an opportunity should be given of making known to the house his great worth & talents. It was so agreed; he moved them, they were agreed to nem. con. [unanimously] and a commee of correspondence appointed of whom Peyton Randolph, the Speaker, was chairman. The Govr. (then Ld. Dunmore) dissolved us, but the Commee met the next day, prepared a circular letter to the Speakers of the other colonies, inclosing to each a copy of the resolns and left it in charge with their chairman to forward them by expresses.

By the time the House was called again in 1774, even more effective methods of resistance were necessary. Boston had greeted the new tea tax with her tea party, and the Crown had retaliated with the notorious Boston Port Act. Again Jefferson left a record of the developing strategy of the defiant group in Williamsburg that met in private to work out a protest plan.

Autobiography, 1821

The next event which excited our sympathies for Massachusets was the Boston port bill, by which that port was to be shut up on the 1st. of June 1774. This arrived while we were in session in the spring of that year. The lead in the house on these subjects being no longer left to the old members, Mr. Henry, R. H. Lee, Fr. L. Lee, 3. or 4. other members, whom I do not recollect, and myself, agreeing that we must boldly take an unequivocal stand in the line with Massachusetts, determined to meet and consult on the proper measures in the Council chamber, for the benefit of the library in that room. We were under conviction of the necessity of arousing our people from the lethargy into which they had fallen as to passing events; and thought that the appointment of a day of general fasting & prayer would be most likely to call up & alarm their attention.... To give greater emphasis to our proposition, we agreed to wait the next morning on Mr. [Robert Carter] Nicholas, whose grave & religious character was more in unison with the tone of our resolution and to sollicit him to move it. We accordingly went to him in the morning. He moved it the same day. The 1st of June was proposed and it passed without opposition. The Governor dissolved us as usual. We retired to the Apollo as before, agreed to an association, and instructed the Commee of correspdce to propose to the corresponding commees of the other colonies to appoint deputies to meet in Congress at such place, *annually*, as should be convenient to direct, from time to time, the measures required by the general interest: and we declared that an attack on any one colony should be considered as an attack on the whole.... We returned home, and in our several counties invited the clergy to meet assemblies of the people on the 1st. of June, to perform the ceremonies of the day, & to address to them discourses suited to the occasion. The people met generally, with anxiety & alarm in their countenances, and the effect of the day thro' the whole colony was like a shock of electricity, arousing every man & placing him erect & solidly on his center.

Seal of Lord Dunmore, Governor of Virginia prior to the Revolution

Virginians responded as Jefferson had thought they would in the latest confrontation with the governor. Dunmore, having dissolved the House of Burgesses in the hope that a newly elected House would be less troublesome, found that the counties had not only reelected the same men but designated them to meet in convention to choose delegates to a proposed Continental Congress. Jefferson outlined a plan of action for the Congress in these resolutions he drafted for signing by the freeholders of Albemarle.

[July 26, 1774]

RESOLVED, that the inhabitants of the several states of British America are subject to the laws which they adopted at their first settlement, and to such others as have been since made by their respective legislatures, duly constituted and appointed with their own consent; that no other legislature whatever may rightfully exercise authority over them, and that these privileges they hold as the common rights of mankind, confirmed by the political constitutions they have respectively assumed, and also by several charters of compact from the crown.

MANUSCRIPT DIVISION, N.Y. PUBLIC LIBRARY

TUESDAY, the 24th of MAY, 14 GEO. III. 1774.

THIS House being deeply impreſſed with Apprehenſion of the great Dangers to be derived to *Britiſh America*, from the hoſtile Invaſion of the City of *Boſton*, in our Siſter Colony of *Maſſachuſetts Bay*, whoſe Commerce and Harbour are on the 1ſt Day of *June* next to be ſtopped by an armed Force, deem it highly neceſſary that the ſaid firſt Day of *June* be ſet apart by the Members of this Houſe as a Day of Faſting, Humiliation, and Prayer, devoutly to implore the divine Interpoſition for averting the heavy Calamity, which threatens Deſtruction to our civil Rights, and the Evils of civil War; to give us one Heart and one Mind firmly. to oppoſe, by all juſt and proper Means, every Injury to *American* Rights, and that the Minds of his Majeſty and his Parliament may be inſpired from above with Wiſdom, Moderation, and Juſtice, to remove from the loyal People of *America* all Cauſe of Danger from a continued Purſuit of Meaſures pregnant with their Ruin.

Ordered, therefore, that the Members of this Houſe do attend in their Places at the Hour of ten in the Forenoon, on the ſaid 1ſt Day of *June* next, in Order to proceed with the Speaker and the Mace to the Church in this City for the Purpoſes aforeſaid; and that the Reverend Mr. *Price* be appointed to read Prayers, and the Reverend Mr. *Gwatkin* to preach a Sermon ſuitable to the Occaſion.

Ordered, that this Order be forthwith printed and publiſhed.

By *the* HOUSE *of* BURGESSES.
 GEORGE WYTHE, C. H. B.

Proclamation by House of Burgesses setting June 1, 1774, as the day of fasting Jefferson and others had urged "to take an unequivocal stand in the line with Massachusetts"

Resolved, that these their natural and legal rights have in frequent instances been invaded by the parliament of Great Britain, and particularly that they were so by an act lately passed to take away the trade of the inhabitants of the town of Boston, in the province of Massachusetts Bay, that all such assumptions of unlawful power are dangerous to the rights of the British empire in general, and should be considered as its common cause, and that we will ever be ready to join with our fellow subjects, in every part of the same, in exerting all those rightful powers, which God has given us, for the re-establishing and guaranteeing such their constitutional rights, when, where, and by whomsoever invaded.

It is the opinion of this meeting, that the most eligible means of effecting these purposes will be to put an immediate stop to all imports from Great Britain (cotton, oznabrigs [osnaburg—coarse cotton], striped duffil [duffel —heavy wool], medicines, gunpowder, lead, books and printed papers, the necessary tools and implements for the handycraft arts and manufactures excepted for a limited time) and to all exports thereto after the 1st day of October, which shall be in the year of our Lord, 1775; and immediately to discontinue all commercial intercourse with every part of the British empire which shall not in like manner break off their commerce with Great Britain.

It is the opinion of this meeting, that we immediately cease to import all commodities from every part of the world which are subjected by the British parliament to the payment of duties in America.

It is the opinion of this meeting that these measures should be pursued until a repeal be obtained of the act for blocking up the harbour of Boston, of the acts prohibiting or restraining internal manufactures in America, of the acts imposing on any commodities duties to be paid in America, and of the acts laying restrictions on the American trade; and that on such repeal it will be reasonable to grant to our brethren of Great Britain such privileges in commerce as may amply compensate their fraternal assistance, past and future.

Jefferson said that an attack of dysentery prevented him from attending the convention that met in Williamsburg on August 1, 1774, but he prepared additional resolutions to be adopted as instructions to the congressmen chosen there. He described the background of this draft.

Autobiography, 1821

They chose universally delegates for the Convention. Being elected one for my own county I prepared a draught of instructions to be given to the delegates whom we should send to the Congress, and which I meant to propose at our meeting. In this I took the ground which, from the beginning I had thought the only one orthodox or tenable, which was that the relation between Gr. Br. and these colonies was exactly the same as that of England & Scotland after the accession of James & until the Union ... having the same Executive chief but no other necessary political connection; and that our emigration from England to this country gave her no more rights over us, than the emigrations of the Danes and Saxons gave to the present authorities of the mother country over England. In this doctrine however I had never been able to get any one to agree with me but Mr. Wythe.... Our other patriots [Peyton] Randolph, the Lees, Nicholas, [Edmund] Pendleton stopped at the half-way house of John Dickinson who admitted that England had a right to regulate our commerce, and to lay duties on it for the purposes of regulation, but not of raising revenue. But for this ground there was no foundation in compact, in any acknoleged principles of colonization, nor in reason: expatriation being a natural right, and acted on as such, by all nations, in all ages. I set out for Wmsbg some days before that appointed for our meeting, but was taken ill of a dysentery on the road, & unable to proceed. I sent on therefore to Wmsbg two copies of my draught, the one under cover to Peyton Randolph, who I knew would be in the chair of the convention, the other to Patrick Henry. Whether Mr. Henry disapproved the ground taken, or was too lazy to read it (for he was the laziest man in reading I ever knew) I never learnt: but he communicated it to nobody. Peyton Randolph informed the Convention he had received such a paper from a member prevented by sickness from offering it in his place, and he laid it on the table for perusal. It was read generally by the members, approved by many, but thought too bold for the present state of things; but they printed it in pamphlet form under the title of 'A Summary view of the rights of British America.'

Although Jefferson explained that there were "some uncertainties and inaccuracies of historical facts" in the *Summary View* that he "neglected at the moment, knowing they could be readily corrected at the meeting," it is possible that he never intended to attend the convention and introduce the instructions himself. He knew he did not have the oratorical eloquence necessary to sway the delegates to such an advanced legal argument and he may have employed an indirect means of achieving his goal, a method thoroughly characteristic of his political style. In this case, he sent a copy of the arguments to Patrick Henry who had so impressed him with his persuasive abilities. He may have hoped Henry would introduce and move them, perhaps employing some of the ardent revolutionary rhetoric Jefferson had provided. Jefferson's dysentery may in fact have been a "diplomatic" illness; his account books show no record of an attempt to get to Williamsburg in time for the convention.

Even though the resolutions were not adopted, they more than served Jefferson's purpose. Published as a twenty-three page pamphlet, the *Summary View* gained wide circulation and brought Jefferson recognition outside his own colony. Ostensibly a guideline for Virginia's delegates to Congress, Jefferson's document went far beyond its avowed goal, setting forth specific grievances that had brought the Congress into existence. It even contained a veiled warning that unless those grievances were remedied, the King might lose the allegiance of his American subjects. Although Jefferson couched his threat in terms of advice to the King, there was no doubt of what he expected to happen if that advice was ignored.

A Summary View of the Rights of British America [July, 1774]

Resolved that it be an instruction to the said deputies when assembled in General Congress with the deputies from the other states of British America to propose to the said Congress that an humble and dutiful address be presented to his majesty begging leave to lay before him as chief magistrate of the British empire the united complaints of his majesty's subjects in America; complaints which are excited by many unwarrantable incroachments and usurpations, attempted to be made by the legislature of one part of the empire, upon those rights which god and the laws have given equally and independently to all. To represent to his majesty that these his states have often individually made humble application to his imperial throne, to obtain thro' it's intervention some redress of their injured rights; to none of which was ever an answer condescended. Humbly to hope that this their joint address, penned in the language of truth, and divested of those expressions of servility which would persuade his majesty that we are asking favors and not rights shall obtain from his majesty a more respectful acceptance. And this his majesty will think we have reason to expect when he reflects that he is no more than the chief officer of the people, appointed by the laws, and circumscribed with definite powers, to assist in working the great machine of government erected for their use, and consequently to their superintendance. And in order that these our rights, as well as the invasions of them, may be laid more fully before his majesty, to take a view of them from the origin and first settlement of these countries.

To remind him that our ancestors, before their emigration to America, were the free inhabitants of the British dominions in Europe, and possessed a right, which nature has given to all men, of departing from the country in which chance, not choice has placed them, of going in quest of new habitations, and of there establishing new societies, under such laws and regulations as to them shall seem most likely to promote public happiness. That their Saxon ancestors had under this universal law, in like manner, left their native wilds and woods in the North of Europe, had possessed themselves of the island of Britain then less charged with inhabitants, and had established there that system of laws which has so long been the glory and protection of that country. Nor was ever any claim of superiority or dependance asserted over them by that mother country from which they had migrated: and were such a claim made it is beleived his majesty's subjects in Great Britain have too firm a feeling of the rights derived to them from their ancestors to bow down the sovereignty of their state before such visionary pretensions. And it is thought that no circumstance has occurred to distinguish materially the British from the Saxon emigration. America was conquered, and her settlements made and firmly established, at the expence of individuals, and not of the British public. Their own blood was spilt in acquiring lands for their settlement, their own fortunes expended in making that settlement effectual. For themselves they fought, for themselves they conquered, and for themselves alone they have right to hold. No shilling was ever issued from the public treasures of his majesty or his ancestors for their assistance, till of very late times, after the colonies had

Title page of the twenty-three page Summary View, *with Jefferson's name filled in as the author*

In July, 1774, as Jefferson was writing the Summary View, The Massachusetts Spy *carried this engraving by Paul Revere of a snake made up of the various colonies defying Great Britain's griffin.*

become established on a firm and permanent footing....

[Jefferson acknowledged the aid Britain had given the Colonies once they had become commercially valuable, but he said the help did not entitle Parliament to any arrogation of authority and could be repaid by granting exclusive trade privileges.]

That settlements having been thus effected in the wilds of America, the emigrants thought proper to adopt that system of laws under which they had hitherto lived in the mother country, and to continue their union with her by submitting themselves to the same common sovereign, who was thereby made the central link connecting the several parts of the empire thus newly multiplied.

But that not long were they permitted, however far they thought themselves removed from the hand of oppression, to hold undisturbed the rights thus acquired at the hazard of their lives and loss of their fortunes. A family of princes [the Stuarts] was then on the British throne, whose treasonable crimes against their people brought on them afterwards the exertion of those sacred and sovereign rights of punishment, reserved in the hands of the people for cases of extreme necessity, and judged by the constitution unsafe to be delegated to any other judicature. While every day brought forth some new and unjustifiable exertion of power over their subjects on that side the water, it was not to be expected that those here, much less able at that time to oppose the designs of despotism, should be exempted from injury. Accordingly that country [British North America]...was by these princes at several times parted out and distributed among the favorites and followers of their fortunes; and by an assumed right of the crown alone were erected into distinct and independent governments; a measure which it is beleived his majesty's prudence and understanding would prevent him from imitating at this day; as no exercise of such a power of dividing and dismembering a country has ever occurred in his majesty's realm of England....

That thus have we hastened thro' the reigns which preceded his majesty's, during which the violation of our rights were less alarming, because repeated at more distant intervals, than that rapid and bold succession of injuries which is likely to distinguish the present from all other periods of American story. Scarcely have our minds been able to emerge from the astonishment into which one stroke of parliamentary thunder has involved us, before another more heavy and more alarming is fallen on us. Single acts of tyranny may be ascribed to the accidental opinion of a day; but a series of oppressions, begun at a distinguished period, and pursued unalterably thro' every change of ministers, too plainly prove a deliberate, systematical plan of reducing us to slavery....

...Not only the principles of common sense, but the common feelings of human nature must be surrendered up, before his majesty's subjects here can be persuaded to beleive that they hold their political existence at the will of a British parliament[.] Shall these governments be dissolved, their property annihilated, and their people reduced to a state of nature, at the imperious breath of a body of men whom they never saw, in whom they never confided, and over whom they have no powers of punishment or removal, let their crimes against the American public be ever so great? Can any one reason be assigned why 160,000 electors in the island of Great Britain should give law to four millions in the states of America, every individual of whom is equal to every individual of them in virtue, in understanding, and in bodily strength? Were this to be admitted, instead of being a free people, as we have hitherto supposed, and mean to continue, ourselves, we should suddenly be found the slaves, not of one, but of 160,000 tyrants, distinguished too from all others by this singular circumstance that they are removed from the reach of fear, the only restraining motive which may hold the hand of a tyrant....

[Jefferson then traced the history of the Boston Port Bill and described other interferences with the Colonies' "glorious right of representation" such as the mother country's habit of dissolving American houses of representatives.]

But your majesty or your Governors have carried this power beyond every limit known or provided for by the laws. After dissolving one house of representatives, they have refused to call another, so that for a great length of time the legislature provided by the laws has been out of existence. From the nature of things, every society must at all times possess within itself the sovereign powers of legislation. The feelings of human nature revolt against the supposition of a state so situated as that it may not in any emergency provide against dangers which perhaps threaten immediate ruin. While those bodies are in existence to whom the people have delegated the powers of legislation, they alone possess and may exercise those powers. But when they are dissolved by the lopping off one or more of their branches, the power reverts to the people, who may use it to unlimited extent, either assembling together in person, sending deputies, or in any other way they may think proper. We forbear to trace consequences further; the dangers are conspicuous with which this practice is replete....

[He then discussed an "error in the nature of our landholdings," that "all lands belong originally to the king." Instead, he said that allotting property was the right of a particular society through legislative action or that each individual "may appropriate to himself such lands as he finds vacant, and occupancy will give him title."]

That, in order to inforce the arbitrary measures before complained of, his majesty has from time to time sent among us large bodies of armed forces, not made up of the people here, nor raised by the authority of our laws. Did his majesty possess such a right as this, it might swallow up all our other rights whenever he should think proper. But his majesty has no right to land a single armed man on our shores; and those whom he sends here are liable to our laws for the suppression and punishment of Riots, Routs, and unlawful assemblies, or are hostile bodies invading us in defiance of law.... To render these proceedings still more criminal against our laws, instead of subjecting the military to the civil power, his majesty has expressly made the civil subordinate to the military. But can his majesty thus put down all law under his feet? Can he erect a power superior to that which erected himself? He has done it indeed by force; but let him remember that force cannot give right.

That these are our grievances which we have thus laid before his majesty with that freedom of language and sentiment which becomes a free people, claiming their rights as derived from the laws of nature, and not as the gift of their chief magistrate. Let those flatter, who fear: it is not an American art. To give praise where it is not due, might be well from the venal, but would ill beseem those who are asserting the rights of human nature. They know, and will therefore say, that kings are the servants, not the proprietors of the people. Open your breast Sire, to liberal and expanded thought. Let not the name of George the third be a blot in the page of history. You are surrounded by British counsellors, but remember that they are parties. You have no ministers for American affairs, because you have none taken from among us, nor amenable to the laws on which they are to give you advice. It behoves you therefore to think and to act for yourself and your people. The great principles of right and wrong are legible to every reader: to pursue them requires not the aid of many counsellors. The whole art of government consists in the art of being honest. Only aim to do your duty, and mankind will give you credit where you fail. No longer persevere in sacrificing the rights of one part of the empire to the inordinate desires of another: but deal out to all equal and impartial right.... This, Sire, is the advice of your great American council, on the observance of which may perhaps depend your felicity and future fame, and the preservation of that harmony which alone can continue both to Great Britain and America the reciprocal advantages of their connection. It is neither our wish nor our interest to separate from her. We are willing on our part to sacrifice every thing which reason can ask to the restoration of that tranquility for which all must wish. On their part let them be ready to establish union on a generous plan.

King George III

The State House in Philadelphia, after a drawing by C. W. Peale

Let them name their terms, but let them be just. Accept of every commercial preference it is in our power to give for such things as we can raise for their use, or they make for ours. But let them not think to exclude us from going to other markets, to dispose of those commodities which they cannot use, nor to supply those wants which they cannot supply. Still less let it be proposed that our properties within our own territories shall be taxed or regulated by any power on earth but our own. The god who gave us life, gave us liberty at the same time: the land of force may destroy, but cannot disjoin them. This, Sire, is our last, our determined resolution: and that you will be pleased to interpose with that efficacy which your earnest endeavors may insure to procure redress of these our great grievances, to quiet the minds of your subjects in British America against any apprehensions of future incroachment, to establish fraternal love and harmony thro' the whole empire, and that that may continue to the latest ages of time, is the fervent prayer of all British America.

The First Continental Congress did adopt a petition to the King, but it went on to employ more practical measures of protest: an association to be signed as a pledge to bar the importation of British goods. Economic boycotts had proved successful in the past, and Americans hoped for some good effect. Jefferson, who had ordered window glass from a London merchant in the summer of 1774, hastened to abide by the new agreement. On December 9 he wrote to the enforcement committees in counties along the James River where he expected his goods to arrive.

Monticello Dec. 9. 1774.

In order therefore that no proceedings of mine might give a handle for traducing our measures I thought it better previously to lay before your committee... a full state of the matter by which it might be seen under what expectations I had failed to give an earlier countermand and to shew that as they come within the prohibitions of the Continental Association (which without the spirit of prophecy could not have been foretold when I ordered them) so I mean they shall be subject to it's condemnation. To your committee therefore if landed within their county I submit the disposal of them, which shall be obeyed as soon as made known to their and your most humble servt.

In the spring of 1775, Jefferson was called on to sacrifice more than a few panes of glass for the American cause. As directed by the First Continental Congress at its adjournment in October, 1774, a second congress was to convene the following May, and Jefferson joined the Virginia delegation in June, replacing Peyton Randolph. A month before leaving for Philadelphia, Jefferson learned of the skirmishes at Lexington and Concord. As he began a letter to Dr. William Small, who had returned to England, he at first confined himself to the details of a shipment of Madeira he had sent his former teacher; but he soon spoke of the disturbing news from Massachusetts.

Virginia May 7. 1775.

Within this week we have received the unhappy news of an action of considerable magnitude between the king's troops and our brethren of Boston, in which it is said 500. of the former with Earl Piercy [Percy] are slain. That such an action has happened is undoubted, tho' perhaps the circumstances may not yet have reached us with truth. This accident has cut off our last hopes of reconciliation, and a phrenzy of revenge seems to have seized all ranks of people. It is a lamentable circumstance that the only mediatory power acknoleged by both parties, instead of leading to a reconciliation his divided people, should pursue the incendiary purpose of still blowing up the flames as we find him constantly doing in every speech and public declaration. This may perhaps be intended to intimidate into acquiescence, but the effect has been most unfortunately otherwise. A little knolege of human nature and attention to it's ordinary workings might have foreseen that the spirits of the people here were in a state in which they were more likely to be provoked than frightened by haughty deportment. And, to fill up the measure of irritation, proscription of individuals has been substituted in the room of just trial. Can it be believed that a grateful people will suffer those to be consigned to execution whose sole crime has been the developing and asserting their rights? Had the parliament possessed the liberty of reflection they would have avoided a measure as impotent as it was inflammatory. When I saw Lord Chatham's bill [a plan for imperial union presented in the House of Lords] I entertained high hope that a reconciliation could have been brought about. The difference between his terms and those offered by our congress might have been accomodated if entered on by both parties with a disposi-

A pencil sketch by Du Simitière, though identified as Jefferson in 1775, is more likely an anonymous British or colonial officer.

tion to accomodate. But the dignity of parliament it seems can brook no opposition to it's power. Strange that a set of men who have made sale of their virtue to the minister should yet talk of retaining dignity!—But I am getting into politics tho' I sat down only to ask your acceptance of the wine, and express my constant wishes for your happiness. This however seems secured by your philosophy and peaceful vocation. I shall still hope that amidst public dissension private friendship may be preserved inviolate, and among the warmest you can ever possess is that of Your obliged humble servt.,

TH. JEFFERSON

Unknown to Jefferson, Small had died some months before: the kindly scholar never learned of the war that split Virginia from Britain or the part his pupil played in the conflict. That role became more important on June 21, 1775, when Jefferson took his seat in the Second Continental Congress. At thirty-two he was one of the youngest members; only John Jay of New York was his junior. Unlike Jay, a veteran of the first congress, Jefferson was a stranger to most of the delegates at Philadelphia. With few skills as an orator he might have had to wait for recognition, but his reputation as a writer had spread quickly. John Adams's recollections of Jefferson as a congressman indicate that it was just as well that Jefferson chose to stay in the background.

Autobiography, 1802-7

Mr. Jefferson had been now about a Year a Member of Congress, but had attended his Duty in the House but a very small part of the time and when there had never spoken in public: and during the whole Time I satt with him in Congress, I never heard him utter three Sentences together. The most of a Speech he ever made in my hearing was a gross insult on Religion, in one or two Sentences, for which I gave him immediately the Reprehension, which he richly merited.

Despite his unorthodox views on religion, Jefferson made a good friend in Adams who confessed that the young Virginian "soon seized upon my heart." A few days after his arrival, Jefferson was added to the important committee charged with preparing a declaration to be issued by General George Washington, the new Commander in Chief of the Continental Army, at camp in Boston. Jefferson recalled the fate of the draft declaration he prepared.

John Dickinson in an engraving after a drawing by Du Simitière

Autobiography, 1821

I prepared a draught of the Declaration committed to us. It was too strong for Mr. [John] Dickinson. He still retained the hope of reconciliation with the mother country, and was unwilling it should be lessened by offensive statements. He was so honest a man, & so able a one that he was greatly indulged even by those who could not feel his scruples. We therefore requested him to take the paper, and put it into a form he could approve. He did so, preparing an entire new statement, and preserving of the former only the last 4. paragraphs & half of the preceding one. We approved & reported it to Congress, who accepted it.

John Dickinson revised the Declaration of the Causes and Necessity for Taking Up Arms, but retained many of Jefferson's fiery phrases. He did not, despite what Jefferson wrote, just add on his last few paragraphs. Like Jefferson in *A Summary View*, he catalogued the unjust acts of the Crown and ministry and the patient response of the Americans in the past. The Declaration, as revised by Dickinson with Jefferson's phrases in italics, continued in this vein.

Declaration of the Causes and Necessity for Taking Up Arms, July 6, 1775

But why should we enumerate our Injuries in detail?...

...[An] Administration sensible that we should regard these oppressive Measures as Freemen ought to do, sent over Fleets and Armies to enforce them. The Indignation of the Americans was roused, it is true; but it was the Indignation of a virtuous, loyal, and affectionate People. A Congress of Delegates from the United Colonies was assembled at Philadelphia, on the fifth Day of last September. We resolved again to offer an humble and dutiful Petition to the King, and also addressed our Fellow Subjects of Great-Britain. *We have pursued every temperate, every respectful Measure; we have even proceeded to break off our commercial Intercourse with our Fellow Subjects, as the last peaceable Admonition, that our Attachment to no Nation upon Earth should supplant our Attachment to Liberty. This, we flattered ourselves, was the ultimate Step of the Controversy: But subsequent Events have shewn, how vain was this Hope of finding Moderation in our Enemies.*

Several threatening Expressions against the Colonies

THE FOUNDING FATHERS

were inserted in His Majesty's Speech; our Petition, tho' we were told it was a Decent one, and that his Majesty had been pleased to receive it graciously, and to promise laying it before his Parliament, was huddled into both Houses among a Bundle of American Papers, and there neglected. The Lords and Commons in their Address, in the Month of February, said, that "a Rebellion at that Time actually existed within the Province of Massachusetts-Bay.... Soon after, the commercial Intercourse of whole Colonies, with foreign Countries, and with each other, was cut off by an Act of Parliament; by another, several of them were intirely prohibited from the Fisheries in the Seas near their Coasts, on which they always depended for their Sustenance; and large Re-inforcements of Ships and Troops were immediately sent over to General Gage.

Fruitless were all the entreaties, arguments, and eloquence of an Illustrious Band of the most distinguished Peers, and Commoners, who nobly and strenuously asserted the Justice of our Cause, to stay, or even to mitigate the heedless fury with which these accumulated and unexampled Outrages were hurried on. Equally fruitless was the interference of the City of London, of Bristol, and many other respectable Towns in our Favour. Parliament adopted an insidious Manoeuvre calculated to divide us, to establish a perpetual Auction of Taxations where Colony should bid against Colony, all of them uninformed what Ransom would redeem their Lives; and thus to extort from us, at the point of the Bayonet, the unknown sums that should be sufficient to gratify, if possible to gratify, ministerial Rapacity, with the miserable indulgence left to us of raising, in our own Mode, the prescribed Tribute. What Terms more rigid and humiliating could have been dictated by remorseless Victors to conquered Enemies? In our circumstances to accept them, would be to deserve them.

Soon after the Intelligence of these proceedings arrived on this Continent, General Gage, who in the course of the last Year had taken Possession of the Town of Boston, in the Province of Massachusetts-Bay, and still occupied it as a Garrison, on the 19th day of April, sent out from that Place a large detachment of his Army, who made an unprovoked Assault on the Inhabitants of the said Province, at the Town of Lexington, as appears by

LIBRARY OF CONGRESS

A view of the green in Lexington, where British troops first clashed with Americans in April, 1775

A French engraving by F. Godefroy of the infamous day at Lexington

the Affidavits of a great Number of Persons, some of whom were Officers and Soldiers of that detachment, murdered eight of the Inhabitants, and wounded many others. From thence the Troops proceeded in warlike Array to the Town of Concord, where they set upon another Party of the Inhabitants of the same Province, killing several and wounding more, until compelled to retreat by the country People suddenly assembled to repel this cruel Aggression. Hostilities, thus commenced by the British Troops, have been since prosecuted by them without regard to Faith or Reputation. . . .

The General, further emulating his ministerial Masters, by a Proclamation bearing date on the 12th day of June, after venting the grossest Falsehoods and Calumnies against the good People of these Colonies, proceeds to "declare them all, either by Name or Description, to be Rebels and Traitors, to supersede the course of the Common Law, and instead thereof to publish and order the use and exercise of the Law Martial." His Troops have butchered our Countrymen, have wantonly burnt Charlestown, besides a considerable number of Houses in other Places; our Ships and Vessels are seized; the necessary supplies of Provisions are intercepted, and he is exerting his utmost Power to spread destruction and devastation around him. . . .

. . . We are reduced to the alternative of chusing an unconditional Submission to the tyranny of irritated Ministers, or resistance by Force. The latter is our choice. We have counted the cost of this contest, and find nothing so dreadful as voluntary Slavery. Honour, Justice, and Humanity, forbid us tamely to surrender that Freedom which we received from our gallant Ancestors, and which our innocent Posterity have a right to receive from us. We cannot endure the infamy and guilt of resigning succeeding Generations to that wretchedness which inevitably awaits them, if we basely entail hereditary Bondage upon them.

Our cause is just. Our union is perfect. Our internal Resources are great, and, if necessary, foreign Assistance is undoubtedly attainable. We gratefully acknowledge, as signal Instances of the Divine Favour towards us, that his Providence would permit us to be called into this severe Controversy, until we were grown up to our present strength, had been previously exercised in war-

Washington had assumed command of the army on July 3, an event depicted in this stylized woodcut.

like Operation, and possessed of the means of defending ourselves. With hearts fortified with these animating Reflections, *we most solemnly, before God and the World, declare, that, exerting the utmost Energy of those Powers, which our beneficent Creator hath graciously bestowed upon us, the Arms we have been compelled by our Enemies to assume, we will, in defiance of every Hazard, with unabating Firmness and Perseverence, employ for the preservation of our Liberties;* being with one Mind resolved to die Freemen rather than to live Slaves.

Lest this Declaration should disquiet the Minds of our Friends and Fellow-Subjects in any part of the Empire, we assure them that we mean not to dissolve that Union which has so long and so happily subsisted between us, and which we sincerely wish to see restored. Necessity has not yet driven us into that desperate Measure, or induced us to excite any other Nation to War against them. We have not raised Armies with ambitious Designs of separating from Great-Britain, and establishing Independent States. *We fight not for Glory or for Conquest. We exhibit to Mankind the remarkable Spectacle of a People attacked by unprovoked Enemies, without any imputation or even suspicion of Offence.* They boast of their Privileges and Civilization, and yet proffer no milder Conditions than Servitude or Death.

In our own native Land, in defence of the Freedom that is our Birthright, and which we ever enjoyed till the late Violation of it—for the protection of our Property, acquired solely by the honest Industry of our fore-fathers and ourselves, *against Violence actually offered, we have taken up Arms. We shall lay them down when Hostilities shall cease on the part of the Aggressors, and all danger of their being renewed shall be removed, and not before.*

With an humble Confidence in the Mercies of the supreme and impartial Judge and Ruler of the Universe, *we most devoutly implore his Divine Goodness to protect us happily through this great Conflict, to dispose our Adversaries to reconciliation on reasonable Terms, and thereby to relieve the Empire from the Calamities of civil War.*

Jefferson may have felt a literary artist's sensitivity to criticism when his draft declaration was rewritten. Certainly he did not care for Dickinson's cautious ways. Two days after the adoption of the Declaration on July 6, Dickinson's draft of a second petition to the King, the Olive Branch Petition, was approved by Congress. Jefferson happily recalled Benjamin Harrison's tart comment on the Pennsylvania conservative's handiwork.

Autobiography, 1821

Congress gave a signal proof of their indulgence to Mr. Dickinson, and of their great desire not to go too fast for any respectable part of our body, in permitting him to draw their second petition to the King according to his own ideas, and passing it with scarcely any amendment. The disgust against it's humility was general; and Mr. Dickinson's delight at its passage was the only circumstance which reconciled them to it. The vote being past, altho' further observn on it was out of order, he could not refrain from rising and expressing his satisfaction and concluded by saying 'there is but one word, Mr. President, in the paper which I disapprove, & that is the word *Congress*,' on which Ben Harrison rose and said 'there is but one word in the paper, Mr. President, of which I approve, and that is the word *Congress*.'

When Congress recessed in early August, Jefferson returned to Virginia with a clearer vision of his and America's future. His work with other leaders from the Colonies had given him a chance to exchange ideas with stimulating men and had helped him refine his own views. Still, he had not abandoned hope for reconciliation. Shortly after arriving at Monticello, Jefferson—in an attempt to influence British opinion more directly—wrote to his kinsman John Randolph, a Loyalist who had fled from Virginia to England.

Monticello. Aug. 25. 1775

I am sorry the situation of our country should render it not eligible to you to remain longer in it. I hope the returning wisdom of Great Britain will e'er long put an end to this unnatural contest. There may be people to whose tempers and dispositions Contention may be pleasing, and who may therefore wish a continuance of confusion. But to me it is of all states, but one, the most horrid. My first wish is a restoration of our just rights; my second a return of the happy period when, consistently with duty, I may withdraw myself totally from the public stage and pass the rest of my days in domestic ease and tranquillity, banishing every desire of afterwards even hearing what passes in the world. Perhaps ardour for the latter may add considerably to the warmth of the former wish. Looking with fondness towards a reconciliation with Great Britain, I cannot help hoping you may be able to contribute towards expediting this good work. I think it must be evident to yourself that the ministry have been deceived by their officers on this side the water, who (for what purposes I cannot tell) have constantly represented the American opposition as that of a small faction, in which the body of the people took little part. This you can inform them of your own knolege to be untrue. They have taken it into their heads too that we are cowards and shall surrender at discretion to an armed force. The past and future operations of the war must confirm or undeceive them on that head. I wish they were thoroughly and minutely acquainted with every circumstance relative to America as it exists in truth. I am persuaded this would go far towards disposing them to reconciliation. Even those in parliament who are called friends to America seem to know nothing of our real determinations. I observe they pronounced in the last parliament that the Congress of 1774 did not mean to insist rigorously on the terms they held out, but kept something in reserve to give up; and in fact that they would give up everything but the article of taxation. Now the truth is far from this, as I can affirm, and put my honor to the assertion; and their continuance in this error may perhaps have very ill consequences. The Congress stated the lowest terms they thought possible to be accepted in order to convince the world they were not unreasonable. They gave up the monopoly and regulation of trade, and all the acts of parliament prior to 1764. leaving to British generosity to render these at some future time as easy to America as the interest of Britain would admit. But this was before blood was spilt. I cannot affirm, but have reason to think, these terms would not now be accepted. I wish no false sense of honor, no ignorance of our real intentions, no vain hope that partial concessions of right will be accepted may induce the ministry to trifle with accomodation till it shall be put even out of our own power to accomodate. If indeed Great Britain, disjoined from her colonies, be a match for the most potent nations of Europe with the colonies thrown into their scale, they may go on securely. But if they are not assured of this, it would be certainly unwise, by trying the event of another campaign, to risque our accepting a foreign aid which perhaps may not be obtainable but on a condition of everlasting avulsion from Great Britain. This would be thought a hard condition to those who still wish for reunion with their parent country. I am sincerely one of those, and would rather be in dependance of Great Britain, properly limited, than on any nation upon earth, or than on no nation. But I am one of those too who rather than submit to the right of legislating for us assumed by the British parliament, and which late experience has shewn they will so cruelly exercise, would lend my hand to sink the whole island in the ocean.

If undeceiving the minister as to matters of fact may change his dispositions, it will perhaps be in your power by assisting to do this, to render service to the whole empire, at the most critical time certainly that it has ever seen. Whether Britain shall continue the head of the greatest empire on earth, or shall return to her original station in the political scale of Europe depends perhaps on the resolutions of the succeeding winter. God send they may be wise and salutary for us all!

But by the time of Jefferson's return to Congress in late September, it was clear that Parliament's resolutions would not lead to peace. Armed resistance to the Crown had broken out in Virginia; Congress had sent out a military expedition to win over Canada. When Jefferson wrote John Randolph in November his tone was far more bitter, and he launched a merciless attack on the "sceptered tyrant" he had once acknowledged as his sovereign.

Philadelphia Nov. 29. 1775.
You will have heard before this reaches you that Ld. Dunmore has commenced hostilities in Virginia. That people bore with every thing till he attempted to burn the town of Hampton. They opposed and repelled him with considerable loss on his side and none on ours. It has raised our country into perfect phrensy. It is an immense misfortune to the whole empire to have a king of such a disposition at such a time. We are told and every thing proves it true that he is the bitterest enemy we have. His minister is able, and that satisfies me that ignorance or wickedness somewhere controuls him. In an earlier part of this contest our petitions told him that

from our king there was but one appeal. The admonition was despised and that appeal forced on us. To undo his empire he has but one truth more to learn, that after colonies have drawn the sword there is but one step more they can take. That step is now pressed upon us by the measures adopted as if they were afraid we would not take it. Beleive me Dear Sir there is not in the British empire a man who more cordially loves a Union with Gr. Britain than I do. But by the god that made me I will cease to exist before I yeild to a connection on such terms as the British parliament propose and in this I think I speak the sentiments of America. We want neither inducement nor power to declare and assert a separation. It is will alone which is wanting and that is growing apace under the fostering hand of our king. One bloody campaign will probably decide everlastingly our future course; I am sorry to find a bloody campaign is decided on. If our winds and waters should not combine to rescue their shores from slavery, and General Howe's reinforcement should arrive in safety we have hopes he will be inspirited to come out of Boston and take another drubbing: and we must drub you soundly before the sceptered tyrant will know we are not mere brutes, to crouch under his hand and kiss the rod with which he deigns to scourge us.

Jefferson's notes on proceedings in the Congress on June 7, 1776, the day Virginia's call for a declaration of independence was moved

A month later Jefferson left Philadelphia to spend the winter at Monticello with Martha and their three-year-old daughter Martha, called Patsy. He found little peace at home. Dunmore had fled the province and now directed naval and military operations against Virginia; Norfolk was burned by Dunmore's forces on New Year's Day and slaves were urged to revolt and join the Crown's forces. Jefferson's mother died at the end of March and his own health was poor.

When he rejoined Congress in early May, he found that independence was no longer a theory to be discussed at leisure. In most colonies royal government had disintegrated as Crown officials prudently withdrew. Provision had to be made for self-government or anarchy would follow. On May 15, the day after Jefferson reached Philadelphia, Congress passed a resolution calling on the colonies to establish new forms of government. But this was not enough. In April John Page had written Jefferson: "For God's sake declare the Colonies independant at once, and save us from ruin." A resolution of the Virginia Convention in May opened the way for debate. Jefferson recorded his delegation's role in Congress on June 7.

THOMAS JEFFERSON

Notes of Proceedings in the
Continental Congress, 1776

Historical Collections of Virginia, BY HENRY HOWE, 1856

A view of Norfolk, which was burned by the British in January, 1776

Friday June 7. 1776. the Delegates from Virginia moved in obedience to instructions from their constituents that the Congress should declare that these United colonies are & of right ought to be free & independant states, that they are absolved from all allegiance to the British crown, and that all political connection between them and the state of Great Britain is & ought to be totally dissolved; that measures should be immediately taken for procuring the assistance of foreign powers, and a Confederation be formed to bind the colonies more closely together.

The house being obliged to attend at that time to some other business the propostition was referred to the next day....

When debate resumed, a sectional division was apparent. Richard Henry Lee, George Wythe, and John Adams pressed for adoption of the resolutions; James Wilson and John Dickinson of Pennsylvania, Robert R. Livingston of New York, and Edward Rutledge of South Carolina argued for caution. The Middle Colonies and South Carolina stood against New England, Virginia, and Georgia in the debates that lasted until Monday, June 10. Congress then hit on a compromise that would win time for public opinion to fall behind independence: a decision on the resolutions themselves would be postponed until July 1, but in the meantime a committee was to draft a declaration of the reasons "which impelled us to this mighty resolution." Jefferson, Adams, Livingston, Benjamin Franklin, and Roger Sherman were appointed to the committee June 11, and the task of actually drafting the declaration fell to Jefferson. In the following seventeen days, Jefferson worked at a desk in his parlor in Graaf's boardinghouse. In years to come, he insisted that his was not a particularly original composition, that the truths he recited were so self-evident that he was merely a reporter rather than a formulator of any new doctrine. He repeated this view in a letter to Henry Lee in 1825.

Jefferson's writing desk
CULVER PICTURES, INC.

Monticello May 8. 1825.
But with respect to our rights, and the acts of the British government contravening those rights, there was but one opinion on this side of the water. All American Whigs thought alike on these subjects.... Not to find out new principles, or new arguments, never before thought of, not merely to say things which had never been said before; but to place before mankind the common sense of

63

The Historic Mansions and Buildings of Philadelphia
BY THOMPSON WESTCOTT, 1877; YALE UNIVERSITY LIBRARY

Jacob Graff's boardinghouse

the subject, [in] terms so plain and firm as to command their assent, and to justify ourselves in the independant stand we [were] compelled to take. Neither aiming at originality of principle or sentiment, nor yet copied from any particular and previous writing, it was intended to be an expression of the American mind, and to give to that expression the proper tone and spirit called for by the occasion. All it's authority rests then on the harmonizing sentiments of the day, whether expressed in conversation, in letters, printed essays or in the elementary books of public right, as Aristotle, Cicero, Locke, Sidney, &c.

Not until July 2 was the question of independence finally met. The original resolution presented by Richard Henry Lee was adopted, and Congress then considered Jefferson's draft declaration itself, which had received some minor revisions in committee. Jefferson recorded his reactions as the delegates debated the declaration for the next three days.

THOMAS JEFFERSON

Committee of Franklin, Jefferson, Adams, Livingston, and Sherman consulting on the Declaration

VIRGINIA HISTORICAL SOCIETY

Notes of Proceedings in the
Continental Congress, 1776

Congress proceeded the same day to consider the declaration of Independance.... the pusillanimous idea that we had friends in England worth keeping terms with, still haunted the minds of many. for this reason those passages which conveyed censures on the people of England were struck out, lest they should give them offence. the clause too, reprobating the enslaving the inhabitants of Africa, was struck out in complaisance to South Carolina & Georgia, who had never attempted to restrain the importation of slaves, and who on the contrary still wished to continue it. our Northern brethren also I believe felt a little tender under those censures; for tho' their people have very few slaves themselves yet they had pretty considerable carriers of them to others. the debates having taken up the greater parts of the 2d. 3d. & 4th. days of July were, in the evening of the last closed. The declaration was reported by the commee., agreed to by the house, and signed by every member present except Mr. Dickinson.

John Adams steadfastly defended every word of the draft in floor debate, while Jefferson—as the inevitable alterations were made—sat by listening to Franklin's anecdotes.

Monticello Dec. 4. [18]18.

Page two of Jefferson's four-page draft of the Declaration; marginal notes identify alterations made by John Adams and Benjamin Franklin.

When the Declaration of Independence was under the consideration of Congress, there were two or three unlucky expressions in it which gave offence to some members.... Altho' the offensive expressions were immediately yielded, these gentlemen continued their depredations on other parts of the instrument. I was sitting by Dr. Franklin who "percieved" that I was not insensible to these mutilations. 'I have made it a rule, said he, whenever in my power, to avoid becoming the draughtsman of papers to be reviewed by a public body. I took my lesson from an incident which I will relate to you. When I was a journeyman printer, one of my companions, an apprentice Hatter, having served out his time, was about to open shop for himself. His first concern was to have a handsome sign-board, with a proper inscription. He composed it in these words 'John Thompson, *Hatter, makes* and *sells hats for*

```
      RARE BOOK DIVISION, N.Y. PUBLIC LIBRARY
  ╔══════════════════════════════╗
  ║        THIRTEEN              ║
  ║   UNITED COLONIES.           ║
  ║   ─────────────              ║
  ║                              ║
  ║ United, we stand---Divided, we fall. ║
  ╚══════════════════════════════╝
```

In May, Alexander Purdie's Virginia Gazette *had replaced its ancient seal of the colony with the new, simple logo shown above.*

ready money,' with a figure of a hat subjoined. But he thought he would submit it to his friends for their amendments. The first he shewed it to thought the word 'Hatter' tautologous, because followed by the words 'makes hats' which shew he was a Hatter. It was struck out. The next observed that the word *'makes'* might as well be omitted, because his customers would not care who made the hats. If good & to their mind, they would buy, by whomsoever made. He struck it out. A third said he thought the words *'for ready money,'* were useless as it was not the custom of the place to sell on credit. Every one who purchased expected to pay. They were parted with, and the inscription now stood 'John Thompson sells hats.' *'sells hats'* says his next friend? 'Why nobody will expect you to give them away. What then is the use of that word?' It was stricken out, and *'hats'* followed it, the rather, as there was one painted on the board. So his inscription was reduced ultimately to 'John Thompson' with the figure of a hat subjoined.

Of the deletions Congress made in Jefferson's draft one, which involved several passages in a long indictment of George III, probably improved the document; but Congress also left out several phrases that might well have been preserved, such as "we must endeavor to forget our former love for them...." and "we might have been a free & a great people together; but a communication of grandeur & of freedom it seems is below their dignity." Jefferson would certainly have preferred to omit the final appeal to Divine Providence. Despite these minor revisions, the basic nobility of his Declaration remained, and it is still one of the most influential political documents of modern times. He had turned philosophic principles into self-evident truths coupled with impassioned pleas for justice similar to those he had presented in the *Summary View* and in his draft of the Declaration of Causes. Finally on July 4 twelve states (New York abstaining) agreed to the amended Declaration, and it was printed that night.

In Congress, July 4, 1776.
A DECLARATION
By the Representatives of the
United States of America
In General Congress Assembled

When in the Course of human events, it becomes necessary for one people to dissolve the political bands which have connected them with another, and to assume

When John Trumbull began a painting of the Declaration's presentation by the Committee of Five, Jefferson drew this floor plan to show him the layout of the room in the State House.

among the powers of the earth, the separate and equal station to which the Laws of Nature and of Nature's God entitle them, a decent respect to the opinions of mankind requires that they should declare the causes which impel them to the separation. We hold these truths to be self-evident, that all men are created equal, that they are endowed by their Creator with certain unalienable Rights, that among these are Life, Liberty and the pursuit of Happiness. That to secure these rights, Governments are instituted among Men, deriving their just powers from the consent of the governed, That whenever any Form of Government becomes destructive of these ends, it is the Right of the People to alter or to abolish it, and to institute new Government, laying its foundation on such principles and organizing its powers in such form, as to them shall seem most likely to effect their Safety and Happiness. Prudence, indeed, will dictate that Governments long established should not be changed for light and transient causes; and accordingly all experience hath shewn, that mankind are more disposed to suffer, while evils are sufferable, than to right themselves by abolishing the forms to which they are accustomed. But when a long train of abuses and usurpations, pursuing invariably the same Object evinces a design to reduce them under absolute Despotism, it is their right, it is their duty, to throw off such Government, and to provide new Guards for their future security. Such has been the patient sufferance of these Colonies; and such is now the necessity which constrains them to alter their former Systems of Government. The history of the present King of Great Britain is a history of repeated injuries and usurpations, all having in direct object the establishment of an absolute Tyranny over these States. To prove this, let Facts be submitted to a candid world. He has refused his Assent to Laws, the most wholesome and necessary for the public good. He has forbidden his Governors to pass Laws of immediate and pressing importance, unless suspended in their operation till his Assent should be obtained; and when so suspended, he has utterly neglected to attend to them. He has refused to pass other Laws for the accommodation of large districts of people, unless those people would relinquish the right of Representation in the Legislature, a right inestimable to them and formidable to tyrants only. He has called to-

Trumbull's pencil sketch, made in 1786, of his original idea for a depiction of the presentation

gether legislative bodies at places unusual, uncomfortable, and distant from the depository of their public Records, for the sole purpose of fatiguing them into compliance with his measures. He has dissolved Representative Houses repeatedly, for opposing with manly firmness his invasions on the rights of the people. He has refused for a long time, after such dissolutions, to cause others to be elected; whereby the Legislative powers, incapable of Annihilation, have returned to the People at large for their exercise; the State remaining in the mean time exposed to all the dangers of invasion from without, and convulsions within. He has endeavoured to prevent the population of these States; for that purpose obstructing the Laws for Naturalization of Foreigners; refusing to pass others to encourage their migrations hither, and raising the conditions of new Appropriations of Lands. He has obstructed the Administration of Justice, by refusing his Assent to Laws for establishing Judiciary powers. He has made Judges dependent on his Will alone, for the tenure of their offices, and the amount and payment of their salaries. He has erected a multitude of New Offices, and sent hither swarms of Officers to harrass our people, and eat out their substance. He has kept among us, in times of peace, standing Armies without the Consent of our legislatures. He has affected to render the Military independent of and superior to the Civil power. He has combined with others to subject us to a jurisdiction foreign to our constitution, and unacknowledged by our laws; giving his Assent to their Acts of pretended Legislation: For Quartering large bodies of armed troops among us: For protecting them, by a mock Trial, from punishment for any Murders which they should commit on the Inhabitants of these States: For cutting off our Trade with all parts of the world: For imposing Taxes on us without our Consent: For depriving us in many cases of the benefits of Trial by Jury: For transporting us beyond Seas to be tried for pretended offences: For abolishing the free System of English Laws in a neighbouring Province, establishing therein an Arbitrary government, and enlarging its Boundaries so as to render it at once an example and fit instrument for introducing the same absolute rule into these Colonies: For taking away our Charters, abolishing our most valuable Laws, and altering fundamentally the Forms of our

Final version of Trumbull's The Declaration of Independence, *which was completed in 1797 in London*

BY JOHN TRUMBULL, 1797; YALE UNIVERSITY ART GALLERY

Governments: For suspending our own Legislatures, and declaring themselves invested with power to legislate for us in all cases whatsoever. He has abdicated Government here, by declaring us out of his Protection and waging War against us. He has plundered our seas, ravaged our Coasts, burnt our towns, and destroyed the Lives of our people. He is at this time transporting large Armies of foreign Mercenaries to compleat the works of death, desolation and tyranny, already begun with circumstances of Cruelty & perfidy scarcely paralleled in the most barbarous ages, and totally unworthy the Head of a civilized nation. He has constrained our fellow Citizens taken Captive on the high Seas to bear Arms against their Country, to become the executioners of their friends and Brethren, or to fall themselves by their Hands. He has excited domestic insurrections amongst us, and has endeavoured to bring on the inhabitants of our frontiers, the merciless Indian Savages, whose known rule of warfare, is an undistinguished destruction of all ages, sexes and conditions. In every stage of these Oppressions We

BEINECKE RARE BOOK AND MANUSCRIPT LIBRARY, YALE UNIVERSITY

**PROPOSALS
BY JOHN TRUMBULL,**
FOR
PUBLISHING BY SUBSCRIPTION
A PRINT
FROM THE ORIGINAL PICTURE, PAINTED BY HIM,
BY ORDER OF THE GOVERNMENT OF THE UNITED STATES, AND
TO BE PLACED IN THE CAPITOL,
REPRESENTING THE
DECLARATION OF INDEPENDENCE,
AND CONTAINING
PORTRAITS
OF MOST OF THE MEMBERS PRESENT IN CONGRESS,
ON THAT MEMORABLE OCCASION.

Trumbull's proposals for raising funds to install a print of his famous painting in the Rotunda of the Capitol, which was done in 1824; subscribers of twenty dollars were to receive copies of the print.

have Petitioned for Redress in the most humble terms: Our repeated Petitions have been answered only by repeated injury. A Prince, whose character is thus marked by every act which may define a Tyrant, is unfit to be the ruler of a free people. Nor have We been wanting in attentions to our Brittish brethren. We have warned them from time to time of attempts by their legislature to extend an unwarrantable jurisdiction over us. We have reminded them of the circumstances of our emigration and settlement here. We have appealed to their native justice and magnanimity, and we have conjured them by the ties of our common kindred to disavow these usurpations, which, would inevitably interrupt our connections and correspondence. They too have been deaf to the voice of justice and of consanguinity. We must, therefore, acquiesce in the necessity, which denounces our Separation, and hold them, as we hold the rest of mankind, Enemies in War, in Peace Friends.

We, therefore, the Representatives of the united States of America, in General Congress, Assembled, appealing to the Supreme Judge of the world for the rectitude of our intentions, do, in the Name, and by Authority of the good People of these Colonies, solemnly publish and declare, That these United Colonies are, and of Right ought to be Free and Independent States; that they are Absolved from all Allegiance to the British Crown, and that all political connection between them and the State of Great Britain, is and ought to be totally dissolved; and that as Free and Independent States, they have full Power to levy War, conclude Peace, contract Alliances, establish Commerce, and to do all other Acts and Things which Independent States may of right do. And for the support of this Declaration, with a firm reliance on the protection of divine Providence, we mutually pledge to each other our Lives, our Fortunes and our sacred Honor.

T he official text of the Declaration was printed and circulated among the Thirteen Colonies and read to a crowd in the State House yard in Philadelphia on July 8. New York's delegates received instructions allowing them to give their assent a week later, and an elaborately engrossed parchment copy was prepared by Timothy Matlack. When it arrived on August 2 those members present added their signatures. Not until November had all those who voted for independence attended and signed their names, which were not made public until January, 1777.

Even though Jefferson remained in Congress until September, serving on several important committees, his attention wandered more and more to his home province. Only two days after his return to Philadelphia in May, he had written to Thomas Nelson in Williamsburg.

Philadelphia May. 16. 1776

Should our Convention propose to establish now a form of government perhaps it might be agreeable to recall for a short time their delegates. It is a work of the most interesting nature and such as every individual would wish to have his voice in. In truth it is the whole object of the present controversy; for should a bad government be instituted for us in future it had been as well to have accepted at first the bad one offered to us from beyond the water without the risk and expence of contest. But this I mention to you in confidence, as in our situation, a hint to any other is too delicate however anxiously interesting the subject is to our feelings....

P.S. In the other colonies who have instituted government they recalled their delegates leaving only one or two to give information to Congress of matters which might relate to their country particularly, and giving them a vote during the interval of absence.

Tradition has it that a few days after the Declaration's adoption Jefferson and others had a private celebration in this garden house in nearby Frankford, Pennsylvania.

Throughout the spring and summer, Jefferson urged his friends to call him back in time to work in the Virginia Convention. The challenge of creating a state government was tantalizing; indeed, Jefferson had found another lifelong preoccupation. He drafted a constitution himself and sent it to Williamsburg with George Wythe in June, but it arrived too late in the convention's sessions to be considered as a whole and it was drawn on only for amendments to the version George Mason presented. If he could have no part in drawing the plan for Virginia's government, Jefferson was nevertheless determined to return home to correct the faults of the newly adopted constitution and to see Virginia launched safely in statehood. He was reelected to Congress but resigned. Reports that his wife was ill prompted him to write Richard Henry Lee, who was to succeed him in Philadelphia: "For God's sake, for your country's sake, and for my sake, come." At last, on September 3, he was able to return to Virginia, a new state with a new, untested frame of government.

Chapter 3

Virginia Reformer

A month after Jefferson's return to Virginia in September, 1776, he was offered a diplomatic appointment by the Continental Congress. Officially he declined this post in Paris because of "circumstances very peculiar in the situation of my family." Certainly his concern for his wife's health was enough to keep him in Virginia, but he confided in his *Autobiography*, "I saw too, that the laboring oar was really at home." The work of transforming Virginia from a colony into a state had begun with the new constitution. Although there seemed to be no marked differences between the political framework suggested by Jefferson and that adopted by the convention on June 29, his version had provided broader citizen participation in government. His property qualifications for voting were so low that they would have resulted in something very close to universal suffrage for white males. In addition, his draft emphasized freedom from maintaining religious establishments, more independence and appointive power for the executive, and a greater portion of legislative control to the more representative lower house of the assembly. Jefferson objected to the fact that the constitution had not been referred to the electorate for approval. He viewed the Declaration of Rights adopted before the constitution, however, as a proper philosophical basis for a government that valued individual liberties.

Even if the constitution was more conservative than Jefferson might have wished, there was still much he could do to implement reforms. For the next three years he worked constantly to enact more democratic laws, beginning in October when he took his seat in the House of Delegates, the successor to the House of Burgesses, at Williamsburg. He would look back upon this period in his life with great satisfaction; for, though many of his proposals were defeated and as many others simply ignored, he was able to begin destroying the vestiges of aristocracy and laying the foundations for a free society. In his *Autobiography*, he recorded the background of his first major campaign that fall, a move to abolish entails and primogeniture.

Part of page one from Jefferson's draft of his "first ideas" for a Virginia constitution, June, 1776

Autobiography, 1821

On the 12th. [of October] I obtained leave to bring [in] a bill declaring tenants in tail to hold their lands in fee simple. In the earlier times of the colony when lands were to be obtained for little or nothing, some provident individuals procured large grants, and, desirous of founding great families for themselves, settled them on their descendants in fee-tail. The transmission of this property from generation to generation in the same name raised up a distinct set of families who, being privileged by law in the perpetuation of their wealth were thus formed into a Patrician order, distinguished by the splendor and luxury of their establishments. From this order too the king habitually selected his Counsellors of State, the hope of which distinction devoted the whole corps to the interests & will of the crown. To annul this privilege, and instead of an Aristocracy of wealth, of more harm and danger, than benefit, to society, to make an opening for the aristocracy of virtue and talent, which nature has wisely provided for the direction of the interests of society, & scattered with equal hand through all it's conditions, was deemed essential to a well ordered republic. To effect it no violence was necessary, no deprivation of natural right, but rather an enlargement of it by a repeal of the law. For this would authorise the present holder to divide the property among his children equally, as his affections were divided; and would place them, by natural generation on the level of their fellow citizens.... The repeal of the laws of entail would prevent the accumulation and perpetuation of wealth in select families, and preserve the soil of the country from being daily more & more absorbed in Mortmain. The abolition of primogeniture, and equal partition of inheritances removed the feudal and unnatural distinctions which made one member of every family rich, and all the rest poor, substituting equal partition, the best of all Agrarian laws.

George Rogers Clark sketched this map of western Virginia on the cover of a bill to divide Fincastle County. Jefferson sponsored the bill at the request of settlers of the region; it passed despite the opposition of land speculators.

Edmund Pendleton, Speaker of the House, led the opponents of Jefferson's bill. Unlike Jefferson, Pendleton had not embarked on revolution in order to create a society in which he might lose his traditional position, and he defended the status quo brilliantly. Jefferson admired an able foe and left this account of Pendleton's part in the debates.

Autobiography, 1821
But this repeal was strongly opposed by Mr. Pendleton, who was zealously attached to ancient establishments;

and who, taken all in all, was the ablest man in debate I have ever met with. He had not indeed the poetical fancy of Mr. Henry, his sublime imagination, his lofty and overwhelming diction; but he was cool, smooth and persuasive; his language flowing, chaste & embellished, his conceptions quick, acute and full of resource; never vanquished; for if he lost the main battle, he returned upon you, and regained so much of it as to make it a drawn one, by dexterous maneuvres, skirmishes in detail, and the recovery of small advantages which, little singly, were important all together. You never knew when you were clear of him, but were harrassed by his perseverance until the patience was worn down of all who had less of it than himself.

In the House of Delegates Jefferson was more active as a leader in floor debates than he had been in the Continental Congress. Nevertheless, in Williamsburg, as in Philadelphia, he valued the aid of friends who helped present and support his views. The first of these "coadjutors in debate" was George Mason.

Autobiography, 1821

In giving this account of the laws of which I was myself the mover & draughtsman, I by no means mean to claim to myself the merit of obtaining their passage. I had many occasional and strenuous coadjutors in debate, and one most steadfast, able, and zealous; who was himself a host. This was George Mason, a man of the first order of wisdom among those who acted on the theatre of the revolution, of expansive mind, profound judgment, cogent in argument, learned in the lore of our former constitution, and earnest for the republican change on democratic principles. His elocution was neither flowing nor smooth, but his language was strong, his manner most impressive, and strengthened by a dash of biting cynicism when provocation made it seasonable.

George Wythe was another ally in the House that autumn, one whose "pure integrity, judgment and reasoning powers gave him great weight." He became the Speaker in 1777. Jefferson also found a new associate in twenty-five-year-old James Madison of Orange County. In 1821 Jefferson paid tribute to the man who had been his closest personal friend and his most able political collaborator for nearly half a century.

Autobiography, 1821

Mr. Madison came into the House in 1776. a new member and young; which circumstances, concurring with his extreme modesty, prevented his venturing himself in debate before his removal to the Council of State in Nov. 77. From thence he went to Congress, then consisting of few members. Trained in these successive schools, he acquired a habit of self-possession which placed at ready command the rich resources of his luminous and discriminating mind, & of his extensive information, and rendered him the first of every assembly afterwards of which he became a member. Never wandering from his subject into vain declamation, but pursuing it closely in language pure, classical, and copious, soothing always the feelings of his adversaries by civilities and softness of expression, he rose to the eminent station which he held in the great National convention of 1787. And in that of Virginia which followed, he sustained the new constitution in all it's parts, bearing off the palm against the logic of George Mason and the fervid declamation of Mr. Henry. With these consummate powers were united a pure and spotless virtue which no calumny has ever attempted to sully. Of the powers and polish of his pen, and of the wisdom of his administration in the highest office of the nation, I need say nothing. They have spoken, and will for ever speak for themselves.

Miniature by Charles W. Peale of James Madison, who still looked very young at the age of thirty-two

Passage of the bills to abolish entail and primogeniture was only the beginning of Jefferson's program to legislate an opening for an aristocracy of virtue and talent. The same day he proposed those changes, Jefferson had introduced a bill calling for a revision of Virginia's code of laws; in November he was named to a committee charged with carrying it out. The legislators doubtlessly expected the committee to correct inequities and discard archaic statutes; few shared Jefferson's conviction that the code "should be corrected, in all its parts, with a single eye to reason, and the good of those for whose government it was framed."

The five members of the committee of revisors conferred at Fredericksburg in January, 1777. George Mason and Thomas Ludwell Lee immediately disqualified themselves from the actual drafting of statutes because they were not lawyers. The other three—Jefferson, George Wythe, and Edmund Pendleton—assumed the monumental task of reworking Virginia's entire legal structure. Jefferson's assignment was to review the common law and English statutes passed before 1607. British laws enacted after the founding of Virginia were committed to Wythe; Pendleton undertook the revision of all laws passed in the colony of Virginia itself. The three worked independently until February, 1779. The report they presented in June, which became known as the *Revisal,* drew little immediate attention from the wartime legislators. But the legislature dipped into what Madison called "a mine of Legislative wealth" over the next few years, and by 1786 fifty-six of the original bills, with amendments, had been adopted. Jefferson described the *Revisal's* history in his *Autobiography.*

In the 1777 cartoon above, "Poor old England" was still trying to "reclaim wicked American Children"; that year the committee of revisors began working on its report (below).

Autobiography, 1821

In the execution of my part I thought it material not to vary the diction of the antient statutes by modernizing it, nor to give rise to new questions by new expressions. The text of these statutes had been so fully explained and defined by numerous adjudications, as scarcely ever now to produce a question in our courts. I thought it would be useful also, in all new draughts, to reform the style of the later British statutes, and of our own acts of assembly, which from their verbosity, their endless tautologies, their involutions of case within case, and parenthesis within parenthesis, and their multiplied efforts at certainty by *saids* and *aforesaids,* by *ors* and by *ands,* to make them more plain, do really render them more perplexed and incomprehensible, not only to common readers, but to the lawyers themselves. We were employed in this work from that time to Feb. 1779, when we met at Williamsburg, that is to say, Mr. Pendleton, Mr. Wythe & myself, and meeting day by day, we examined critically our several parts, sentence by sentence, scrutinizing and amending until we had agreed on the whole.... We had in this work brought so much of the Common law as it was thought necessary to alter, all the British statutes from Magna charta to the present day, and all the laws of Virginia, from the establishment of our legislature, in [1607] to the present time, which we thought should be retained, within the compass of 126 bills, making a printed folio of 90 pages only. Some bills were taken out occasionally, from time to time, and past; but the main body of the work was not entered on by the legislature until after the general peace, in 1785. when by the unwearied exertions of Mr. Madison, in opposition to the endless quibbles, chicaneries, perversions, vexations and delays of lawyers and demi-lawyers, most of the bills were passed by the legislature, with little alteration.

Many of the statutes Jefferson revised required little work, merely the deletion of references to the authority of the Crown and the substitution of references to state authority. But legislation in four areas was especially important to him. He hoped to introduce two humanitarian reforms in Virginia: the abolition of slavery and the modernization of the criminal codes. Jefferson had spent his life in a slave-owning society, and in his *Notes on Virginia* he offered a now famous indictment of this way of life and its tragic consequences for both master and slave.

Notes on Virginia, 1782

There must doubtless be an unhappy influence on the manners of our people produced by the existence of slavery among us. The whole commerce between master and slave is a perpetual exercise of the most boisterous passions, the most unremitting despotism on the one part, and degrading submissions on the other. Our children see this, and learn to imitate it; for man is an imitative animal. This quality is the germ of all education in him. From his cradle to his grave he is learning to do what he sees others do. If a parent could find no motive either in his philanthropy or his self-love, for restraining the intemperance of passion towards his slave, it should always be a sufficient one that his child is present. But generally it is not sufficient. The parent storms, the child looks on, catches the lineaments of wrath, puts on the same airs in the circle of smaller slaves, gives a loose to his worst of passions, and thus nursed, educated, and daily exercised in tyranny, cannot but be stamped by it with odious peculiarities. The man must be a prodigy who can retain his manners and morals undepraved by such circumstances. And with what execration should the statesman be loaded, who permitting one half the citizens thus to trample on the rights of the other, transforms those into despots, and these into enemies, destroys the morals of the one part, and the amor patriæ of the other. For if a slave can have a country in this world, it must be any other in preference to that in which he is born to live and labour for another: in which he must lock up the faculties of his nature, contribute as far as depends on his individual endeavours to the evanishment of the human race, or entail his own miserable condition on the endless generations proceeding from him. With the morals of the people, their industry also is destroyed. For in a warm climate, no man will labour for himself who can make another labour for him. This

Broadside for a slave auction held at Charleston in August, 1769

In 1769 Jefferson advertised for a runaway slave in the Gazette.

is so true, that of the proprietors of slaves a very small proportion indeed are ever seen to labour. And can the liberties of a nation be thought secure when we have removed their only firm basis, a conviction in the minds of the people that these liberties are of the gift of god? That they are not to be violated but with his wrath? Indeed I tremble for my country when I reflect that God is just: that his justice cannot sleep for ever: that considering numbers, nature and natural means only, a revolution of the wheel of fortune, an exchange of situation, is among possible events: that it may become probable by supernatural interference! The Almighty has no attribute which can take side with us in such a contest.

Jefferson was also convinced, however, that if the slaves were freed, there would be no hope for their integration into American society as full citizens.

Notes on Virginia, 1782

Deep rooted prejudices entertained by the whites; ten thousand recollections, by the blacks, of the injuries they have sustained; new provocations; the real distinctions which nature has made; and many other circumstances, will divide us into parties, and produce convulsions, which will probably never end but in the extermination of the one or the other race.

Thus, instead of advocating the simple abolition of slavery, Jefferson favored gradual emancipation and a carefully planned program to establish colonies for the freed slaves in areas distant from their former places of bondage. In 1779 public opinion in Virginia seemed ready to accept some modifications in the system; the assembly had already passed a law barring the further importation of slaves. Jefferson moved cautiously for more extensive reform and forty years later recalled the fate of the revisors' plan for an amendment to the bill they recommended.

Autobiography, 1821

The bill on the subject of slaves was a mere digest of the existing laws respecting them, without any intimation of a plan for a future & general emancipation. It was thought better that this should be kept back, and attempted only by way of amendment whenever the bill should be brought on. The principles of the amendment however were agreed on, that is to say, the freedom of

Louisiana slaves cutting sugar cane

all born after a certain day, and deportation at a proper age. But it was found that the public mind would not yet bear the proposition, nor will it bear it even at this day. Yet the day is not distant when it must bear and adopt it, or worse will follow. Nothing is more certainly written in the book of fate than that these people are to be free. Nor is it less certain that the two races, equally free, cannot live in the same government. Nature, habit, opinion has drawn indelible lines of distinction between them. It is still in our power to direct the process of emancipation and deportation peaceably and in such slow degree as that the evil will wear off insensibly, and their place be pari passu filled up by free white laborers. If on the contrary it is left to force itself on, human nature must shudder at the prospect held up.

Jefferson's other projected reform proved equally unsuccessful. He had anticipated opposition to his plan to end slavery, but he does not seem to have realized how controversial his program for a revised system of criminal law would be. His work on the portion of the Virginia code dealing with "the scale of punishments" probably took more of his time than any other statute assigned to him. His letter to George Wythe, written shortly before their final conference with Pendleton on the *Revisal*, not only gives Jefferson's views on criminal justice but also shows the system worked out by the committee for cooperating on their report.

Monticello Nov. 1. 1778.
I have got thro' the bill 'for proportioning crimes and punishments in cases heretofore capital,' and now inclose it to you with a request that you will be so good as scrupulously to examine and correct it, that it may be presented to our committee with as few defects as possible. In it's style I have aimed at accuracy, brevity and simplicity, preserving however the very words of the established law, wherever their meaning had been sanctioned by judicial decisions, or rendered technical by usage.... And I must pray you to be as watchful over what I have not said as what is said; for the omissions of this bill have all their positive meaning. I have thought it better to drop in silence the laws we mean to discontinue, and let them be swept away by the general negative words of this, than to detail them in clauses of express repeal. By the side of the text I have written the notes I made, as I went along, for the benefit of my

Portion from a printed version of the "Bill for proportioning crimes and punishments" in the Revisal

own memory. They may serve to draw your attention to questions to which the expressions or the omissions of the text may give rise....

I have strictly observed the scale of punishments settled by the Committee, without being entirely satisfied with it. The lex talionis [the law of punishment equivalent to the offense], altho' a restitution of the Common law, to the simplicity of which we have generally found it so advantageous to return will be revolting to the humanised feelings of modern times. An eye for an eye, and a hand for a hand will exhibit spectacles in execution whose moral effect would be questionable; and even the...punishment of the offending member, altho' long authorised by our law, for the same offence in a slave, has you know been not long since repealed in conformity with public sentiment. This needs reconsideration.

The committee apparently chose not to reconsider its decision on the principle of *lex talionis,* and this produced an odd dichotomy in Jefferson's final Bill for Proportioning Crimes and Punishments. His bill, in general, provided for less severe punishments than those dictated in old statutes, the death penalty being exacted only in cases of treason and murder. Other offenses that had been capital crimes would now be punished by hard labor. Grafted onto this modern, realistic bill was the committee's proposal that the rule of "an eye for an eye" be revived. When Jefferson's bill was finally considered by the legislature in 1784, however, it was not the *lex talionis* that drew criticism, but the plan for limiting crimes punishable by death. After the bill was defeated, James Madison wrote sadly, "Our old bloody code is...fully restored."

Neither slaves nor felons were to benefit from Jefferson's work on the revised statutes; public opinion had blocked reform in both areas. Jefferson believed, however, in the wisdom of Solon's remark, "that no more good must be attempted than the nation can bear." In later years he cited two other sections of the *Revisal* as his most important contributions: those on religious freedom and public education. They would lay the groundwork, he hoped, for an informed electorate.

Jefferson saw the alliance between Church and State as the enemy of personal freedom and a barrier to free inquiry. Thus, the protection of an individual's right to his own beliefs was essential to the enlightened society he hoped to see in Virginia. "In every country and in every age," he wrote, "the priest has been hostile to liberty. He is always in alliance with the despot, abetting his abuses in return for protection of his own." His determination to destroy the alliance already existing in his own state and his contempt for those who sought to control the thoughts of others were expounded in the book he wrote three years later.

Notes on Virginia, 1782

The error seems not sufficiently eradicated, that the operations of the mind, as well as the acts of the body, are subject to the coercion of the laws. But our rulers can have no authority over such natural rights, only as we have submitted to them. The rights on conscience we never submitted, we could not submit. We are answerable for them to our god. The legitimate powers of government extend to such acts only as are injurious to others. But it does me no injury for my neighbor to say there are twenty gods, or no god. It neither picks my pocket nor breaks my leg. If it be said his testimony in a court of justice cannot be relied on; reject it then, and be the stigma on him. Constraint may make him worse by making him a hypocrite, but it will never make him a truer man. It may fix him obstinately in his errors, but will not cure them. Reason and free enquiry are the only effectual agents against error. Give a loose to them, they will support the true religion by bringing every false one to their tribunal, to the test of their investigation. They are the natural enemies of error, and of error only. Had not the Roman government permitted free enquiry, Christianity could never have been introduced. Had not free enquiry been indulged, at the aera of the reformation, the corruptions of Christianity could not have been purged away. If it be restrained now, the present corruptions will be protected and new ones encouraged. Was the government to prescribe to us our medicine and diet, our bodies would be in such keeping as our souls are now. Thus in France the emetic was once forbidden as a medicine and the potatoe as an article of food. Government is just as infallible too when it fixes systems in Physics. Galileo was sent to the inquisition for affirming that the earth was a sphere: the government had declared it to be as flat as a trencher, and Galileo was obliged to abjure his error. This error however at length prevailed, the earth became a globe, and Descartes declared it was whirled round it's axis by a vortex. The government in which he lived was wise enough to see that this was no question of civil jurisdiction or we should all have been involved by authority in vortices. In fact, the vortices have been exploded, and the Newtonian principle of gravitation is now more firmly established on the basis of reason than it would be were the government to step in and to make it an article of necessary faith. Reason and experiment have been indulged, and error has fled before them. It is error alone which needs the support of government. Truth can stand by itself. Subject opinion to coercion: whom will you make your inquisitors? Fallible men; men governed by bad passions, by private as well as public reasons. And why subject it to coercion? To produce uniformity. But is uniformity of opinion desireable? No more than of face and stature. Introduce the bed of Procrustes then, and as there is danger that the large men may beat the small, make us all of a size by lopping the former and stretching the latter. Difference of opinion is advantageous in religion. The several sects perform the office of a Censor morum over each other. Is uniformity attainable? Millions of innocent men, women and children since the introduction of Christianity have been burnt, tortured, fined, imprisoned. Yet have we not advanced one inch towards uniformity. What has been the effect of coercion? To make one half the world fools and the other half hypocrites. To support roguery and error all over the earth....

But every state, says an inquisitor, has established some religion. No two, say I, have established the same. Is this a proof of the infallibility of establishments? Our sister states of Pennsylvania and New York however have long subsisted without any establishment at all. The experiment was new and doubtful when they made it.

Virginia, HOWE

The legislature met in the old capitol in Williamsburg until 1780.

It has answered beyond conception. They flourish infinitely. Religion is well supported; of various kinds, indeed, but all good enough; all sufficient to preserve peace and order: or if a sect arises whose tenets would subvert morals, good sense has fair play and reasons and laughs it out of doors, without suffering the state to be troubled with it. They do not hang more malefactors than we do. They are not more disturbed with religious dissensions. On the contrary, their harmony is unparalleled, and can be ascribed to nothing but their unbounded tolerance, because there is no other circumstance in which they differ from every nation on earth. They have made the happy discovery that the way to silence religious disputes, is to take no notice of them. Let us too give this experiment fair play, and get rid while we may, of those tyrannical laws.

In Virginia an especially inequitable system had developed. In Jefferson's *Autobiography* he recited the history of religion in the colony. The first settlers, colonial Anglicans, had simply transplanted their homeland's established church, with all its legal privileges and special status. Soon, however, new immigrants had come: English dissenters, Scotch Presbyterians, and German Lutherans who resented contributing to the support of a faith to which they did not subscribe.

Autobiography, 1821
By the time of the revolution, a majority of the inhabitants had become dissenters from the established church, but were still obliged to pay contributions to support the Pastors of the minority. This unrighteous compulsion to maintain teachers of what they deemed religious errors was grievously felt during the regal government, and without a hope of relief. But the first republican legislature which met in 76. was crouded with petitions to abolish this spiritual tyranny. These brought on the severest contests in which I have ever been engaged. Our great opponents were Mr. Pendleton & Robert Carter Nicholas, honest men, but zealous churchmen. The petitions were referred to the Commee of the whole house on the state of the country; and after desperate contests in that Committee, almost daily from the 11th. of Octob. to the 5th. of December, we prevailed so far only as to repeal the laws which rendered criminal the maintenance of any religious opinions, the forbearance of repairing

THOMAS JEFFERSON

to church, or the exercise of any mode of worship: and further, to exempt dissenters from contributions to the support of the established church; and to suspend, only until the next session levies on the members of that church for the salaries of their own incumbents. For altho' the majority of our citizens were dissenters, as has been observed, a majority of the legislature were churchmen. Among these however were some reasonable and liberal men, who enabled us, on some points, to obtain feeble majorities. But our opponents carried in the general resolutions of the Commee of Nov. 19. a declaration that religious assemblies ought to be regulated, and that provision ought to be made for continuing the succession of the clergy, and superintending their conduct. And in the bill now passed was inserted an express reservation of the question Whether a general assessment should not be established by law, on every one, to the support of the pastor of his choice; or whether all should be left to voluntary contributions; and on this question, debated at every session from 76. to 79. (some of our dissenting allies, having now secured their particular object, going over to the advocates of a general assessment) we could only obtain a suspension from session to session until 79. when the question against a general assessment was finally carried, and the establishment of the Anglican church entirely put down.

THE COLLEGE OF WILLIAM AND MARY

Colonial Anglicans established churches such as the one above in Williamsburg's Bruton Parish.

The disestablishment of the Church, however, was only a necessary first step, for the end of one state religion did not protect free inquiry for future generations. To protect his fellow citizens in their right to worship, or not to worship, as they chose, Jefferson drafted a Bill for Establishing Religious Freedom, which appeared as the eighty-second bill in the *Revisal*. The preamble opened with a sweeping declaration of man's right to freedom from coercion in matters of conscience. The bill went far beyond advocates of toleration and proclaimed full religious liberty. (The italicized words were not part of the version adopted by the legislature.)

A Bill for Establishing Religious Freedom [1779]
Well aware that the opinions and belief of men depend not on their own will, but follow involuntarily the evidence proposed to their minds; that Almighty God hath created the mind free, *and manifested his supreme will that free it shall remain by making it altogether insusceptible of restraint;* that all attempts to influence it by

85

temporal punishments, or burthens, or by civil incapacitations, tend only to beget habits of hypocrisy and meanness, and are a departure from the plan of the holy author of our religion, who being lord both of body and mind, yet chose not to propagate it by coercions on either, as was in his Almighty power to do, *but to extend it by its influence on reason alone;* that the impious presumption of legislators and rulers, civil as well as ecclesiastical, who, being themselves but fallible and uninspired men, have assumed dominion over the faith of others, setting up their own opinions and modes of thinking as the only true and infallible, and as such endeavoring to impose them on others, hath established and maintained false religions over the greatest part of the world and through all time: That to compel a man to furnish contributions of money for the propagation of opinions which he disbelieves *and abhors,* is sinful and tyrannical; that even the forcing him to support this or that teacher of his own religious persuasion, is depriving him of the comfortable liberty of giving his contributions to the particular pastor whose morals he would make his pattern, and whose powers he feels most persuasive to righteousness; and is withdrawing from the ministry those temporary rewards, which proceeding from an approbation of their personal conduct, are an additional incitement to earnest and unremitting labours for the instruction of mankind; that our civil rights have no dependance on our religious opinions, any more than our opinions in physics or geometry; that therefore the proscribing any citizen as unworthy the public confidence by laying upon him an incapacity of being called to offices of trust and emolument, unless he profess or renounce this or that religious opinion, is depriving him injuriously of those privileges

Earliest printed text of the "Bill for establishing Religious Freedom"

and advantages to which, in common with his fellow citizens, he has a natural right; that it tends also to corrupt the principles of that *very* religion it is meant to encourage, by bribing, with a monopoly of worldly honours and emoluments, those who will externally profess and conform to it; that though indeed these are criminal who do not withstand such temptation, yet neither are those innocent who lay the bait in their way; *that the opinions of men are not the object of civil government, nor under its jurisdiction;* that to suffer the civil magistrate to intrude his powers into the field of opinion and to restrain the profession or propagation of principles on supposition of their ill tendency is a dangerous falacy, which at once destroys all religious liberty, because he being of course judge of that tendency will make his opinions the rule of judgment, and approve or condemn the sentiments of others only as they shall square with or differ from his own; that it is time enough for the rightful purposes of civil government for its officers to interfere when principles break out into overt acts against peace and good order; and finally, that truth is great and will prevail if left to herself; that she is the proper and sufficient antagonist to error, and has nothing to fear from the conflict unless by human interposition disarmed of her natural weapons, free argument and debate; errors ceasing to be dangerous when it is permitted freely to contradict them.

[The heart of the bill followed, concluding with an attempt to safeguard religious liberty from incursions by future legislators.]

We the General Assembly of Virginia do enact that no man shall be compelled to frequent or support any religious worship, place, or ministry whatsoever, nor shall be enforced, restrained, molested, or burthened in his body or goods, nor shall otherwise suffer, on account of his religious opinions or belief; but that all men shall be free to profess, and by argument to maintain, their opinions in matters of religion, and that the same shall in no wise diminish, enlarge, or affect their civil capacities.

And though we well know that this Assembly, elected by the people for the ordinary purposes of legislation only, have no power to restrain the acts of succeeding

Assemblies, constituted with powers equal to our own, and that therefore to declare this act irrevocable would be of no effect in law; yet we are free to declare, and do declare, that the rights hereby asserted are of the natural rights of mankind, and that if any act shall be hereafter passed to repeal the present or to narrow its operation, such act will be an infringement of natural right.

When this bill was first introduced in 1779, many Virginians saw it as a diabolical scheme, and it, too, waited several years for passage, aided by the "unwearied exertions" of James Madison. Jefferson was in France when his friend informed him that the bill had at last been approved, and he reported to Madison the enthusiasm aroused in the Old World by news of the statute. "It is honorable for us," he wrote Madison, "to have produced the first legislature which had the courage to declare that the reason of man may be trusted with the formation of his own opinions."

The reason of man, left in ignorance, would be imprisoned as cruelly as it had been by religious bigotry. Jefferson's Bill for the More General Diffusion of Knowledge, along with two others in the *Revisal*—one for a reform of William and Mary College and another for the creation of a public library—would have established an educational system designed to ensure an enlightened commonwealth of free men. In the Bill for the More General Diffusion of Knowledge, Jefferson proposed a pyramidal plan of educational opportunities. At the broad base, elementary schooling would be offered to all, regardless of ability to pay; higher levels of the system would be open to those selected for their outstanding performance in the lower levels.

Notes on Virginia, 1782

Another object of the Revisal is to diffuse knowledge more generally through the mass of the people. This bill proposes to lay off every county into small districts of five or six miles square called hundreds, and in each of them to establish a school for teaching reading, writing and arithmetic. The tutor to be supported by the hundred, and every person in it entitled to send their children three years gratis, and as much longer as they please, paying for it. These schools to be under a visitor, who is annually to chuse the boy, of best genius in the school, of those whose parents are too poor to give them further education, and to send him forward to one of the Grammar schools, of which twenty are proposed to be erected in different parts of the country, for teaching Greek, Latin,

An important part of Jefferson's educational plan was the "Bill for establishing a public Library."

geography, and the higher branches of numerical Arithmetic. Of the boys thus sent in any one year, trial is to be made at the grammar schools one or two years, and the best genius of the whole selected and continued six years, and the residue dismissed. By this means twenty of the best geniusses will be raked from the rubbish annually, and be instructed, at the public expence so far as the Grammar schools go. At the end of six years instruction, one half are to be discontinued (from among whom the Grammar schools will probably be supplied with future masters); and the other half, who are to be chosen for the superiority of their parts and disposition, are to be sent and continued three years in the study of such sciences as they shall chuse, at William and Mary college, the plan of which is proposed to be enlarged, as will be hereafter explained, and extended to all the useful sciences. The ultimate result of the whole scheme of education would be the teaching all children of the state reading, writing, and common arithmetic: turning out ten annually, of superior genius, well taught in Greek, Latin, geography, and the higher branches of arithmetic: turning out ten others annually, of still superior parts, who, to those branches of learning, shall have added such of the sciences as their genius shall have led them to: the providing to the wealthier part of the people convenient schools, at which their children may be educated, at their own expence. — The general objects of this law are to provide an education adapted to the years, to the capacity, and the condition of every one, and directed to their freedom and happiness.... By that part of our plan which prescribes the selection of the youths of genius from among the classes of the poor, we hope to avail the state of those talents which nature has sown as liberally among the poor as the rich, but which perish without use, if not sought for and cultivated. — But of all the views of this law none is more important, none more legitimate, than that of rendering the people safe, as they are the ultimate, guardians of their own liberty. For this purpose the reading in the first stage, where *they* will receive their whole education, is proposed, as has been said, to be chiefly historical. History by apprising them of the past will enable them to judge of the future; it will avail them of the experience of other times and other nations; it will qualify them as judges of the actions

Virginia, HOWE

Liberty Hall, one of the oldest literary academies south of the Potomac, received an endowment and a new name—Washington Academy—in honor of George Washington in 1796; that year part of Jefferson's plan for public education was finally adopted.

and designs of men; it will enable them to know ambition under every disguise it may assume; and knowing it, to defeat its views. In every government on earth is some trace of human weakness, some germ of corruption and degeneracy, which cunning will discover, and wickedness insensibly open, cultivate, and improve. Every government degenerates when trusted to the rulers of the people alone. The people themselves therefore are its only safe depositories. And to render even them safe their minds must be improved to a certain degree.... The influence over government must be shared among all the people. If every individual which composes their mass participates of the ultimate authority, the government will be safe; because the corrupting the whole mass will exceed any private resources of wealth: and public ones cannot be provided but by levies on the people. In this case every man would have to pay his own price. The government of Great-Britain has been corrupted, because but one man in ten has a right to vote for members of parliament. The sellers of the government therefore get nine-tenths of their price clear. It has been thought that corruption is restrained by confining the right of suffrage to a few of the wealthier of the people: but it would be more effectually restrained by an extension of that right to such numbers as would bid defiance to the means of corruption.

Seven years after submitting the bill, Jefferson had come to believe that it was the most important bill in the *Revisal,* and he wrote to George Wythe from France concerning his hopes for its passage. His experience in Europe had confirmed his belief that no democracy could survive without an educated public.

Paris Aug. 13. 1786.
I think by far the most important bill in our whole code is that for the diffusion of knowlege among the people. No other sure foundation can be devised for the preservation of freedom, and happiness. If any body thinks that kings, nobles, or priests are good conservators of the public happiness, send them here. It is the best school in the universe to cure them of that folly. They will see here with their own eyes that these descriptions of men are an abandoned confederacy against the happiness of the mass of people. The omnipotence of their effect

cannot be better proved than in this country particularly, where notwithstanding the finest soil upon earth, the finest climate under heaven, and a people of the most benevolent, the most gay, and amiable character of which the human form is susceptible, where such a people I say, surrounded by so many blessings from nature, are yet loaded with misery by kings, nobles and priests, and by them alone. Preach, my dear Sir, a crusade against ignorance; establish and improve the law for educating the common people. Let our countrymen know that the people alone can protect us against these evils, and that the tax which will be paid for this purpose is not more than the thousandth part of what will be paid to kings, priests and nobles who will rise up among us if we leave the people in ignorance.

Virginians were not yet ready for public responsibility for education in the Confederation period. In 1796 a modified and fairly ineffective version of his plan for elementary schools was finally adopted, but the other provisions of the bill were ignored, as were his proposals for the reorganization of William and Mary and for the creation of a state-supported library.

Jefferson's early attempts to shape the development of Virginia government had met with little immediate success. His draft constitution had been all but ignored, and the most important sections of his contribution to the *Revisal* would be adopted piecemeal over the succeeding years or defeated. Shortly before the committee of revisors submitted its report on June 18, 1779, however, Jefferson's legislative efforts were rather abruptly curtailed. The assembly chose him to succeed Patrick Henry as Virginia's second governor. Henceforth, fundamental reform would be temporarily shelved as Jefferson concentrated all of his energy on meeting the daily crises of a wartime government.

List of articles purchased for the Governor's Palace at Williamsburg by Patrick Henry on May 29, 1779

Chapter 4

Wartime Governor

Jefferson certainly did not seek the opportunity to serve as Virginia's second governor. Under the constitution, the office had narrowly defined powers that would limit the executive's ability to implement any personal program for state policy. The thirty-six-year-old legislator probably did no more than allow his name to be put in nomination; he did not campaign among the assembly members who made the final selection in June, 1779. Any reluctance Jefferson may have felt over assuming the responsibilities of the governorship was justified. The next two years were to be an ordeal no one would have chosen to undergo, and the generally accepted view of Jefferson as a wartime governor is a critical one. It has been charged that he did not anticipate the problems that arose; that he was a poor administrator; that he hesitated to exceed the limits of his constitutional powers; that he exposed his state to invasion, humiliation, and the collapse of civil authority; in short, that he left office thoroughly discredited.

But the documentary record of his two one-year terms shows determined efforts to meet a military situation that would have strained the limits of the best equipped civil government. Despite the limits of his office, Jefferson devised a strategy for the defense of Virginia's frontier in the Northwest and an early warning system of communications in eastern Virginia. Despite the poor quality and inexperience of much of the military leadership sent to the Southern Department, Jefferson used his own knowledge of methods of frontier fighting and the ways of militia to organize what human and material resources Virginia did have. But he was continually hampered by the unwillingness and inability of Congress to provide adequate support and military leadership for the state's defense. Virginia had contributed to the "common cause," as Jefferson described it, with a flow of men, money, and supplies northward when the war centered in New England and the Middle States; but when British strategy shifted to the South in 1778, there seemed to be no reciprocal reinforcement. With scant assistance, the new governor was called on to preside over the most extensive territory in the new nation, bounded by a weakly defended western frontier and a particularly vulnerable coastline.

His term began with some personal embarrassment. On the first ballot in the legislature, he had received only a plurality of the votes; his two friends John Page and Thomas Nelson had won the rest. On the second ballot Jefferson narrowly defeated Page by a vote of sixty-seven to sixty-one. Both candidates were chagrined by this appearance of political rivalry, and Page immediately wrote to assure the governor-elect that he was not "influenced by some low dirty feelings" and promised to "do every thing in my Power to make your Administration easy and agreeable to you." Jefferson responded with equal warmth.

[Williamsburg, June 3, 1779]
It had given me much pain that the zeal of our respective friends should ever have placed you and me in the situation of competitors. I was comforted however with the reflection that it was their competition, not ours, and that the difference of the numbers which decided between us, was too insignificant to give you a pain or me a pleasure [had] our dispositions towards each other been such as to have admitted those sensations.

Jefferson's first message to the assembly seemed to reflect modest confidence as he assumed office.

[June 2, 1779]
In a virtuous and free state, no rewards can be so pleasing to sensible minds, as those which include the approbation of our fellow citizens. My great pain is, lest my poor endeavours should fall short of the kind expectations of my country; so far as impartiality, assiduous attention, and sincere affection to the great American cause, shall enable me to fulfill the duties of any appointment, so far I may, with confidence undertake; for all beyond, I must rely on the wise counsels of the General Assembly....

In a letter to Richard Henry Lee two weeks later, however, Jefferson betrayed his fears of what the governorship might hold for him. Virginia was not threatened by British arms in the summer of 1779, but her economy, like those of all the other states, was endangered by depreciation of the Continental currency and by the assembly's desperate efforts to curb inflation with new and higher taxes.

Memorandum in Governor Jefferson's handwriting of "our forces supposed to be now in field," October, 1779

Williamsburgh June 17 1779
In a virtuous government, and more especially in times like these, public offices are, what they should be, burthens to those appointed to them which it would be wrong to decline, though foreseen to bring with them intense labor and great private loss....

It is a cruel thought that when we feel ourselves standing on the firmest ground in every respect, the cursed arts of our secret enemies combining with other causes, should effect, by depreciating our money, what the open arms of a powerful enemy could not. What is to be done? Taxation is become of no account, for it is foreseen that notwithstanding it's increased amount there will still be a greater deficiency than ever. I own I see no assured hope but in peace or a plentiful loan of hard money.

Three months after Jefferson took office, Congress voted to stop issuing new Continental currency. This was the first step in a program that would soon place the burden of supplying the army on individual states. Jefferson tried to cooperate fully with General Washington's requests for additional troops despite growing demands on the state.

Williamsburgh Nov. 28. 1779.
We have at present very pressing calls to send additional numbers of men to the Southward. No inclination is wanting in either the legislative or Executive powers to aid them, or to strengthen you: but we find it very difficult to procure men.

By the close of 1779, the state was hard pressed. Crops had failed, and for the first time Virginia had to import provisions. Jefferson and his Council of State sought relief by purchasing goods in Maryland, only to learn that their neighbor had seized the foodstuffs to insure adequate local supplies. On January 30 Jefferson made a vain appeal to Maryland authorities to release the desperately needed flour.

Wmsburg Jan. 30th. 1780.
A most distressing harvest in this State having reduced us to the necessity of either disbanding our military force or seeking subsistence for them else where we asked permission from Governor [Thomas] Johnson to purchase a quantity of flour in your State. He was pleased to grant it to the extent of two thousand Barrels. Mr. Smith who was intrusted with the purchase informed

THOMAS JEFFERSON

Jefferson made this plan, probably during 1779, for a proposed Governor's House in Richmond.

us at different times of purchases to the amount of sixteen hundred Barrels, of which about two hundred Barrels I believe have been forwarded.... we are now informed that the residue not forwarded has been seised by your State. Should it be detained we shall be in very great distress having absolutely no other means of supporting our military till harvest. The object of the act [of Maryland]...is patriotic and laudable. But I refer to your Excellency to consider whether the supply of the troops of the several states may not be considered as comprehended in the spirit of the act. The defence of the States severally makes up the general defence, no matter whether fed and paid at the generall or separate charge. Indeed I am induced to hope your Excellency will think our Stores not seizable within the Letter of the Law.... Accustomed at all other times to furnish Subsistence to others, it is the first instance wherein providence has exposed us to the necessity of asking leave to purchase it among our friends.

But as Jefferson's first term ended, Virginia's position became even more precarious. By April, 1780, when the state's capital was moved inland to Richmond, the British had opened a massive new campaign against Virginia's southern neighbors. A few days before Jefferson's reelection on June 2, he learned of the surrender of Charleston and the loss of the Virginia regiments garrisoned there. Adjusting quickly to his new role as leader of a state in danger of armed attack, he offered Washington a plan for improving the flow of military intelligence.

Richmond June 11th. 1780.
Our intelligence from the Southward is most lamentably defective. Tho' Charlestown has now been in the hands of the enemy a month, we hear nothing of their movements which can be relied on. Rumours are that they are penetrating Northward. To remedy this defect I shall immediately establish a line of expresses from hence to the neighborhood of their army, and send thither a sensible judicious gentleman to give us information of their movements.... There is really nothing to oppose the progress of the enemy Northward but the cautious principles of the military art. North Caroline is without arms. We do not abound. Those we have are freely imparted to them, but such is the state of their resources that they have not yet been able to move a single musket from this state

Sir Henry Clinton congratulates troops on South Carolina successes.

95

to theirs. All the waggons we can collect have been furnished to the Marquis de Kalb, and are assembling for the march of 2500 militia under Genl. Stevens of Culpeper who will move on the 19th, inst. I have written to Congress to hasten supplies of arms and military stores for the Southern states, and particularly to aid us with Cartridge paper and Cartridge boxes, the want of which articles, small as they are, renders our stores useless. The want of money cramps every effort.

By midsummer Lord Cornwallis's forces were camped near the North Carolina-Virginia border. With only the state militia left to guard Virginia, Jefferson had little reason to feel secure. Still he went about the routine of his office, acknowledging letters and searching for supplies for troops at the front. When the Chevalier de La Luzerne, the French minister at Philadelphia, announced the arrival of a French fleet, Jefferson replied that some force would be helpful in protecting Chesapeake Bay. But he kept the common cause uppermost, only hinting at the "temporary misfortunes" besetting the South.

Richmond August 31. 1780.
The interest of this State is intimately blended so perfectly the same with that of the others of the confederacy that the most effectual aid it can at any time receive is where the general cause most needs it. Of this yourself, Congress, and General Washington are so perfect judges that it is not for me to point it out. You can as well, and will as impartially judge whether the late disasters in the south call for any of those future aids so generously tendered in your Excellency's Letter. If their action in the north will have more powerful influence towards establishing our Independence, they ought not to be wished for in the south be the temporary misfortunes there what they will.

Engraving of the Battle of Camden

Among those "temporary misfortunes" was Horatio Gates's humiliating defeat at Camden, South Carolina, on August 16. The American commander's hurried retreat overshadowed his earlier triumphs in the war, and Virginia's troops had shared fully in the disgrace. Jefferson wrote ruefully to their commander, General Edward Stevens.

Richmond Septemr. 3rd. 1780
I sincerely condole with you on our late Misfortune which sits the heavier on my mind as being produced by

my own Country Men. Instead of considering what is past, however, we are to look forward and prepare for the future.

The Continental government continued to demand reinforcements from Virginia but seemed disinclined to provide arms or supplies for these same troops. Vainly, Jefferson urged the president of Congress, Samuel Huntington, to come to terms with the situation.

Richmond Sep. 3. 1780.
Almost the whole of the small arms having been unfortunately lost in the last defeat, the men proposed for the feild will be unarmed, unless it is in your power to furnish arms. Indeed not only a sufficient number is wanting to arm the men now raising, but, as our stores will be exhausted in effecting that as far as they will go towards it, it seems indispensible that Congress should form a plentiful magazine of small arms, and other military stores that we may not be left an unarmed prey to the enemy, should our Southern misfortunes be not yet ended. Should any disaster like the late one, befal that army which is now collecting, and which will be so much weaker in regulars as that brave corps is lessened in the unequal conflict which was put upon them, the consequences will be really tremendous if we be found without arms. With a sufficiency of these, there can be no danger in the end. The losses of our brethren in the mean time may be great, the distresses of individuals in the neighborhood of the war will be cruel, but there can be no

Jefferson's responsibilities as war governor included commissioning an officer to recruit men (right) and urging Samuel Huntington (above) to replace the arms lost at Camden.

Richard Henry Lee by C. W. Peale

doubt of an ultimate recovery of the country. The scene of military operations has been hitherto so distant from these states, that their militia are strangers to the actual presence of danger. Habit alone will enable them to view this with familiarity, to face it without dismay; a habit which must be purchased by calamity, but cannot be purchased too dear. In the acquisition of this, other misfortunes may yet be to be incurred, for which we should be prepared. I am earnestly therefore to sollicit Congress for plentiful supplies of small arms, powder, flints, cartridge boxes and paper; and to pray that no moment may be lost in forwarding them.

In his public correspondence, Jefferson remained the determined, if hard-pressed, executive. But as he faced the autumn of 1780, he was privately near despair, and he confided his feelings to Richard Henry Lee.

Richmond Sep. 13. 1780.
The application requisite to the duties of the office I hold is so excessive, and the execution of them after all so imperfect, that I have determined to retire from it at the close of the present campaign. I wish a successor to be thought of in time who to sound whiggism can join perseverance in business, and an extensive knowlege of the various subjects he must superintend. Such a one may keep us above water even in our present moneyless situation.

Fortunately, Cornwallis was unable to take advantage of his position after his successes of the summer. His advance north from strongholds in South Carolina and Georgia was halted in the fall, and, except for a British coastal raid in October, Virginia would be safe for the rest of the year. In an effort to reorganize the shaken American army in the South, Washington named Nathanael Greene to replace Gates. Baron von Steuben, the famed drillmaster of Valley Forge, was left in charge of forces in Virginia for the winter.

In this comparatively stable situation, Jefferson found time to consider expanding military operations on another front; the lands claimed by Virginia to the north and west, a vast territory stretching to the Mississippi and the Great Lakes. Concerned by rumors of a secessionist movement in Kentucky and of a spring attack by Britain's Indian allies, Jefferson prepared instructions for young George Rogers Clark, Virginia's commander in the Northwest. Threatened by Cornwallis to the south and the British fleet to the east, Virginia would open a daring attack on the frontier.

Richmond december 25th. 1780.
A powerful army forming by our enemies in the south renders it necessary for us to reserve as much of our militia as possible free to act in that quarter. At the same time we have reason to believe that a very extensive combination of British and Indian savages is preparing to invest our western frontier. To prevent the cruel murders and devastations which attend the latter species of war and at the same time to prevent it's producing a powerful diversion of our force from the southern quarter in which they mean to make their principal effort and where alone success can be decisive of their ultimate object, it becomes necessary that we aim the first stroke in the western country and throw the enemy under the embarrassments of a defensive war rather than labour under them ourselves. We have therefore determined that an expedition shall be undertaken under your command in a very early season of the approaching year into the hostile country beyond the Ohio, the principal object of which is to be the reduction of the British post at Detroit, and incidental to it the acquiring possession of Lake Erie....

...If that Post be reduced we shall be quiet in future on our frontiers, and thereby immense Treasures of blood and Money be saved; we shall be at leizure to turn our whole force to the rescue of our eastern Country from subjugation, we shall divert through our own Country a branch of commerce which the European States have thought worthy of the most important struggles and sacrifices, and in the event of peace on terms which have been contemplated by some powers we shall form to the American union a barrier against the dangerous extension of the British Province of Canada and add to the Empire of liberty an extensive and fertile Country thereby converting dangerous Enemies into valuable friends.

George Rogers Clark (above) defended Virginia's western frontier while Lord Cornwallis (below) threatened from the south.

Jefferson's dreams of securing the Northwest were superseded a few days later when a British fleet commanded by the traitor Benedict Arnold was sighted in Chesapeake Bay. As the fleet moved up the James River, Jefferson called out the militia. It was obvious, however, that it was too late to organize a defense, and he arranged for the transfer of public stores and state records from Richmond. When he learned of the British landing at Westover on January 4, Jefferson took personal charge of these operations and then withdrew to await the next British move. In a report to Washington, he described the subsequent raid on the capital.

> Richmond Jany 10. 1781.
> They marched from Westover at 2 o Clock in the afternoon of the 4th. and entered Richmond at 1 o Clock in the afternoon of the 5th. A regiment of infantry and about 30 horse continued on without halting to the Foundery. They burnt that, the boring mill the magazine and two other houses, and proceeded to Westham, but nothing being in their power there they retired to Richmond. The next morning they burnt some buildings of public and some of private property, with what Stores remained in them, destroyed a great quantity of private Stores and about 12 o Clock retired towards Westover where they encamped within the neck the next day. The loss sustained is not yet accurately known. As far as I have been able to discover it consisted at this place in about 300 musquets, some soldiers clothing to a small amount some quarter masters Stores of which 120 sides of leather was the principal article, part of the artificers tools and 3 waggons, besides which 5 brass 4 [pounders] which we had sunk in the river were discovered to them, raised and carried off. At the Foundery we lost the greater part of the papers belonging to the auditors office, and of the books and papers of the Council office. About 5 or 6 tons as we conjecture of powder was thrown into the canal of which there will be a considerable saving by remanufacturing it. The roof of the foundery was burnt but the Stacks of Chimnies and furnaces not at all injured. The boring mill was consumed. Within less than 48 hours from the time of their landing and 19 from our knowing their destination they had penetrated 33 miles, done the whole injury and retired.

Heading of a 1780 proclamation Benedict Arnold issued in New York inviting members of the Continental Army "to join His Majesty's Arms"

The Continental cause could survive the loss of some supplies and powder, but the reputation of Virginia and the state's new government was seriously damaged. After returning to Richmond, Jefferson conceived a plan for Arnold's capture. His letter outlining this scheme to General John Muhlenberg, second-in-command in Virginia, betrayed his feelings of personal humiliation at the turncoat general's hands. He deleted the material in italics before sending the instructions.

Richmond Jan. 31. 1781.
Acquainted as you are with the treasons of Arnold, I need say nothing for your information, or to give you a proper sentiment of them. You will readily suppose that it is above all things desireable to drag him from those under whose wing he is now sheltered. On his march to and from this place I am certain it might have been done with facility by men of enterprize and firmness. I think it may still be done though perhaps not quite so easily. Having peculiar confidence in the men from the Western side of the mountains, I meant as soon as they should come down to get the enterprize proposed to a chosen number of them, such whose courage and whose fidelity would be above all doubt. Your perfect knowlege of those men personally, and my confidence in your discretion, induce me to ask you to pick from among them proper characters, in such number as you think best, to reveal to them our desire, and engage them [to] undertake to seize and bring off this greatest of all traitors.... *I shall be sorry to suppose that any circumstances may put it out of their power to bring him off alive after they shall have taken him and of course oblige them to put him to death. Should this happen, however, and America be deprived of the satisfaction of seeing him exhibited as a public spectacle of infamy, and of vengeance, I must give my approbation to their putting him to death. I do this considering him as a deserter from the American army, who has incurred the pain of death by his desertion, which we have a right to inflict on him and against which he cannot be protected by any act of our enemies. I distinguish him from an honourable enemy, who, in his station, would never be considered by me as a justifiable object of such an enterprize.*

German engraving of Arnold

Arnold remained at liberty while Jefferson did his best to meet Nathanael Greene's demands for men and supplies for the Southern Department. He hinted to Greene that the general might use his influence to gain aid from the other states.

Richmond Feb. 10. 1781.
Every moment however brings us new proofs that we must be aided by our Northern brethren. Perhaps they are aiding us, and we may be uninformed of it. I think near half the enemy's force are now in Virginia and the

states South of that. Is half the burthen of opposition to rest on Virginia and N. Carolina? I trust you concur with us in crying aloud to Congress on this head.

A week later, Jefferson outlined the situation to Horatio Gates who had retired to his Berkeley County farm.

Richmond Feb. 17. 1781.
The situation of affairs here and in Carolina is such as must shortly turn up important events one way or the other. By letter from Genl. Greene dated Guilford C[ourt]house Feb. 10. Ld. Cornwallis rendered furious by the affair at the Cowpens [a British defeat] and surprise of George town [an American raid] had burnt his own waggons to enable himself to move with facility, had pressed on to the vicinities of the Moravian towns and was still advancing. The prisoners taken at the Cowpens were saved by a hair's breadth accident, and Greene was retreating. His force 2000 regulars and no militia, Cornwallis's 3000. Genl. [William] Davidson was killed in a skirmish. Arnold lies still at Portsmouth with 1500 men. A French 64. gun ship and 2 frigates of 36 each arrived in our bay three days ago. They would suffice to destroy the British shipping here (a 40., four frigates and a 20) could they get at them. But these are withdrawn up Elizabeth river which the 64. cannot enter. We have ordered about 700 riflemen from Washington Montgomery and Bedford and 500 common militia from Pittsylva. and Henry to reinforce Genl. Greene, and 500 new levies will march from Chestfd. C. H. in a few days. I have no doubt however that the Southwestern counties will have turned out in greater numbers before our orders reach them. I have been knocking at the door of Congress for aids of all kinds, but especially of arms ever since the middle of summer. The Speaker [of the House of Delegates, Benjamin] Harrison is gone to be heard on that subject. Justice indeed requires that we should be aided powerfully. Yet if they would repay us the arms we have lent them we should give the enemy trouble tho' abandoned to ourselves.

In March, as a response to Arnold's raid, the young Marquis de Lafayette was sent to Virginia in command of a detachment of

Broadside from Jefferson to county lieutenants in April, 1781, urged action against militia delinquents.

the Continental Army. In a letter of welcome, Jefferson gave the French aristocrat fair warning of the problems he would face.

Richmond March 10th. 1781

Mild Laws, a People not used to war and prompt obedience, a want of the Provisions of War and means of procuring them render our orders often ineffectual, oblige us to temporize and when we cannot accomplish an object in one way to attempt it in another. Your knowledge of the Circumstances with a temper accomodated to them ensure me your Cooperation in the best way we can when we shall not be able to pursue the Way we would wish.

Lafayette adapted well to local customs and militiamen. At the end of April he helped turn back a British raid on Richmond, but his small force could not defend the capital against a major attack. Those members of the legislature who appeared for the May session promptly adjourned to the safety of Charlottesville. Jefferson remained in Richmond for a time, but any effective government ended in the face of Cornwallis's renewed march north from South Carolina. Added to this was the threat of another British force moving west from Petersburg. Even with invasion at hand, militia quotas were unfilled, and Jefferson gave Lafayette a discouraging report.

Richmond May 14th. 1781

I inclose you a State of the Counties who have been called on to come into the Field, some of them to perform a full Tour of Duty and others to make a present Opposition to the Junction of the two hostile Armies. The Delay and Deficiencies of the first are beyond all expectation and if the Calls on the latter do not produce sufficient Reinforcements to you, I shall candidly acknowledge that it is not in my power to do any thing more than to represent to the General Assembly that unless they can provide more effectually for the Execution of the Law it will be vain to call on Militia. I could perhaps do something by Reprimands to the County Lieutenants by repeating and even increasing the Demands on them by way of penalty, if you would be so good as to have returns made to me once a week or at any other stated periods of the particular number of men from each County. Without these we can never know what Counties obey our Calls or how long your men are to continue with you so as to provide in time.

Sketch by Dupré for a medal in honor of Daniel Morgan, who led the defeat of the British at Cowpens

The next day Jefferson joined his family at Tuckahoe. The legislature had failed to reorganize at Charlottesville, and in the last weeks of his governorship, Jefferson presided over a state without any effective legislative or executive program to meet Cornwallis's advance. On May 28 the assembly finally made a quorum, but in a letter to Washington of that date, Jefferson made it clear that Virginia could not survive without substantial aid from her kindred states and he pleaded for Washington himself to help defend his native state.

> Charlottsville May 28th. 1781.
> I make no doubt you will have heard, before this shall have the honour of being presented to Your Excellency, of the junction of Lord Cornwallis with the force at Petersburg under Arnold who had succeeded to the command on the death of Major General Philips. I am now advised that they have evacuated Petersburg, joined at Westover a Reinforcement of 2000 Men just arrived from New York, crossed James River, and on the 26th. Instant were three Miles advanced on their way towards Richmond.... Your Excellency will judge from this state of things and from what you know of your own Country what it may probably suffer during the present Campaign. Should the Enemy be able to produce no opportunity of annihilating the Marquis's Army a small proportion of their force may yet restrain his movements effectually while the greater part is employed in detachment to waste an unarmed Country and to lead the minds of the people to acquiesence under those events which they see no human power prepared to ward off. We are too far removed from the other scenes of war, to say whether the main force of the Enemy be within this State, but I suppose they cannot any where spare so great an Army for the operations of the field: Were it possible for this Circumstance to justify in Your Excellency a determination to lend us Your personal aid, it is evident from the universal voice that the presence of their beloved Countryman, whose talents have been so long successfully employed in establishing the freedom of kindred States, to whose person they have still flattered themselves they retained some right, and have ever looked up as their dernier resort in distress, that your appearance among them I say would restore full confidence of salvation, and would render them equal to whatever is not impossible.... A few days will bring to me that period of relief which the Constitution has prepared for those

oppressed with the labours of my office, and a long declared resolution of relinquishing it to abler hands has prepared my way for retirement to a private station: still however as an individual citizen I should feel the comfortable effects of your presence....

Five days later Jefferson's second term as governor expired. The legislature neglected to choose a successor, and he remained in Charlottesville to finish up official business before returning to nearby Monticello on Sunday, June 3. That same day Banastre Tarleton, Cornwallis's brilliant cavalry commander, began a forced march from Hanover to Charlottesville to execute a surprise attack that Cornwallis hoped would destroy what remained of Virginia's government. Colonel John Jouett happened on Tarleton's party and began a legendary ride to warn Jefferson and the assembly of the danger. Jouett outraced Tarleton, reaching Monticello before dawn on June 5, and then covered the three miles to Charlottesville to warn the drowsy assemblymen. All but seven made their escape to Staunton—still without a governor. Jefferson arranged for his family to take refuge at a friend's estate at Blenheim and followed them there that evening. Seven years later Jefferson gave his account of Tarleton's raid to the historian William Gordon.

Paris July 16. 1788.
You ask, in your letter of Apr. 24. details of my sufferings by Colo. Tarleton. I did not suffer by him. On the contrary he behaved very genteelly with me. On his approach to Charlottesville which is within 3. miles of my house at Monticello, he dispatched a troop of his horse under Capt. Mc.leod with the double object of taking me prisoner with the two Speakers of the Senate and Delegates who then lodged with me, and remaining there. in vedette, my house commanding a view of 10. or 12 counties round about. He gave strict orders to Capt. Mc.leod to suffer nothing to be injured. The troop failed in one of their objects, as we had notice so that the two speakers had gone off about two hours before their arrival at Monticello, and myself with my family about five minutes. But Captn. Mc.leod preserved every thing with sacred care during about 18. hours that he remained there. Colo. Tarleton was just so long at Charlottesville being hurried from thence by news of the rising of the militia, and by a sudden fall of rain which threatened to swell the river and intercept his return. In general he did little injury to the inhabitants on that short and hasty excur-

Silhouette of John Jouett

sion, which was of about 60. miles from their main army then in Spotsylvania, and ours in Orange.

[But Jefferson's admiration for Tarleton did not extend to Cornwallis, who joined the advance party of raiders a few days later.]

Lord Cornwallis then proceeded to the point of fork, and encamped his army from thence all along the main James river to a seat of mine called Elkhill, opposite to Elk island and a little below the mouth of the Byrd creek.... He remained in this position ten days, his own head quarters being in my house at that place. I had had time to remove most of the effects out of the house. He destroyed all my growing crops of corn and tobacco, he burned all my barns containing the same articles of the last year, having first taken what corn he wanted, he used, as was to be expected, all my stocks of cattle, sheep, and hogs for the sustenance of his army, and carried off all the horses capable of service: of those too young for service he cut the throats, and he burnt all the fences on the plantation, so as to leave it an absolute waste. He carried off also about 30. slaves: had this been to give them freedom he would have done right, but it was to consign them to inevitable death from the small pox and putrid fever then raging in his camp. This I knew afterwards to have been the fate of 27. of them. I never had news of the remaining three, but presume they shared the same fate. When I say that Lord Cornwallis did all this, I do not mean that he carried about the torch in his own hands, but that it was all done under his eye, the situation of the house, in which he was, commanding a view of every part of the plantation, so that he must have seen every fire. I relate these things on my own knowlege in a great degree, as I was on the ground soon after he left it. He treated the rest of the neighborhood somewhat in the same stile, but not with that spirit of total extermination with which he seemed to rage over my possessions. Wherever he went, the dwelling houses were plundered of every thing which could be carried off. Lord Cornwallis's character in England would forbid the belief that he shared in the plunder. But that his table was served with the plate thus pillaged from private houses can be proved by many hundred eye witnesses. From an

VIRGINIA HISTORICAL SOCIETY

Banastre Tarleton

estimate I made at that time on the best information I could collect, I supposed the state of Virginia lost under Ld. Cornwallis's hands that year about 30,000 slaves, and that of these about 27,000 died of the small pox and camp fever, and the rest were partly sent to the West Indies and exchanged for rum, sugar, coffee and fruits, and partly sent to New York, from whence they went at the peace either to Nova Scotia, or England. From this last place I believe they have been lately sent to Africa. History will never relate the horrors committed by the British army in the *Southern* states of America. They raged in Virginia 6. months only, from the middle of April to the middle of October 1781. when they were all taken prisoners, and I give you a faithful specimen of their transactions for 10. days of that time and in one spot only.... I suppose their whole devastations during those 6. months amounted to about three millions sterling.

Thomas Nelson, Jr.

In later years Jefferson's enemies blamed him for the interruption in effective state government that occurred, and critics charged him with abdicating official duty in his last-minute escape from Monticello. But as one Jefferson biographer, Dumas Malone, has pointed out, "It would be nearer the truth to say that the government abandoned him than that he abandoned the government." Even after the legislators reached Staunton, they seemed in no hurry to choose a new executive: five days passed before they elected Thomas Nelson, Jr.

Jefferson was less concerned about attacks on his behavior during the crisis of June, 1781, than he was by another result of Tarleton's raid: a move in the assembly for the creation of a dictator. Many of Patrick Henry's supporters argued that only this resort would give Virginia the leadership her governors had failed to provide by constitutional methods. Jefferson had no patience with those who argued that democracy could not function in an emergency or that such a crisis justified suspending the constitution. His ideal of a free society was not one that could be casually abandoned in time of peril and effectively resurrected on the return of safety. In his *Notes on Virginia*, Jefferson recalled the history of the attempts to impose temporary tyranny in Virginia.

Notes on Virginia, 1782

In December 1776, our circumstances being much distressed, it was proposed in the house of delegates to create a *dictator,* invested with every power legislative, executive and judiciary, civil and military, of life and of

Listing of Jefferson's traveling expenses and payment for "13 days attendance" at the December, 1781, session of the House of Delegates

death, over our persons and over our properties: and in June 1781, again under calamity, the same proposition was repeated, and wanted a few votes only of being passed. — One who entered into this contest from a pure love of liberty, and a sense of injured rights, who determined to make every sacrifice, and to meet every danger, for the re-establishment of those rights on a firm basis, who did not mean to expend his blood and substance for the wretched purpose of changing this master for that, but to place the powers of governing him in a plurality of hands of his own choice, so that the corrupt will of no one man might in future oppress him, must stand confounded and dismayed when he is told, that a considerable portion of that plurality had meditated the surrender of them into a single hand, and, in lieu of a limited monarch, to deliver him over to a despotic one! ... Necessities which dissolve a government, do not convey its authority to an oligarchy or a monarchy. They throw back, into the hands of the people, the powers they had delegated, and leave them as individuals to shift for themselves. A leader may offer, but not impose himself, nor be imposed on them. Much less can their necks be submitted to his sword, their breath be held at his will or caprice. The necessity which should operate these tremendous effects should at least be palpable and irresistible. Yet in both instances, where it was feared, or pretended with us, it was belied by the event.... The very thought alone was treason against the people; was treason against mankind in general; as rivetting for ever the chains which bow down their necks, by giving to their oppressors a proof, which they would have trumpeted through the universe, of the imbecility of republican government, in times of pressing danger, to shield them from harm. Those who assume the right of giving away the reins of government in any case, must be sure that the herd, whom they hand on to the rods and hatchet of the dictator, will lay their necks on the block when he shall nod to them. But if our assemblies supposed such a resignation in the people, I hope they mistook their character.

The scheme's narrow defeat did not end Jefferson's tribulations that summer. By late June he had moved his wife and daughters to Poplar Forest, an estate he had inherited from his father-in-law in Bedford County, so that he could recuperate there from a fall from a horse. One of his first tasks after his recovery was meeting a proposed inquiry "into the Conduct of the Executive of this State for the last twelve Months." He sent a curt note to young George Nicholas, who had introduced the inquiry resolution in the assembly.

> Monticello July 28, 1781.
> I am informed that a resolution on your motion passed the House of Delegates requiring me to render account of some part of my administration without specifying the act to be accounted for. As I suppose that this was done under the impression of some particular instance or instances of ill conduct, and that it could not be intended just to stab a reputation by a general suggestion under a bare expectation that facts might be afterwards hunted up to boulster it, I hope you will not think me improper in asking the favor of you to specify to me the unfortunate passages in my conduct which you mean to adduce against me, that I may be enabled to prepare to yield obedience to the house while facts are fresh in my memory and witnesses and documents are in existence.

Silhouette of George Nicholas

Nicholas did present some charges, but he did not even attend the House session in December when Jefferson presented his defense. The legislature closed the matter by passing a resolution of "sincere thanks" to Jefferson "for his impartial, upright, and attentive administration whilst in office." Despite this public vindication, Jefferson remained bitter, and he confided to a friend that he suspected Patrick Henry of having engineered the attack on his integrity.

> Richmond Dec. 24. [1781]
> You have heard probably of the vote of the H. of Delegates at the last session of assembly. I came here in consequence of it, and found neither accuser nor accusation. They have acknowledged by an express vote that the former one was founded on *rumours* only, for which no foundation can be discovered: they have thanked &c. The trifling body who moved this matter was below contempt; he was more an object of pity. His natural ill-temper was the tool worked with by another hand. He [Nicholas] was like the minners which go in and out of the fundament of the whale [Henry]. But the whale himself was discoverable enough by the turbulence of the water under which he moved.

Months before he was given a chance to defend his administration, Jefferson had decided to retire from public life. He confessed to Edmund Randolph in Congress that not even a diplomatic appointment could shake his determination to withdraw.

> Monticello Sep. 16. 1781.
>
> Were it possible for me to determine again to enter into public business there is no appointment whatever which would have been so agreeable to me. But I have taken my final leave of every thing of that nature, have retired to my farm, my family and books from which I think nothing will ever more separate me. A desire to leave public office with a reputation not more blotted than it has deserved will oblige me to emerge at the next session of our assembly and perhaps to accept of a seat in it, but as I go with a single object, I shall withdraw when that shall be accomplished.

Jefferson's withdrawal seemed justified. Five years of service to Virginia had brought him little gratitude or popular recognition. At the end of 1781, his efforts to reform the state's legal system had stalled and his wartime efforts had brought sharp criticism from his fellow Virginians. A man as conscientious as he could not excuse the apparent failure of his administration by citing the obvious fact that probably no one else could have done more to prepare Virginia for invasion or contribute to the common cause.

Indeed Jefferson's commitment to that cause doubtless irritated many who placed local above national interests. Jefferson did not see Virginia as an isolated political entity, divorced from the needs of the other states. He had hoped to give the commonwealth laws that would have made it a model of progressive ideas and liberal policies. But few had shared his vision, and too few other state leaders had acknowledged or acted on a community of interests. In the short-term view, Jefferson had failed as a state political leader more because of his commitment to his ideals than because he had forsaken his responsibilities.

A Picture Portfolio

America's Renaissance Man

SON OF VIRGINIA

No one who came into contact with Thomas Jefferson could fail to be impressed by the wide range of his interests and knowledge. The Marquis de Chastellux, after a visit to Monticello, summed it up: "No object had escaped Mr. Jefferson; it seemed as if from his youth he had placed his mind, as he had done his house, on an elevated situation, from which he might contemplate the universe." His classic *Notes on Virginia*, written in 1781, answered twenty-three specific questions about his native state and securely established Jefferson's reputation as a universal scholar and perhaps the most learned man in America. He presented a published copy with an inscription (below, left) to the Marquis de Barbé-Marbois who had originally posed the questions on behalf of the French government which was eager to learn about the new country. The subjects listed on the title page (below, right) reveal the vast scope of his knowledge. Among the natural wonders of Virginia, the Natural Bridge (right), rising 215 feet over Cedar Creek, was described as "the most sublime." Jefferson had owned it since 1773 and extolled it further: "so beautiful an arch, so elevated, so light, and springing, as it were, up to heaven, the rapture of the Spectator is really indiscribable!"

Th: Jefferson having had a few copies of these Notes printed to be offered to some of his friends and to some other estimable characters beyond that line, presents one to Mons.' de Marbois, under the most just of all titles, his right to the original. unwilling to expose them to the public eye, he asks the favour of Mons.' de Marbois to put them into the hands of no person on whose care & fidelity he cannot rely to guard them against publication.

NOTES on the ſtate of VIRGINIA;
written in the year 1781, ſomewhat corrected and enlarged in the winter of 1782, for the uſe of a Foreigner of diſtinction, in anſwer to certain queries propoſed by him reſpecting

1. Its boundaries	page 1
2. Rivers	3
3. Sea ports	27
4. Mountains	28
5. Caſcades and caverns	33
6. Productions mineral, vegetable and animal	41
7. Climate	134
8. Population	151
9. Military force	162
10. Marine force	165
11. Aborigines	166
12. Counties and towns	171
13. Conſtitution	173
14. Laws	135
15. Colleges, buildings, and roads	275
16. Proceedings as to tories	285
17. Religion	287
18. Manners	298
19. Manufactures	301
20. Subjects of commerce	304
21. Weights, Meaſures and Money	311
22. Public revenue and expences	313
23. Hiſtories, memorials, and ſtate-papers	312

MDCCLXXXII

HOME ON A MOUNTAINTOP

When Jefferson was twenty-six, he began a project that was to give him great pleasure throughout a long life. Picking the highest site on his Albemarle County land, he began to build; the sketch at right, above, is the first version of the house. "Of prospect I have a rich profusion...," he wrote: "mountains distant & near, smooth & shaggy, single & in ridges, a little river hiding itself among the hills so as to shew in lagoons only, cultivated grounds under the eye and two small villages." The watercolor above shows the view from the north front of the house he called Monticello, Italian for little mountain. Surrounding this summit home lay five thousand acres of Jefferson's land on which he lavished his agricultural and horticultural skills. The sketch at right is of a plan he made in 1772 of the house and garden; additions to it were continued after he retired from public office in 1809. He adored gardening and wrote to Charles Willson Peale in 1811 that "no occupation is so delightful to me as the culture of the earth, and no culture comparable to that of the garden.... though an old man, I am but a young gardener."

PRIVATE COLLECTION

THOMAS JEFFERSON MEMORIAL FOUNDATION

MASSACHUSETTS HISTORICAL SOCIETY

115

BEAUTY AND UTILITY

"Mr. Jefferson is the first American who has consulted the fine arts to know how he should shelter himself from the weather," observed a foreign visitor after seeing Monticello (right) for the first time. The interior, too, reflected Jefferson's appreciation for beautiful things, among them a magnificent silver coffee urn made from his own design (above). But Jefferson was also a highly practical man and loved to devise ways to improve the workings of things and thereby make life easier and more enjoyable. His house contained dumbwaiters that brought wine from the cellars and a wall panel with a revolving buffet from the kitchen to the dining room. Jefferson sat in a modified form of a swivel chair of his design with his feet on a chaise lounge over which a work table could be comfortably drawn. He had built for himself an adjustable music stand and architect's drafting desk. A notable improvement in moldboard plows resulted from his sketch at far right, bottom, of one "of least resistance." Above it are his designs for an apple mill and a fireplace that could be used to heat every apartment in a house. He even turned his fertile mind to the design of a "hominy beater," as shown in the detail at right from a letter to Charles Willson Peale. Inside and out, Monticello reflected to an extraordinary extent the taste and ingenuity of its architect, landscaper, builder, cabinetmaker, and proud owner.

116

MANUSCRIPT DIVISION, LIBRARY OF CONGRESS

MASSACHUSETTS HISTORICAL SOCIETY

MANUSCRIPT DIVISION, LIBRARY OF CONGRESS

LOUVRE

THE PAPERS OF BENJAMIN HENRY LATROBE, MARYLAND HISTORICAL SOCIETY

"ARCHITECTURE IS MY DELIGHT"

In the *Notes on Virginia* Jefferson had written that "the only public buildings worthy of mention are the capitol, the palace, the college, and the hospital for lunatics, all of them in Williamsburg." He became a one-man task force to rectify that situation and was the first in America, and indeed one of the first anywhere, to make use of classical models. While serving as a minister in Paris he was asked to submit a design for a state capitol in Richmond; he took for his model "what is called the Maison Quarré of Nismes [left, above], one of the most beautiful, if not the most beautiful and precious morsel of architecture left us by antiquity." When Benjamin Latrobe made the watercolor sketch at left of Richmond in 1796, Jefferson's graceful building dominated the landscape, and one could gaze at it "like a lover at his mistress," which is how Jefferson had described his first encounter with the Maison Carrée in 1787. Not all of Jefferson's designs were successful, however. When a national capital was planned on the banks of the Potomac, Jefferson anonymously submitted a design (right, above) in the competition for the President's House. But it lost out to the simpler one of James Hoban. "Architecture is my delight," Jefferson admitted, "and putting up and pulling down one of my favorite amusements." Near the end of his long life he planned and executed the beautiful University of Virginia at Charlottesville. The Rotunda (right, below) housed the library and was first used as a banquet hall to honor the Marquis de Lafayette when he visited America in 1824.

MARYLAND HISTORICAL SOCIETY

MANUSCRIPTS DEPARTMENT, ALDERMAN LIBRARY, UNIVERSITY OF VIRGINIA

119

DEPARTMENT OF GRAPHICS, UNIVERSITY OF VIRGINIA

"ACADEMICAL VILLAGE"

Jefferson's election as Rector of the University of Virginia in 1819 capped four decades of his efforts to establish "a system of general instruction, which shall reach every description of our citizens from the richest to the poorest." The "academical village" (above) which he designed was only two miles from Monticello, visible on its mountaintop right of center.

MASSACHUSETTS HISTORICAL SOCIETY

Exhuming the First American Mastodon BY CHARLES WILLSON PEALE; THE PEALE MUSEUM, BALTIMORE

NATURAL HISTORIAN

In 1792, when Jefferson was Secretary of State, he had the honor of having a plant named for him, the *Jeffersonia diphylla* (above, right). The citation stated in part that "in botany and zoology, the information of this gentleman is equalled by that of few persons in the United States." He had been elected to membership in the prestigious American Philosophical Society in 1780 (the date on the copy of his certificate above, far left, is in error) and served as its third president for seventeen years. Jefferson succeeded David Rittenhouse (above, left), whom he considered "second to no astronomer living" and who, along with Washington and Franklin, he felt offered proof to doubting Europeans that America could indeed produce geniuses. While he was its head, the Society provided Charles Willson Peale with financial support to undertake the excavation of some mammoth bones in Ulster County, New York, a scene the versatile artist later put on canvas (left). The success of the venture can be surmised from the drawing (above) of the "first fossil skeleton ever mounted in America." Thirty feet long, it was displayed in Peale's Natural History Museum in Philadelphia and was an instant sensation.

OBSERVANT TRAVELER

Jefferson's inquisitive mind was constantly rewarded during his years in France. Sitting on a balustrade of the Tuileries, he watched with fascination the building of the elegant Hôtel de Salm (above). Declaring himself "violently smitten," he filed away his impressions to recall when making additions to Monticello. He witnessed the balloon craze that swept Paris and reported on the first disaster when two Frenchmen tried to cross the English Channel only to have their balloon catch fire and fall, crushing them "to atoms" (above, right). Following his romance with Maria Cosway, during which he had dislocated his wrist in an accident, doctors advised a trip to Aix-en-Provence (right) to partake of the waters. Jefferson took this opportunity to make a three-month journey to southern France and northern Italy. He made detailed notes of his travels and wrote friends that "architecture, painting, sculpture, antiquities [such as the Roman aqueduct at Lyon (far right)], agriculture, the condition of the labouring poor fill all my moments."

MUSÉE CARNAVALET

Histoire des Ballons BY GASTON TISSANDIER, 1783; YALE UNIVERSITY LIBRARY

127

MUSÉE DE CHERBOURG

NEW-YORK HISTORICAL SOCIETY

CONNOISSEUR OF THE ARTS

Although music for Jefferson was "the favorite passion of my soul" and the operas and concerts of Paris his delight, he derived considerable pleasure, too, in expanding his knowledge of the other fine arts in the magnificent museums and ateliers surrounding him. He was quick to recommend the sculptor Jean Antoine Houdon for the commission by the Virginia assembly to carve a heroic statue of Washington, for he considered him "unrivalled in Europe." Houdon, seen in his atelier (left), not only did Washington but also made the excellent bust of Jefferson himself (left, above) and, among many others, one of his predecessor as Minister to France, the venerable Benjamin Franklin. Jefferson's bust can be seen in the painting at left on the rear shelf; Franklin and a small bust of Washington, on the shelf to the right. Jefferson visited the biennial expositions held in the salon of the Louvre where paintings were exhibited from ceiling to floor (above), and he thoroughly enjoyed the soirées attended by the leading arbiters of artistic taste of this most cosmopolitan of cities. He wrote of France, after his five years packed full of experiences he was uniquely able to enjoy and absorb: "Ask the travelled inhabitant of any nation, in what country on earth would you rather live?—Certainly in my own, where are all my friends, my relations, and the earliest & sweetest affections and recollections of my life. Which would be your second choice? France."

Chapter 5

Public Service and Private Misery

By the summer of 1781, Jefferson's services to Virginia had apparently been repudiated and he returned to Albemarle to superintend Monticello in the company of his wife and daughters, who had often suffered by his absences in earlier years. Certainly he would eventually have overcome his resentment of the attacks by his political enemies, but had he been left to recover slowly from his harrowing experiences as governor and had his personal happiness at Monticello continued uninterrupted, he might well have been a figure of less imposing historical importance. Instead, his personal life was shattered by tragedy, and his deep-rooted impulse to serve "the holy cause of liberty" became dominant once again. His dedication to the new order was firm, stifled only momentarily by sorrow and disillusionment.

None of this could be foreseen in 1781, and Jefferson began his retirement by declining an appointment to the commission to negotiate peace with Britain, citing among other reasons his "indispensable obligation of being within this state till a later season of the present year" to defend himself in the assembly. Renouncing that diplomatic post caused him some personal anguish, however, as he revealed in a letter to the Marquis de Lafayette.

> Monticello Aug. 4. 1781.
> I thank you also for your kind sentiments and friendly offers on the occasion, which th[at] I cannot avail myself of has given me more mortification than al[most] any occurrence of my life. I lose an opportunity, the only one I ever had and perhaps ever shall have of combining public service with private gratification, of seeing count[ries] whose improvements in science, in arts, and in civilization it has been my fortune to [ad]mire at a distance but never to see and at the same

time of lending further aid to a cause which has been handed on from it's first origination to [its] present stage by every effort of which my poor faculties were capable. These however have not been such as to give satisfaction to some of my countrymen and [it] has become necessary for me to remain in the state till a later period in the present [year] ....

Shortly thereafter, Jefferson turned to a project which would keep that cause alive in his heart and mind and which helped him refine his ideas about America: his *Notes on the State of Virginia.* The project was set in motion at the end of the summer of 1780 when François de Barbé-Marbois, secretary of the French legation in Philadelphia, distributed twenty-two questions from his government on the government, economics, and customs of the thirteen states. Congressman Joseph Jones delivered a set to Governor Jefferson, who assigned himself the task of answering the questions for Virginia and began work as early as November, 1780. Wartime emergencies forced him to postpone his major research and writing, however, until the summer of 1781. At Poplar Forest, ninety miles west of Monticello, and later in his own library, Jefferson prepared the manuscript that would become the only full-length book he ever published. He explained some of his methods in his *Autobiography.*

Autobiography, 1821

I had always made it a practice whenever an opportunity occurred of obtaining any information of our country, which might be of use to me in any station public or private, to commit it to writing. These memoranda were on loose papers, bundled up without order, and difficult of recurrence when I had occasion for a particular one. I thought this a good occasion to embody their substance, which I did in the order of Mr. Marbois' queries, so as to answer his wish and to arrange them for my own use.

Floor plan of Poplar Forest

By the end of the year, when he traveled to Richmond to answer Nicholas's charges, Jefferson had completed the manuscript. Marbois probably expected brief but useful answers that would give the French government a guide to local conditions. Instead, Jefferson's months of labor with his books and memoranda produced a profound study of the state's history and customs, detailed descriptions of its scenic beauty, and scholarly analyses of the political and economic factors that would shape the future not only of Virginia but of the United States as well. But Jefferson apologized to Marbois for troubling him with a manuscript so "imperfect." Although Jefferson did not intend to have the document publicized, he was too conscientious to allow its imperfections to remain. Over the next few years he revised and expanded the *Notes* until they had "swelled nearly to treble bulk" by mid-1784. In 1785 he arranged for the printing of two hundred copies, but his name did not appear on the title page and the books were only for distribution to carefully chosen friends and associates. Were the *Notes* "to go to the public at large," Jefferson feared that his frank comments might damage the political fortunes of two reforms he favored: the abolition of slavery and the revision of the state constitution. By the fall of 1785, he admitted that he might not long be able to keep the book secret. "I have been obliged to give so many...that I fear their getting published." Early in 1786, Jefferson found that his apprehensions were justified.

Autobiography, 1821

An European copy, by the death of the owner, got into the hands of a bookseller, who engaged it's translation, & when ready for the press, communicated his intentions & Manuscript to me, without any other permission than that of suggesting corrections. I never had seen so wretched an attempt at translation. Interverted, abridged, mutilated, and often reversing the sense of the original, I found it a blotch of errors from beginning to end. I corrected some of the most material, and in that form it was printed in French. A London bookseller, on seeing the translation, requested me to permit him to print the English original. I thought it best to do so to let the world see that it was not really so bad as the French translation had made it appear.

Early engraving of Natural Bridge

The book opened with a factual description of Virginia's geography, with subsequent topics following the order of Marbois's original queries. The Frenchman's question concerning "Cascades and Caverns" allowed Jefferson to depart from a discussion of rivers, mountains, and seaports to describe the famous Natural Bridge. Although this local wonder did not really fall under the question, Jefferson could not resist including it—especially since he was the proud owner of the land on which it stood.

Notes on Virginia, 1782

The *Natural bridge,* the most sublime of Nature's works, though not comprehended under the present head, must not be pretermitted. It is on the ascent of a hill, which seems to have been cloven through its length by some great convulsion....Though the sides of this bridge are provided in some parts with a parapet of fixed rocks, yet few men have resolution to walk to them and look over into the abyss. You involuntarily fall on your hands and feet, creep to the parapet and peep over it. Looking down from this height about a minute, gave me a violent head ach. This painful sensation is relieved by a short, but pleasing view of the Blue ridge along the fissure downwards, and upwards by that of the Short hills, which, with the Purgátory mountain is a divergence from the North ridge; and, descending then to the valley below, the sensation becomes delightful in the extreme. It is impossible for the emotions, arising from the sublime, to be felt beyond what they are here: so beautiful an arch, so elevated, so light, and springing, as it were, up to heaven, the rapture of the Spectator is really indiscribable!

Jefferson's drawing, c. 1767

Other selections from the *Notes on Virginia* reveal the work's breadth. It remains the most complete record of Jefferson's vision of America, not only of his home state, but also of his broader philosophical convictions. It was in reply to Marbois's question concerning "The present state of manufactures, commerce, interior and exterior trade," for example, that Jefferson outlined his theory of the moral superiority of agriculture as an occupation and hinted at his fear of the corrupting effects of a dependence on manufactures.

Notes on Virginia, 1782

Those who labour in the earth are the chosen people of god, if ever he had a chosen people, whose breasts he has made his peculiar deposit for substantial and genuine virtue. It is the focus in which he keeps alive that sacred fire, which otherwise might escape from the face of the earth. Corruption of morals in the mass of cultivators is a phænomenon of which no age nor nation has furnished an example. It is the mark set on those, who not looking up to heaven, to their own soil and industry, as does the husbandman, for their subsistance, depend for it on the casualties and caprice of customers. Dependance begets subservience and venality, suffocates the germ of virtue, and prepares fit tools for the designs of ambition. This, the natural progress and consequence of the arts, has sometimes perhaps been retarded by accidental circumstances: but, generally speaking, the proportion which the aggregate of the other classes of citizens bears in any state to that of its husbandmen, is the proportion of its unsound to its healthy parts, and is a good-enough

Authorized London edition of Notes, *printed in 1787 by John Stockdale*

barometer whereby to measure its degree of corruption. While we have land to labour then, let us never wish to see our citizens occupied at a work-bench, or twirling a distaff. Carpenters, masons, smiths, are wanting in husbandry: but, for the general operations of manufacture, let our work-shops remain in Europe. It is better to carry provisions and materials to workmen there, than bring them to the provisions and materials, and with them their manners and principles.

Jefferson also used the opportunity to dispel myths that had grown up about America. He was particularly incensed by the theories of the French naturalist Buffon who had asserted that "the animals common both to the old and new world are smaller in the latter, that those peculiar to the new are in a smaller scale, that those which have been domesticated in both have degenerated in America." Another French author, the Abbé Raynal, had applied Buffon's theories to the descendants of European settlers in America. Jefferson not only debunked Raynal's charges, but claimed that the New World possessed boundless potential for development and even for attaining superiority to Europe.

Notes on Virginia, 1782

So far the Count de Buffon has carried this new theory of the tendency of nature to belittle her productions on this side of the Atlantic. Its application to the race of whites, transplanted from Europe, remained for the Abbé Raynal. '...l'Amerique n'ait pas encore produit un bon poëte...un homme de genie dans un seul art, ou seule Science....America has not yet produced one good poet.' When we shall have existed as a people as long as the Greeks did before they produced a Homer, the Romans a Virgil, the French a Racine and Voltaire, the English a Shakespeare and Milton, should this reproach be still true, we will enquire from what unfriendly causes it has proceeded, that the other countries of Europe and quarters of the earth shall not have inscribed any name in the roll of poets. But neither has America produced 'one able mathematician, one man of genius in a single art or a single science.' In war we have produced a Washington, whose memory will be adored while liberty shall have votaries, whose name will triumph over time, and will in future ages assume its just station among the most celebrated worthies of the world, when that wretched philosophy shall be forgotten which would have arranged

The Comte de Buffon

A Pictorial Geography BY S. G. GOODRICH, 1840

Comparative sizes of North American animals from A Pictorial Geography, *published in United States in 1840*

David Rittenhouse's observatory in Norriton, Pennsylvania, built to watch the transit of Venus in 1769

The History of Philadelphia
BY J. THOMAS SCHARF AND THOMPSON WESTCOTT, 1884

him among the degeneracies of nature. In physics we have produced a Franklin, than whom no one of the present age has made more important discoveries, nor has enriched philosophy with more, or more ingenious solutions of the phænomena of nature. We have supposed Mr. [David] Rittenhouse second to no astronomer living: that in genius he must be the first, because he is self-taught. As an artist he has exhibited as great a proof of mechanical genius as the world has ever produced. He has not indeed made a world; but he has by imitation approached nearer its Maker than any man who has lived from the creation to this day. As in philosophy and war, so in government, in oratory, in painting, in the plastic art, we might shew that America, though but a child of yesterday, has already given hopeful proofs of genius, as well of the nobler kinds, which arouse the best feelings of man, which call him into action, which substantiate his freedom, and conduct him to happiness, as of the subordinate, which serve to amuse him only. We therefore suppose, that this reproach is as unjust as it is unkind; and that, of the geniuses which adorn the present age, America contributes its full share. For comparing it with those countries, where genius is most cultivated, where are the most excellent models for art, and scaffoldings for the attainment of science, as France and England for instance, we calculate thus. The United States contain three millions of inhabitants; France twenty millions; and the British islands ten. We produce a Washington, a Franklin, a Rittenhouse. France then should have half a dozen in each of these lines, and Great-Britain half that number, equally eminent. It may be true, that France has: we are but just becoming acquainted with her, and our acquaintance so far gives us high ideas of the genius of her inhabitants.... The present war having so long cut off all communication with Great-Britain, we are not able to make a fair estimate of the state of science in that country. The spirit in which she wages war is the only sample before our eyes, and that does not seem the legitimate offspring either of science or of civilization. The sun of her glory is fast descending to the horizon. Her philosophy has crossed the Channel, her freedom the Atlantic, and herself seems passing to that awful dissolution, whose issue is not given human foresight to scan.

THE FOUNDING FATHERS

The dismemberment of the British Empire seemed near as Jefferson completed drafting his manuscript for Marbois. Two months before the finished *Notes* were sent to the French diplomat, Cornwallis's surrender at Yorktown brought peace to Virginia and the promise of peace and security to the United States. With the vindication of his administration by the legislature in December, 1781, Jefferson could more comfortably withdraw to the privacy for which he longed. He even declined a seat in the Virginia legislature as a representative from Albemarle, and his refusal of service prompted considerable criticism. James Monroe wrote from Richmond: "It is publickly said here that the people of your county inform'd you they had frequently elected you in times of less difficulty and danger than the present to please you, but that now they had call'd you forth into publick office to serve themselves." Jefferson's reply cited his need to repair the "disorder and ruin" of his private affairs and his obligations to his daughters and to the six children of his late brother-in-law Dabney Carr. But the letter showed, as well, that Jefferson was still bitter about the attacks from his political enemies.

Dutch cartoon of the surrender at Yorktown (in distance) has British lion howling in pain next to an Englishman on his knees in despair.

Monticello May 20. 1782.

I am much obliged by the kind wishes you express of seeing me also in Richmond, and am always mortified when any thing is expected from me which I cannot fulfill, and more especially if it relate to the public service. Before I ventured to declare to my countrymen my determination to retire from public employment I examined well my heart to know whether it were thoroughly cured of every principle of political ambition, whether no lurking particle remained which might leave me uneasy when reduced within the limits of mere private life. I became satisfied that every fibre of that passion was thoroughly eradicated. I examined also in other views my right to withdraw. I considered that I had been thirteen years engaged in public service, that during that time I had so totally abandoned all attention to my private affairs as to permit them to run into great disorder and ruin, that I had now a family advanced to years which require my attention and instruction, that to this was added the hopeful offspring of a deceased friend whose memory must be for ever dear to me..., that by a constant sacrifice of time, labour, loss, parental and friendly duties, I had been so far from gaining the affection of my countrymen which was the only reward I ever asked or could have felt, that I had even lost the small estimation I before possessed: that however I might have comforted myself under the dis-

Page from the Virginia Almanac *listing the members of government in 1782, one of the few years Jefferson held no public office*

Jefferson's sketch for a circular stand with three shelves, probably designed for use at Monticello

approbation of the well-meaning but uninformed people yet that of their representatives was a shock on which I had not calculated: that this indeed had been followed by an exculpatory declaration, but in the mean time I had been suspected and suspended in the eyes of the world without the least hint then or afterwards made public which might restrain them from supposing I stood arraigned for treasons of the heart and not mere weaknesses of the head. And I felt that these injuries, for such they have been since acknowleged, had inflicted a wound on my spirit which will only be cured by the all-healing grave. If reason and inclination unite in justifying my retirement, the laws of my country are equally in favor of it.... Nothing could so completely divest us of ... liberty as the establishment of the opinion that the state has a *perpetual* right to the services of all it's members. This to men of certain ways of thinking would be to annihilate the blessing of existence; to contradict the giver of life who gave it for happiness and not for wretchedness, and certainly to such it were better that they had never been born. However with these I may think public service and private misery inseparably linked together, I have not the vanity to count myself among those whom the state would think worth oppressing with perpetual service. I have received a sufficient memento to the contrary. I am persuaded that having hitherto dedicated to them the whole of the active and useful part of my life I shall be permitted to pass the rest in mental quiet.... I preferred a simple act of renunciation to the taking sanctuary under those many disqualifications (provided by the law for other purposes indeed but) which afford asylum also for rest to the wearied. I dare say you did not expect by the few words you dropped on the right of renunication to expose yourself to the fatigue of so long a letter, but I wished you to see that if I had done wrong I had been betrayed by a semblance of right at least.

[The closing paragraph of this long letter contained a further explanation of Jefferson's reluctance to leave Monticello.]

...Mrs. Jefferson has added another daughter to our family. She has been ever since and still continues very dangerously ill.

After visiting Jefferson in the spring of 1782, the Marquis de Chastellux had written of the master of Monticello: "it seemed as if from his youth he had placed his mind, as he had done his house, on an elevated situation, from which he might contemplate the universe." But his personal universe was shattered abruptly a few months later. The daughter born in May was Martha Jefferson's sixth child in ten years; a son and two daughters had died in infancy. Although Jefferson jealously guarded the details of his private life, it is clear that his wife had never enjoyed good health and she failed to recover from the delivery of Lucy Elizabeth. For four months Thomas Jefferson lived with the growing knowledge that his thirty-three-year-old wife was dying. His eldest daughter, Patsy, was only ten at the time, but nearly fifty years later she recalled that terrible summer and fall at Monticello.

Martha Jefferson Carr, Jefferson's widowed sister

"Reminiscences of Th. J. by MR," [*c.* 1832] As a nurse no female ever had more tenderness or anxiety; he nursed my poor Mother in turn with aunt Carr and her own sisters setting up with her and administring her medecines and drink to the last. For four months that she lingered he was never out of Calling. When not at her bed side he was writing in a small room which opened immediately at the head of her bed. A moment before the closing scene he was led from the room almost in a state of insensibility by his sister Mrs. Carr who with great difficulty got him into his library where he fainted and remained so long insensible that they feared he never would revive. The scene that followed I did not witness but the violence of his emotion, of his grief when almost by stealth I entered his room at night to this day I dare not trust myself to describe. He kept his room for three weeks and I was never a moment from his side. He walked almost incessantly night and day only lying down occasionally when nature was completely exhausted on a pallet that had been brought in during his long fainting fit. My Aunts remained constantly with him for some weeks, I do not remember how many. When at last he left his room he rode out and from that time he was incessantly on horseback rambling about the mountain in the least frequented roads and just as often through the woods; in those melancholy rambles I was his constant companion, a solitary witness to many a violent burst of grief, the remembrance of which has consecrated particular scenes of that lost home beyond the power of time to obliterate.

"There is a time in human suffering," Jefferson wrote in a small pocket notebook at the time, "when exceeding sorrows are but like snow falling on an iceberg." Despite his wife's long illness, he seemed unprepared for her death and the tragedy was too great for him to describe. His account book, usually reserved for the most impersonal notes, carried a simple entry: "September 6—My dear wife died this day at 11:45 A.M." He noted in his *Autobiography* that he had "lost the cherished companion of my life, in whose affections, unabated on both sides, I had lived the last ten years in unchequered happiness."

Even in preparing an epitaph, Jefferson tried to provide some privacy for his grief. A simple slab of white marble was placed over her grave in the family cemetery on the mountainside with a quotation from the *Iliad* in the original Greek. In Pope's translation it read:

> If in the melancholy shades below,
> The flames of friends and lovers cease to glow,
> Yet mine shall sacred last; mine undecayed
> Burn on through death and animate my shade.

Fortunately, Jefferson was not allowed to remain long at Monticello. His friends realized that he needed something to occupy his mind and new ideas and new surroundings to distract him from his grief. On November 12, 1782, he was unanimously reappointed to the peace commission. Madison noted that "the act took place in consequence of its being suggested that the death of Mrs. J. had probably changed the sentiments of Mr. J. with regard to public life, and that all the reasons which led to his original appointment still existed."

Jefferson's colleagues in Philadelphia had judged his mood with uncanny accuracy. He welcomed the opportunity to get away from his saddened home and fulfill his ambition to visit Europe. Jefferson himself best described his mood in one of the first letters he wrote after Martha's death, while visiting a friend's estate, to the Marquis de Chastellux.

Detail of a page from Jefferson's account book has entry of wife's death at 11:45 on September 6.

Ampthill Nov. 26. 1782.
[Your letter] found me a little emerging from that stupor of mind which had rendered me as dead to the world as she was whose loss occasioned it. Your letter recalled to my memory, that there were persons still living of much value to me. If you should have thought me remiss in not testifying to you sooner how deeply I had been impressed with your worth in the little time I had the happiness of being with you you will I am sure ascribe it to it's true cause the state of dreadful suspence in which I had been kept all the summer and the catastrophe which closed it. Before that event my scheme of life had been determined. I had folded myself in the arms of retirement, and rested all prospects of future happiness on domestic and literary

objects. A single event wiped away all my plans and left me a blank which I had not the spirits to fill up. In this state of mind an appointment from Congress found me requiring me to cross the Atlantic, and that temptation might be added to duty I was informed at the same time from his Excy. the Chevalier de la Luzerne that a vessel of force would be sailing about the middle of Dec. in which you would be passing to France. I accepted the appointment and my only object now is so to hasten over those obstacles which would retard my departure as to be ready to join you in your voiage, fondly measuring your affections by my own and presuming your consent. It is not certain that by any exertions I can be in Philadelphia by the middle of December. The contrary is most probable. But hoping it will not be much later and counting on those procrastinations which usually attend the departure of vessels of size I have hopes of being with you in time. This will give me full Leisure to learn the result of your observations on the Natural bridge, to communicate to you my answers to the queries of Monsr. de Marbois, to receive edification from you on these and on other subjects of science, considering chess too as a matter of science.

Jefferson needed only a little more than three weeks to put his affairs in order in Virginia. His friends Francis Eppes and Nicholas Lewis would superintend his business interests in his absence, and Eppes and his wife Elizabeth, Martha's sister, also agreed to care for four-year-old Mary and the infant Lucy. Patsy would accompany her father and continue her education abroad under his direction.

On December 27, the Jeffersons arrived in Philadelphia. Patsy was put in school while her father made arrangements for their voyage. Bad weather delayed the sailing of the French vessel *Romulus,* however, and Jefferson waited out the delay in James Madison's company at a boarding-house owned by Mrs. Mary House. Mrs. House's daughter, Elizabeth Trist, befriended young Patsy and entertained her while Jefferson shopped for books and maps to take to Europe. At the end of January, Jefferson rode to Baltimore to confer with the captain of the ice-locked *Romulus.* The weather had improved, but a small British fleet had taken advantage of the thaw to station itself in Chesapeake Bay. Jefferson sought instructions from Congress since, "I must acknolege that they [the ships] appear such as to render a capture certain were we to hazard" a voyage. While Congress considered this new development, Jefferson amused himself in Baltimore as best he could by corresponding with his friends. In a letter to Madison, he considered the problems he might encounter serving as a minister plenipotentiary with John Adams in Paris.

Detail from unfinished painting by Benjamin West of commission: Jay, Adams, Franklin, Henry Laurens; William Temple Franklin, secretary

Baltimore Feb. 14. 1783.
I am nearly at a loss to judge how he will act in the negotiation. He hates Franklin, he hates Jay, he hates the French, he hates the English. To whom will he adhere? His vanity is a lineament in his character which had entirely escaped me. His want of taste I had observed. Notwithstanding all this he has a sound head on substantial points, and I think he has integrity. I am glad therefore that he is of the commission and expect he will be useful in it. His dislike of all parties, and all men, by balancing his prejudices, may give the same fair play to his reason as would a general benevolence of temper. At any rate honesty may be extracted even from poisonous weeds.

The next day Jefferson received word from Madison of unofficial reports that a preliminary peace treaty had already been concluded. Jefferson suspended his plans to sail and returned to Philadelphia. Not until April 1 did Congress release him from his commission so that he might return to Virginia. His journey to Monticello with Patsy was interrupted by a stop in Richmond where he conferred with members of the legislature. Two matters of great interest to Jefferson were to be considered at that session, and he probably used the opportunity to lobby on their behalf. The first proposal was for the states to grant Congress the right to impose an import tax or "impost" and to assume state debts which could then be met by this duty. The second was to call a popularly elected convention to revise the state constitution. After his return to Monticello on May 15, Jefferson prepared a draft constitution, drawing on the one he had written in 1776 and adding some new provisions. The convention was not called, but drafting the constitution and journeying to Philadelphia and Baltimore had helped bring Jefferson back to a full and active life. He would never forget his beloved wife, but he was beginning to learn to live with his loss. The assembly took notice of this fact in June, 1783, when they named him to the state's congressional delegation. The appointment would not take place until November, however, and Jefferson spent the summer and early autumn at home, superintending nine youngsters and organizing his personal library. His collection of 2,640 volumes, painstakingly assembled after the fire at Shadwell in 1770, was probably the finest of its kind in America. Arranging the items according to Lord Bacon's "table of sciences" was a labor of love for their owner.

The pleasant interlude at Monticello ended with Jefferson's departure in search of a wandering Congress, which had adjourned from Philadelphia when mutinous, unpaid troops threatened the State House. First leaving Patsy with Mrs. Trist in Philadelphia, Jefferson rode to New Jersey expecting to find his fellow delegates at Princeton, their most recent meeting place, but they had adjourned again to meet in Annapolis the following month. Jefferson returned to Philadelphia and spent the next few weeks attending to Patsy's education and care. Mrs. Trist was soon to leave the city, and he found a home for his eleven-year-old daughter with Mrs. Thomas Hopkinson, the mother of a congressional colleague of 1776. Determined to guide Patsy's development carefully, Jefferson continued to offer her stern fatherly lectures even after he left the city late in November. His letters combined deep affection with instructions on matters ranging from study habits to moral philosophy.

Annapolis Nov. 28. 1783.

My dear Patsy

After four days journey I arrived here without any accident and in as good health as when I left Philadelphia. The conviction that you would be more improved in the situation I have placed you than if still with me, has solaced me on my parting with you, which my love for you has rendered a difficult thing. The acquirements which I hope you will make under the tutors I have provided for you will render you more worthy of my love, and if they cannot increase it they will prevent it's diminution. Consider the good lady who has taken you under her roof, who has undertaken to see that you perform all your exercises, and to admonish you in all those wanderings from what is right or what is clever to which your inexperience would expose you, consider her I say as your mother, as the only person to whom, since the loss with which heaven has been pleased to afflict you, you can now look up; and that her displeasure or disapprobation on any occasion will be an immense misfortune which should you be so unhappy as to incur by any unguarded act, think no concession too much to regain her good will. With respect to the distribution of your time the following is what I should approve.

from 8. to 10 o'clock practise music.
from 10. to 1. dance one day and draw another
from 1. to 2. draw on the day you dance, and write a letter the next day.
from 3. to 4. read French.
from 4. to 5. exercise yourself in music.

First page of Jefferson's 1783 draft constitution, which he had printed and appended to some copies of the Notes on Virginia

Jefferson himself read widely in French as evidenced by books such as this history of Rome, translated from Lucius Florus, in his library.

from 5. till bedtime read English, write &c. Communicate this plan to Mrs. Hopkinson and if she approves of it pursue it.... I expect you will write to me by every post. Inform me what books you read, what tunes you learn, and inclose me your best copy of every lesson in drawing. Write also one letter every week either to your aunt Eppes, your aunt Skipwith [her mother's sister], your aunt Carr, or the little lady from whom I now inclose a letter, and always put the letter you so write under cover to me. Take care that you never spell a word wrong. Always before you write a word consider how it is spelt, and if you do not remember it, turn to a dictionary. It produces great praise to a lady to spell well. I have placed my happiness on seeing you good and accomplished, and no distress which this world can now bring on me could equal that of your disappointing my hopes. If you love me then, strive to be good under every situation and to all living creatures, and to acquire those accomplishments which I have put in your power, and which will go far towards ensuring you the warmest love of your affectionate father,

TH: JEFFERSON

P.S. keep my letters and read them at times that you may always have present in your mind those things which will endear you to me.

In a letter to Marbois, Jefferson explained his reasons for imposing this demanding schedule on Patsy. He hoped to prepare her for the heavy responsibilities she might face as a grown woman in America.

Annapolis Dec. 5. 1783.

Your very obliging letter of Nov. 22. was put into my hands just in the moment of my departure from Philadelphia, which put it out of my power to acknolege in the same instant my obligations for the charge you were so kind as to undertake of presenting a French tutor to my daughter.... The same cause prevented my procuring her the books you were so kind as to recommend, but this shall be supplied by orders from hence.... The plan of reading which I have formed for her is considerably different from what I think would be most proper for her sex in any other country than America. I am obliged in it to extend my views beyond herself, and consider her as possibly at the head of a little family of her own.

The chance that in marriage she will draw a blockhead I calculate at about fourteen to one, and of course that the education of her family will probably rest on her own ideas and direction without assistance. With the best poets and prosewriters I shall therefore combine a certain extent of reading in the graver sciences. However I scarcely expect to enter her on this till she returns to me. Her time in Philadelphia will be chiefly occupied in acquiring a little taste and execution in such of the fine arts as she could not prosecute to equal advantage in a more retired situation.

Jefferson was also determined that his motherless daughter would not lack guidance in the feminine graces or advice on the fashions that would most please the opposite sex.

Annapolis Dec. 22. 1783
I omitted in that [letter] to advise you on the subject of dress, which I know you are a little apt to neglect. I do not wish you to be gayly clothed at this time of life, but that what you wear should be fine of it's kind; but above all things, and at all times let your clothes be clean, whole, and properly put on. Do not fancy you must wear them till the dirt is visible to the eye. You will be the last who will be sensible of this. Some ladies think they may under the privileges of the dishabille be loose and negligent of their dress in the morning. But be you from the moment you rise till you go to bed as cleanly and properly dressed as at the hours of dinner or tea. A lady who has been seen as a sloven or slut in the morning, will never efface the impression she then made with all the dress and pageantry she can afterwards involve herself in. Nothing is so disgusting to our sex as a want of cleanliness and delicacy in yours. I hope therefore the moment you rise from bed, your first work will be to dress yourself in such a stile as that you may be seen by any gentleman without his being able to discover a pin amiss, or any other circumstance of neatness wanting.

The new State House in Annapolis

There was ample time for letter writing during Jefferson's first weeks in Annapolis. Although Congress was supposed to have opened sessions on November 26, only six states were represented by December 11. Under the Confederation, seven states were required to conduct the most routine business, and nine were necessary to consider extraordinary matters. Jefferson complained ruefully to James Madison who had retired temporarily to his home in Orange County.

> Annapolis Dec. 11. 1783.
> It is now above a fortnight since we should have met, and six states only appear. We have some hopes of Rhodeisland coming in to-day, but when two more will be added seems as insusceptible of calculation as when the next earthquake will happen.

It was essential that Congress be able to act quickly in December, 1783. The definitive treaty of peace, which ended the war and recognized American independence, had been signed in Paris on September 3, 1783. The treaty provided that ratifications be exchanged among the parties to the agreement within six months. Jefferson, as chairman of a committee charged with considering ratification, recommended approval of the articles on December 16, but by then more than half of the prescribed time had passed. A week later a seventh state had arrived; urgent appeals went out to governors of the unrepresented states warning that the delegates' absence might endanger the treaty. Jefferson recalled those tedious, frustrating weeks of arguing and waiting for a response.

Detail from ink sketch by Trumbull of presentation of the preliminary peace treaty in the House of Lords

> *Autobiography*, 1821
> Our body was little numerous, but very contentious. Day after day was wasted on the most unimportant questions. My colleague [John Francis] Mercer was one of those afflicted with the morbid rage of debate, of an ardent mind, prompt imagination, and copious flow of words, he heard with impatience any logic which was not his own. Sitting near me on some occasion of a trifling but wordy debate, he asked how I could sit in silence hearing so much false reasoning which a word should refute? I observed to him that to refute indeed was easy, but to silence impossible. That in measures brought forward by myself, I took the laboring oar, as was incumbent on me; but that in general I was willing to listen. If every sound argument or objection was used by some one or other of the numerous debaters, it was enough: if not, I thought it sufficient to suggest the omission, without going into a repetition of what had been already said by others. That this was a waste and abuse of the time and patience of the house which could not be justified. And I believe that if the members of deliberative bodies were to observe this course generally, they would do in a day

what takes them a week, and it is really more questionable, than may at first be thought, whether Bonaparte's dumb legislature which said nothing and did much, may not be preferable to one which talks much and does nothing. I served with General Washington in the legislature of Virginia before the revolution, and, during it, with Dr. Franklin in Congress. I never heard either of them speak ten minutes at a time, nor to any but the main point which was to decide the question. They laid their shoulders to the great points, knowing that the little ones would follow of themselves. If the present Congress errs in too much talking, how can it be otherwise in a body to which the people send 150. lawyers, whose trade it is to question everything, yield nothing, & talk by the hour? That 150. lawyers should do business together ought not to be expected.

At last, on January 14, delegates from New Jersey and New Hampshire arrived to take their seats. Some members of Congress, to Jefferson's dismay, had been ready to ratify the treaty with only seven states voting, but this desperate measure proved unnecessary. The treaty was duly ratified, and congressmen soon began to find excuses to leave: not until March would nine states again be represented. The problems that remained were those of peace, not war, but they were equally vital for America's future. First was the question of western lands. After years of argument over legal technicalities, Virginia's cession of the Northwest Territory had been accepted in a form agreeable to the other states. Jefferson was appointed to chair the committee that prepared a plan for the area's temporary government. His final report of March 22, which formed the basis for the Ordinance of 1784, was one of his most important state papers. It provided a new legal structure for territorial expansion: the formation not of subject colonies, but of territories with temporary governments that would prepare them to join the older states as full partners.

[March 22, 1784]

Provided that both the temporary and permanent governments be established on these principles as their basis. 1. That they shall for ever remain a part of this confederacy of the United States of America. 2. That in their persons, property and territory they shall be subject to the government of the United states in Congress assembled, and to the articles of Confederation in all those cases in which the original states shall be so subject. 3. That they shall be subject to pay a part

The Critical Period of American History BY JOHN FISKE, 1897

Copy of a map made in 1784 of the proposed states in the Northwest

of the federal debts...to be apportioned on them by Congress.... 4. That their respective governments shall be in republican forms, and shall admit no person to be a citizen who holds any hereditary title. 5. That after the year 1800. of the Christian æra, there shall be neither slavery nor involuntary servitude in any of the said states, otherwise than in punishment of crimes....

That whensoever any of the said states shall have, of free inhabitants, as many as shall then be in any one of the least numerous of the thirteen original states, such state shall be admitted...into the Congress of the United states, on an equal footing with the said original states: provided nine states agree to such admission according to the...11th of the articles of Confederation. And in order to adapt the said articles of confederation to the state of Congress when it's numbers shall be thus increased, it shall be proposed to the legislatures of the states originally parties thereto, to require the assent of two thirds of the United states in Congress assembled in all those cases wherein by the said articles the assent of nine states is now required.... Until such admission by their delegates into Congress, any of the said states, after the establishment of their temporary government, shall have authority to keep a sitting member in Congress, with a right of debating, but not of voting.

Congress did not accept all of Jefferson's report: the sections barring slavery and citizenship for people holding hereditary titles were deleted. But by then Jefferson was accustomed to introducing reforms that were too radical for many of his colleagues. The fundamental provision of the report remained—the creation of self-governing territories that would be guaranteed republican government in all stages of their progress to full statehood. He had succeeded in giving America a form of territorial expansion appropriate to a democracy, not one borrowed from monarchical colonialism.

A variety of other projects occupied Jefferson during his six-month stint at Annapolis. He was placed on every important committee, served as chairman of most of them, and wrote almost all of the significant public papers to emerge from that session of Congress. In addition to his efforts in behalf of the peace treaty and the organization of governments in the Northwest, Jefferson arranged the state occasion for Washington's renunciation of his command, proposed canal routes, and developed a decimal system of coinage—making the Spanish dollar the base unit, with a gold piece worth ten dollars, a silver dime, and a copper cent. His insistence on this simplification earned for him the title "Father of the Dollar." Another matter had been of special interest to Jefferson: the plan to negotiate commercial treaties with European nations. In his *Notes,* Jefferson had written of the need not only to "cultivate the peace and friendship of every nation" but also "to throw open the doors of commerce."

Jefferson's expenses as a delegate to Congress, submitted to the Treasurer of Virginia, May 11, 1784

Notes on Virginia, 1782

Young as we are, and with such a country before us to fill with people and with happiness, we should point in that direction the whole generative force of nature, wasting none of it in efforts of mutual destruction. It should be our endeavour to cultivate the peace and friendship of every nation, even of that which has injured us most, when we shall have carried our point against her. Our interest will be to throw open the doors of commerce, and to knock off all its shackles, giving perfect freedom to all persons for the vent of whatever they may chuse to bring into our ports, and asking the same in theirs. Never was so much false arithmetic employed on any subject, as that which has been employed to persuade nations that it is their interest to go to war. Were the money which it has cost to gain, at the close of a long war, a little town, or a little territory, the right to cut wood here, or to catch fish there, expended in improving what they already possess, in making roads, opening rivers, building ports, improving the arts, and finding employment for their idle poor, it would render them much stronger, much wealthier and happier. This I hope will be our wisdom.

Commercial treaties, properly negotiated, would lay the foundations for free trade, and in May, 1784, Jefferson was named a commissioner with Franklin and Adams, who were already abroad, to accomplish this task. At last he would have his chance to visit Europe, not to negotiate an end to the war for political independence, but to help establish what he hoped would be the beginning of commercial independence for the young Republic.

Chapter 6

Seasoning of a Diplomat

On July 5, 1784, Jefferson and his daughter Patsy sailed from Boston for Paris, via West Cowes, England and Le Havre. America's newest minister plenipotentiary had carefully arranged his affairs to permit an absence of two years, the time limit placed on his joint commission with Franklin and Adams to negotiate commercial treaties. Like many of Jefferson's carefully made plans, this one would be upset: his stay abroad would be not for two years, but for more than five years; it would be not for a mission limited to the negotiation of trade concessions and commercial regulations, but for a wide-ranging adventure in European diplomacy and politics. Excitement seemed unlikely when he arrived in Paris the first week in August. During the first few months suitable lodging had to be found for himself and his official family. Patsy had to be properly dressed in Parisian style and then enrolled in the convent school at the Abbaye Royale de Panthémont. Jefferson's friendship with Adams and Franklin was reestablished as the trio was reunited for the first time since 1776.

Despite his obligations as householder, father, and diplomat, Jefferson found some time to behave like any tourist in a new country. His friends in America were kept informed of foreign curiosities that Jefferson felt would interest them, as well as of political events that it was his duty to report. He interrupted a report to James Madison on French politics and trade to give him a description of "Phosphoretic matches" and an Argand lamp.

> Paris Nov. 11. 1784.
> By having them [matches] at your bedside with a candle, the latter may be lighted at any moment of the night without getting out of bed. By keeping them on your writing table, you may seal three or four letters with one of them, or light a candle if you want to seal more which in the summer is convenient. In the woods they supply the want of steel, flint and punk.... There is a new lamp

invented here lately which with a very small consumption of oil (of olives) is thought to give a light equal to six or eight candles. The wick is hollow in the middle of the form of a hollow cylinder, and permits the air to pass up thro' it. It requires no snuffing. They make shade candlesticks of them at two guineas price, which are excellent for reading and are much used by studious men.

Jefferson's fascination with the latest practical advances in European technology was far more than mere interest in gadgets; it was part of his personal mission to Europe. As he explained to President Joseph Willard of Harvard, America had a special need to cultivate scientific knowledge and a special opportunity for contributing to that field.

The Grille de Chaillot, near Jefferson's residence in Paris, looking down the Champs-Elysées

Paris Mar. 24. 1789.
What a feild have we at our doors to signalize ourselves in! The botany of America is far from being exhausted: it's Mineralogy is untouched, and it's Natural history or Zoology totally mistaken and misrepresented. As far as I have seen there is not one single species of terrestrial birds common to Europe and America, and I question if there be a single species of quadrupeds. (Domestic animals are to be excepted.) It is for such institutions as that over which you preside so worthily, Sir, to do justice to our country, it's productions, and it's genius. It is the work to which the young men, whom you are forming, should lay their hands. We have spent the prime of our lives in procuring them the precious blessing of liberty. Let them spend theirs in shewing that it is the great parent of science and of virtue; and that a nation will be great in both always in proportion as it is free.

It was Jefferson's public mission, however, that consumed most of his time in the fall and winter of 1784. As soon as John Adams had returned from welcoming his wife and daughter in London, the three commissioners began their work.

Autobiography, 1821
Mr. Adams soon joined us at Paris, & our first employment was to prepare a general form to be proposed to such nations as were disposed to treat with us. During the negotiations for peace with the British Commissioner David Hartley, our Commissioners had proposed, on the suggestion of Doctr. Franklin, to insert an article exempt-

The Hôtel de Langeac, where he lived from 1785 to 1789, is also at far left in the picture opposite.

ing from capture by the public or private armed ships of either belligerent, when at war, all merchant vessels and their cargoes, employed merely in carrying on the commerce between nations. It was refused by England, and unwisely, in my opinion. For in the case of a war with us, their superior commerce places infinitely more at hazard on the ocean than ours; and as hawks abound in porportion to game, so our privateers would swarm in proportion to the wealth exposed to their prize, while theirs would be few for want of subjects of capture. We inserted this article in our form, with a provision against the molestation of fishermen, husbandmen, citizens unarmed and following their occupations in unfortified places, for the humane treatment of prisoners of war, the abolition of contraband of war, which exposes merchant vessels to such vexatious & ruinous detentions and abuses; and for the principle of free bottoms, free goods.

At the beginning of his mission, Jefferson was optimistic about prospects for favorable trade treaties. The Austrian Empire had reopened an old dispute with the Netherlands over the Scheldt River, and Jefferson wrote James Monroe of the advantages American diplomats might gain from a European war. He also outlined what he thought United States policy should be in dealing with the Barbary pirates.

Paris Nov. 11. 1784.

The die is thrown here and has turned up war. Doubts whether an accomodation may not yet take place are still entertained by some, but I hold it impossible.... Supposing we are not involved in a new contest with Great Britain, this war may possibly renew that disposition in the powers of Europe to treat with us on liberal principles, a disposition which blazed out with enthusiasm on the conclusion of peace, but which had subsided as far below the just level in consequence of the anarchy, and depravation of principle which the British papers have constantly held forth as having taken place among us. I think when it shall become certain that war is to take place, that those nations at least who are engaged in it will be glad to ensure our neutrality and friendly dispositions by a just treaty. Such a one, or none is our business.

Engraving of David Hartley after a portrait by George Romney

[But, he warned Congressman Monroe, there was little

Jefferson made this drawing of the Hôtel de Langeac and its gardens.

John Paul Jones by Charles Willson Peale

chance of success in forcing commercial concessions from Britain, the commissioners' main goal, until Congress enforced the principle that "there should be no trade where there is no treaty."]

With England nothing will produce a treaty but an enforcement of the resolutions of Congress proposing that there should be no trade where there is no treaty. The infatuation of that nation seems really preternatural. If any thing will open their eyes it will be an application to the avarice of their merchants who are the very people who have opposed the treaty first meditated, and who have excited the spirit of hostility at present prevailing against us. Deaf to every principle of common sense, insensible of the feelings of man, they firmly beleive they shall be permitted by us to keep all the carrying trade and that we shall attempt no act of retaliation because they are pleased to think it our interest not to do so.... We have taken some pains to find out the sums which the nations of Europe give to the Barbary states to purchase their peace. They will not tell this; yet from some glimmerings it appears to be very considerable; and I do expect that they would tax us at one, two, or perhaps three hundred thousand dollars a year. Surely our people will not give this. Would it not be better to offer them an equal treaty. If they refuse, why not go to war with them? Spain, Portugal, Naples and Venice are now at war with them. Every part of the Mediterranean therefore would offer us friendly ports. We ought to begin a naval power, if we mean to carry on our own commerce. Can we begin it on a more honourable occasion or with a weaker foe? I am of opinion Paul Jones with half a dozen frigates would totally destroy their commerce: not by attempting bombardments as the Mediterranean states do wherein they act against the whole Barbary force brought to a point, but by constant cruising and cutting them to peices by peicemeal.

As the winter wore on, progress on trade agreements was slow, despite the threat of war. Subsequently the commissioners decided, for strategic reasons, to propose no new treaties.

Autobiography, 1821
In a conference with the Count de Vergennes [Foreign

Minister of France], it was thought better to leave to legislative regulation on both sides such modifications of our commercial intercourse as would voluntarily flow from amicable dispositions. Without urging, we sounded the ministers of the several European nations at the court of Versailles, on their dispositions towards mutual commerce, and the expediency of encouraging it by the protection of a treaty. Old Frederic of Prussia met us cordially and without hesitation, and appointing the Baron de Thulemeyer, his minister at the Hague, to negotiate with us, we communicated to him our Project, which with little alteration by the King, was soon concluded. Denmark and Tuscany entered also into negociations with us. Other powers appearing indifferent we did not think it proper to press them. They seemed in fact to know little about us, but as rebels who had been successful in throwing off the yoke of the mother country. They were ignorant of our commerce, which had been always monopolized by England, and of the exchange of articles it might offer advantageously to both parties. They were inclined therefore to stand aloof until they could see better what relations might be usefully instituted with us. The negotiations therefore begun with Denmark & Tuscany we protracted designedly until our powers had expired; and abstained from making new propositions to others having no colonies; because our commerce being an exchange of raw for wrought materials, is a competent price for admission into the colonies of those possessing them: but were we to give it, without price, to others, all would claim it without price on the ordinary ground of gentis amicissimae [most favored nation].

Bill of exchange made out to Jefferson for first payment on proposed statue of Washington

Gradually Jefferson's responsibilities increased. William Short, a young protégé Jefferson had invited to join him in France, arrived from Virginia at the end of November, 1784, with a letter from Governor Benjamin Harrison. Harrison asked Jefferson and Franklin to select a sculptor for a statue of Washington commissioned by the Virginia assembly. At first this seemed a simple enough matter, and Jefferson replied to Harrison after conferences with the famed Jean Antoine Houdon.

Paris Jan. 12. 1785

There could be no question raised as to the Sculptor who should be employed, the reputation of Monsr. Houdon of

Houdon's statue of Washington for Virginia state capitol in Richmond

this city being unrivalled in Europe. He is resorted to for the statues of most of the sovereigns in Europe. On conversing with him, Doctr. Franklin and myself became satisfied that no statue could be executed so as to obtain the approbation of those to whom the figure of the original is known, but on an actual view by the artist. Of course no statue of Genl. Washington, which might be a true evidence of his figure to posterity could be made from his picture. Statues are made every day from portraits but if the person be living, they are always condemned by those who know him for a want of resemblance, and this furnishes a conclusive presumption that similar representations of the dead are equally unfaithful. Monsr. Houdon whose reputation is such as to make it his principal object, was so anxious to be the person who should hand down the figure of the General to future ages, that without hesitating a moment he offered to abandon his business here, to leave the statues of kings unfinished, and to go to America to take the true figure by actual inspection and mensuration.

The artistic commission proved unexpectedly complicated, and Jefferson would have to correspond for several years with Harrison's successor, his old political enemy Patrick Henry. It was no wonder that the statue was not completed until 1796, for every detail was the subject of endless discussion and debate. In 1787 Jefferson wrote Washington of the expert opinion sought concerning Washington's decision to be represented in modern dress.

Paris Aug. 14. 1787.
I was happy to find by the letter of Aug. 1. 1786. which you did me the honour to write me, that the modern dress for your statue would meet your approbation. I found it strongly the sentiment of [Benjamin] West, [John Singleton] Copeley, [John] Trumbul and [Mather] Brown in London, after which it would be ridiculous to add that it was my own. I think a modern in an antique dress as *just* an object of ridicule as an Hercules or Marius with a periwig and chapeau bras.

In January another friend was reunited with Jefferson when the Marquis de Lafayette returned to France from a triumphal American tour. Lafayette had to break the unhappy news that Jefferson's youngest daughter, Lucy, had died at the age of two and a half of whooping cough. Jefferson ended his first winter in Paris mourning the death of the last child born to his wife. In this mood, he wrote bitterly to Monroe of new demands made by the Barbary pirates.

[Paris, February 6, 1785]

The attempts heretofore made to suppress these powers have been to exterminate them at one blow. They are too numerous and powerful by land for that. A small effort, but long continued, seems to be the only method. By suppressing their marine and trade totally and continuing this till the present race of seamen should be pretty well out of the way and the younger people betaken to husbandry for which their soil and climate is well fitted, these nests of banditti might be reformed. I am not well enough acquainted with the present dispositions of the European courts to say whether a general confederacy might be formed for suppressing these pyracies. Such as should refuse would give us a just right to turn pyrates also on their West India trade, and to require an annual tribute which might reimburse what we may be obliged to pay to obtain a safe navigation in their seas. Were we possessed even of a small naval force what a bridle would it be in the mouths of the West India powers and how respectfully would they demean themselves toward us. Be assured that the present disrespect of the nations of Europe for us will inevitably bring on insults which must involve us in war. A coward is much more exposed to quarrels than a man of spirit.

Jefferson's compilation of his salary for several years in Paris; he wrote to James Monroe that meeting his diplomatic expenses required "rigid economy bordering...on meanness."

Fortunately, the mild spring brought a fresh assignment sure to return him to his usual energy and good humor. In May the aging Franklin was granted leave to return to America; Jefferson and Adams would become America's ministers at Paris and London, respectively. Their joint commission had produced only one successful negotiation, an agreement with Prussia; but Jefferson would henceforth be free to function more independently. One of his main objects was to open up the subject of fundamental reciprocity; he immediately wrote to Adams suggesting that they negotiate a treaty granting virtually unlimited reciprocity of rights to nationals among the contracting powers. He knew that Britain would reject it, but France might go along. It was really beyond their powers, but Jefferson was willing to risk proposing it; Adams never replied.

As Adams and Franklin made arrangements to leave France, Jefferson hurried to work out necessary details for his own responsibilities. Now certain that he would be abroad for some time, he decided to bring his younger daughter Mary, or Polly, to live with him. He began a campaign to persuade the nine-year-old girl to leave her beloved Aunt Eppes through letters that blended outright bribery with stern moral lessons.

Paris Sep. 20. 1785.
I know, my dear Polly, how sorry you will be, and ought to be, to leave them and your cousins but your [sister and m]yself cannot live without you, and after a while we will carry you back again to see your friends in Virginia. In the meantime you shall be taught here to play on the harpsichord, to draw, to dance, to read and talk French and such other things as will make you more worthy of the love of your friends. But above all things, by our care and love of you, we will teach you to love us more than you will do if you stay so far from us.... when you come here you shall have as many dolls and playthings as you want for yourself....I hope you are a very good girl, that you love your uncle and aunt very much, and are very thankful to them for all their goodness to you; that you never suffer yourself to be angry with any body, that you give your playthings to those who want them, that you do whatever any body desires of you that is right, that you never tell stories, never beg for any thing, mind your book and your work when your aunt tells you, never play but when she permits you, nor go where she forbids you. Remember too as a constant charge not to go out without your bonnet because it will make you very ugly and then we should not love you so much....We shall hope to have you with us next summer....

Miniature of Martha Jefferson at age seventeen, by Joseph Boze

By June Jefferson's melancholy had disappeared. Even in reporting a fatal ballooning accident to Joseph Jones, he emphasized the scientific significance of the ascension rather than its tragic outcome.

Paris, June 19, 1785.

An accident has happened here which will probably damp the ardour with which aerial navigation has been pursued. Monsr. Pilatre de Rosiere had been attending many months at Boulogne a fair wind to cross the channel in a baloon which was compounded of one of inflammable air and another called a Montgolfier with rarefied air only. He at length thought the wind fair and with a companion ascended. After proceeding in a proper direction about two leagues the wind changed and brought them again over the French coast. Being at the height of about 6000 feet some accident, unknown, burst the balloon of inflammable air and the Montgolfier being unequal alone to sustain their weight they precipitated from that height to the earth and were crushed to atoms. Though navigation by water is attended with frequent accidents, and in it's infancy must have been attended with more, yet these are now so familiar that we think little of them, while that which has signalised the two first martyrs to the aeronautical art will probably deter very many from the experiments they would have been disposed to make.

Jefferson made these calculations on his rate of walking from the Grille de Chaillot to various spots, noting that he walked a "French mile [1¼ English miles] in 17½ minutes."

Summer also brought an artistic assignment more to Jefferson's taste than the long negotiations with Houdon.

Autobiography, 1821

I was written to in 1785 (being then in Paris) by Directors appointed to superintend the building of a Capitol in Richmond, to advise them as to a plan, and to add to it one of a prison. Thinking it a favorable opportunity of introducing into the state an example of architecture in the classic style of antiquity, and the Maison quarrée of Nismes, an antient Roman temple, being considered as the most perfect model existing of what may be called Cubic architecture, I applied to M. Clerissault, who had published drawings of the Antiquities of Nismes, to have me a model of the building made in stucco, only changing the order from Corinthian to Ionic, on account of the difficulty of the Corinthian capitals. I yielded with reluctance to the taste of Clerissault, in his preference of the modern capital of Scamozzi to the more noble capital of antiquity. This was executed by the artist whom Choiseul Gouffier [a Frenchman who had traveled in the Ottoman Empire] had carried with him to Constantinople, and employed while Ambassador, there, in making those beautiful models of the remains of Grecian architecture which are to be seen at Paris. To adapt the exterior to our use, I drew a plan for the interior, with the apartments necessary for legislative, executive & judiciary purposes, and accommodated in their size and distribution to the form and dimensions of the building.

Jefferson's drawing of the front elevation of the Virginia capitol

As this fascinating project went forward, Jefferson received alarming news from Virginia: construction of the capitol had begun before his design was completed. He wrote indignantly to Madison.

Paris Sep. 20. 1785.
I have been much mortified with information which I received two days ago from Virginia that the first brick of the Capitol would be laid within a few days. But surely the delay of this peice of a summer would have been repaid by the savings in the plan preparing here, were we to value it's other superiorities as nothing. But how is a taste in this beautiful art to be formed in our countrymen, unless we avail ourselves of every occasion when public buildings are to be erected, of presenting to them models for their study and imitation? Pray try if you can effect the stopping of this work.... The loss will be only of the laying the bricks already laid, or a part of them.... This loss is not to be weighed against the saving of money which will arise, against the comfort of laying out the public money for something honourable, the satisfaction of seeing an object and proof of national good taste, and the regret and mortification of erecting a monument of our barbarism which will be loaded with execrations as long as it shall endure.

Plan Jefferson had made c. 1782–85 for extending the town of Richmond

The construction already started in Richmond was not irreversible and Jefferson continued his work on the plans. In January the drawings were ready, and he forwarded them to a friend, Dr. James Currie, with a touch of justifiable pride.

Paris Jan. 28. 1786.
I send by this conveiance designs for the Capitol. They

are not the brat of a whimsical conception never before brought to light, but copied from the most precious the most perfect model of antient architecture remaining on earth; one which has received the approbation of near 2000 years, and which is sufficiently remarkable to have been visited by all travellers.

With minor alterations, Jefferson's plans were used for the completion of the capitol, giving his state a splendid example of neoclassical architecture to symbolize the commonwealth. Even as he was collaborating with the French architectural expert Charles-Louis Clérisseau on the designs, Jefferson had begun assuming his duties as Minister to France. His position was a delicate one, due to Benjamin Franklin's overwhelming personal popularity with the French court and nation. Jefferson explained how he had successfully dealt with one aspect of this problem after Franklin's departure for the United States in July, 1785.

Houdon's bust of Benjamin Franklin

Philadelphia, Feb. 19. 1791

I can only therefore testify in general that there appeared to me more respect & veneration attached to the character of Doctor Franklin in France than to that of any other person in the same country, foreign or native....

When he left Passy, it seemed as if the village had lost it's Patriarch. On taking leave of the court, which he did by letter, the king ordered him to be handsomely complimented, & furnished him with a litter & mules of his own, the only kind of conveyance the state of his health could bear....

The succession to Dr. Franklin at the court of France, was an excellent school of humility. On being presented to any one as the Minister of America, the common-place question, used in such cases was *'c'est vous, Monsieur, qui remplace le Docteur Franklin?'* 'It is you, Sir, who replace Doctor Franklin?' I generally answered 'no one can replace him, Sir: I am only his successor.'

Jefferson never sought to rival his predecessor's popularity. Franklin had been an excellent representative for America during wartime, and he had been, in a sense, an advertisement for the new nation with his witty anecdotes and conscious role-playing. Jefferson, on the other hand, preferred to work quietly, often doggedly, behind the scenes—a method far better suited to the needs of America's diplomatic interests in the Confederation period. Jefferson's major task was to win concessions from France's powerful Minister of Foreign Affairs, the Comte de Vergennes, who, Jefferson once remarked, was guided by "devotion to the principles of pure despotism" and had no love for the American Republic. But the Count's "fear of England" made him "value us as a make weight." The elderly nobleman and the young American diplomat found each other surprisingly congenial colleagues, for they shared a dislike of intrigues.

Autobiography, 1821

The Count de Vergennes had the reputation with the diplomatic corps of being wary & slippery in his diplomatic intercourse; and so he might be with those whom he knew to be slippery and double-faced themselves. As he saw that I had no indirect views, practised no subtleties, meddled in no intrigues, pursued no concealed object, I found him as frank, as honorable, as easy of access to reason as any man with whom I had ever done business; and I must say the same for his successor Montmorin, one of the most honest and worthy of human beings.

In the summer of 1785, Jefferson had begun arranging for the personal direction of his embassy. William Short was named as his secretary, an appointment that gave Jefferson an invaluable and trusted aide during his remaining years in Paris. John Jay, in the Department for Foreign Affairs, received Jefferson's outline of his views on America's long-term commercial goals and the role of diplomacy in promoting them.

Paris Aug. 23, 1785.

We have now lands enough to employ an infinite number of people in their cultivation. Cultivators of the earth are the most valuable citizens. They are the most vigorous, the most independant, the most virtuous, and they are tied to their country and wedded to it's liberty and interests by the most lasting bands. As long therefore as they can find emploiment in this line, I would not convert them into mariners, artisans, or any thing else. But our citizens will find emploiment in this line till their numbers, and of course their productions, become too great for the demand both internal and foreign. This is not the case as yet, and probably will not be for a considerable time. As soon as it is, the surplus of hands must be turned to something else. I should then perhaps wish to turn them to the sea in preference to manufactures, because comparing the characters of the two classes I find the former the most valuable citizens. I consider the class of artificers as the panders of vice and the instruments by which the liberties of a country are generally overturned. However we are not free to decide this question on principles of theory only. Our people are decided in the opinion that it is necessary for us to take a share in the occupation of the ocean, and their established habits induce them to require that the sea be kept open to them, and that that line of policy be pursued which will render the use of that element as great as possible to them. I think it a duty in those entrusted with the administration of their affairs to conform themselves to the decided choice of their constituents: and that therefore we should in every instance preserve an equality of right to them in the transportation of commodities, in the right of fishing, and in the other uses of the sea. But what will be the consequence? Frequent wars without a doubt. Their property will be violated on the sea, and in foreign ports, their persons will be insulted, emprisoned &c. for pretended debts, contracts, crimes, contraband &c. &c. These insults must be resented, even if we had no feelings, yet to prevent their eternal repetition. Or in other words, our commerce on the ocean and in other countries must be paid for by frequent war. The justest dispositions possible in ourselves will not secure us against it. It would be necessary that all other nations were just also. Justice indeed on our part will save us from those wars which would have been produced by a contrary disposition. But how to prevent those produced by the wrongs of other nations? By putting ourselves in a condition to punish them. Weakness provokes insult and injury, while a condition to punish it often prevents it. This reasoning leads to the necessity of some naval force, that being the only weapo[n] with which we can reach an enemy. I think it to our interest to punis[h] the first insult: because an insult unpunished is the parent of many oth[ers]. We are not at this moment in a condition to do it, but we should put ourselv[es] into it as soon as possible. If a war with England should take place it see[ms] to me that the first thing necessary would be a resolution to abandon the carrying trade because we cannot protect it. Foreign nations must in that case be invited to bring us what we want and to take our productions in their own bottoms. This alone could prevent the loss of those productions to us and the acquisition of them to our enemy. Our seamen

Secretary Jay, to whom Jefferson reported, did not support his policy of multiplying diplomatic and commercial bonds with France; he once leaked part of the Minister's dispatches to the press.

Office of Secretary for Foreign Affairs, John Jay, in Philadelphia

might be emploied in depredations on their trade. But how dreadfully we shall suffer on our coasts, if we have no force on the water, former experience has taught us. Indeed I look forward with horror to the very possible case of war with an European power, and think there is no protection against them but from the possession of some force on the sea. Our vicinity to their West India possessions and to the fisheries is a bridle which a small naval force on our part would hold in the mouths of the most powerful of these countries. I hope our land office will rid us of our debts, and that our first attention then will be to the beginning a naval force of some sort. This alone can countenance our people as carriers on the water, and I suppose them to be determined to continue such.

In France, Jefferson could do little to further his proposal for developing an American navy; his own contribution to strengthening American commerce was to attempt to remove foreign restrictions on American goods and ships. He described his duties at Paris as "the receipt of our whale-oils, salted fish, and salted meats on favorable terms, the admission of our rice on equal terms with that of Piedmont, Egypt, & the Levant, a mitigation of the monopolies of our tobacco by the Farmers-general, and a free admission of our productions into their islands [the West Indies]...." His campaign began with a letter to Vergennes suggesting that the King abolish the monopoly held by the Farmers General, which had the sole right to purchase tobacco imports.

Paris August 15. 1785.
In truth no two countries are better calculated for the exchanges of commerce. France wants rice, tobacco, potash, furs, ship-timber. We want wines, brandies, oils and manufactures. There is an affection too between the two people which disposes them to favour one another. If they do not come together then to make the exchange in their own ports, it shews there is some substantial obstruction in the way. We have had the benefit of too many proofs of his majesty's friendly disposition towards the United states, and know too well his affectionate care of his own subjects, to doubt his willingness to remove these obstructions, if they can be unequivocally pointed out. It is for his wisdom to decide whether the [tobacco] monopoly which is the subject of this letter be deservedly classed with the principal of these.

Even as he cautiously introduced Vergennes to his theories of commercial reciprocity, Jefferson knew that his own nation could nullify his efforts. The American states, free to adopt individual trade restrictions, made it virtually impossible for a United States envoy in Europe to promise that a consistent American policy on trade existed. While his experiences abroad confirmed his dissatisfaction with the halting American Confederation, continued exposure to European society produced a subtle change in his reports home. As soon as he reached Europe, he had obliged friends in America with observations on politics and excited descriptions of scientific advances and the latest inventions. But Jefferson was primarily a student of the human condition; as a careful observer and conscientious reporter, he did not record his feelings on such complicated matters as the nature of the French people and their society until he was sure of his conclusions. Perhaps the best known of his analyses was contained in a 1785 letter to Carlo Bellini, William and Mary's first professor of modern languages. Jefferson had fought for Bellini's appointment at the college and he fulfilled a promise to give the Florentine savant his impressions of Europe with this famous and sometimes biting critique of the Old World.

Paris Sep. 30. 1785.

Behold me at length on the vaunted scene of Europe! It is not necessary for your information that I should enter into details concerning it. But you are perhaps curious to know how this new scene has struck a savage of the mountains of America. Not advantageously I assure you. I find the general fate of humanity here most deplorable. The truth of Voltaire's observation offers itself perpetually, that every man here must be either the hammer or the anvil. It is a true picture of that country to which they say we shall pass hereafter, and where we are to see god and his angels in splendor, and crouds of the damned trampled under their feet. While the great mass of the people are thus suffering under physical and moral oppression, I have endeavored to examine more nearly the condition of the great, to appreciate the true value of the circumstances in their situation which dazzle the bulk of the spectators, and especially to compare it with that degree of happiness which is enjoyed in America by every class of people. Intrigues of love occupy the younger, and those of ambition the more elderly part of the great. Conjugal love having no existence among them, domestic happiness, of which that is the basis, is utterly unknown. In lieu of this are substituted pursuits which nourish and invigorate all our bad passions, and which offer only moments of extasy amidst days and months

The Comte de Vergennes

of restlessness and torment. Much, very much inferior this to the tranquil permanent felicity with which domestic society in America blesses most of it's inhabitants, leaving them to follow steadily those pursuits which health and reason approve, and rendering truly delicious the intervals of these pursuits. In science, the mass of people is two centuries behind ours, their literati half a dozen years before us. Books, really good, acquire just reputation in that time, and so become known to us and communicate to us all their advances in knowlege. Is not this delay compensated by our being placed out of the reach of that swarm of nonsense which issues daily from a thousand presses and perishes almost in issuing? With respect to what are termed polite manners, without sacrificing too much the sincerity of language, I would wish [my] countrymen to adopt just so much of European politeness as to be ready [to] make all those little sacrifices of self which really render European manners amiable, and relieve society from the disagreeable scenes to which rudeness often exposes it. Here it seems that a man might pass a life without encountering a single rudeness. In the pleasures of the table they are far before us, because with good taste they unite temperance. They do not terminate the most sociable meals by transforming themselves into brutes. I have never yet seen a man drunk in France, even among the lowest of the people. Were I to proceed to tell you how much I enjoy their architecture, sculpture, painting, music, I should want words. It is in these arts they shine. The last of them particularly is an enjoiment, the deprivation of which with us cannot be calculated. I am almost ready to say it is the only thing which from my heart I envy them, and which in spight of all the authority of the decalogue I do covet.—But I am running on in an estimate of things infinitely better known to you than to me, and which will only serve to convince you that I have brought with me all the prejudices of country, habit and age.

One of the calling cards Jefferson used in France

Yet Jefferson's unfavorable reactions to French society were mitigated by a sincere affection for the French people, whose inbred gentility and courtesy were so like his own. He described their congenial temperament to Elizabeth Trist.

Paris Aug. 18. 1785.
I am much pleased with the people of this country. The roughnesses of the human mind are so thoroughly rubbed off with them that it seems as if one might glide thro' a whole life among them without a justle. Perhaps too their manners may be the best calculated for happiness to a people in their situation. But I am convinced they fall far short of effecting a happiness so temperate, so uniform and so lasting as is generally enjoyed with us. The domestic bonds here are absolutely done away. And where can their compensation be found? Perhaps they may catch some moments of transport above the level of the ordinary tranquil joy we experience, but they are separated by long intervals during which all the passions are at sea without rudder or compass. Yet fallacious as these pursuits of happiness are, they seem on the whole to furnish the most effectual abstraction from a contemplation of the hardness of their government. Indeed it is difficult to conceive how so good a people, with so good a king, so well disposed rulers in general, so genial a climate, so fertile a soil, should be rendered so ineffectual for producing human happiness by one single curse, that of a bad form of government. But it is a fact. In spite of the mildness of their governors the people are ground to powder by the vices of the form of government.

Jefferson's love for the common people of France was deepened by his compassion for their plight under the monarchy. In America he had written much of the evils of tyranny, but he had seen nothing of the human suffering of the subjects of a king until he came to Europe. The reality of despotism was far worse than anything he had imagined. "Of twenty millions of people supposed to be in France," he wrote an American correspondent, "I am of opinion there are nineteen millions more wretched, more accursed in every circumstance of human existence, than the most conspicuously wretched individual of the whole United States." Jefferson recounted to Madison an incident during a visit to Fountainebleau that illustrated the hopeless conditions under which the French lived.

Fontainebleau Oct. 28. 1785.
As soon as I had got clear of the town I fell in with a poor woman walking at the same rate with myself and going the same course. Wishing to know the condition of the labouring poor I entered into conversation with her, which I began by enquiries for the path which would lead

BOTH: *Geography*, GOODRICH

The lives of French peasants such as the above aroused Jefferson's compassion; below, women washing their clothes in the Seine.

me into the mountain: and thence proceeded to enquiries into her vocation, condition and circumstance. She told me she was a day labourer, at 8. sous [about eight cents] or 4 d. sterling the day; that she had two children to maintain, and to pay a rent of 30 livres [600 sous a year] for her house (which would consume the hire of 75 days), that often she could get no emploiment, and of course was without bread. As we had walked together near a mile and she had so far served me as a guide, I gave her, on parting 24 sous. She burst into tears of a gratitude which I could perceive was unfeigned, because she was unable to utter a word. She had probably never before received so great an aid. This little attendrissement, with the solitude of my walk led me into a train of reflections on that unequal division of property which occasions the numberless instances of wretchedness which I had observed in this country and is to be observed all over Europe. The property of this country is absolutely concentered in a very few hands, having revenues of from half a million of guineas a year downwards.... I asked myself what could be the reason that so many should be permitted to beg who are willing to work, and in a country where there is a very considerable proportion of uncultivated lands?... Whenever there is in any country, uncultivated lands and unemployed poor, it is clear that the laws of property have been so far extended as to violate natural right. The earth is given as a common stock for man to labour and live on.

Such experiences confirmed Jefferson's conviction that America was especially fortunate in being isolated from European influences and that those born American were blessed by Providence. He confessed his own homesickness to a Hessian friend, the Baron de Geismar, who had been a prisoner of war in Charlottesville during the Revolution.

Paris Sep. 6. 1785.

I am now of an age which does not easily accomodate itself to new manners and new modes of living: and I am savage enough to prefer the woods, the wilds, and the independance of Monticello, to all the brilliant pleasures of this gay capital. I shall therefore rejoin myself to my native country with new attachments, with exaggerated esteem for it's advantages, for tho' there is less wealth there, there is more freedom, more ease and less misery.

He disapproved of wealthy Americans who sent their sons to Europe for an education and warned friends not to endanger their children's morals by sending them abroad. He dismissed the supposed advantages of such travel in a letter to John Banister, Jr., the son of an old friend in Williamsburg.

Paris Oct. 15. 1785.

Let us view the disadvantages of sending a youth to Europe. To enumerate them all would require a volume. I will select a few. If he goes to England he learns drinking, horse-racing and boxing. These are the peculiarities of English education. The following circumstances are common to education in that and the other countries of Europe. He acquires a fondness for European luxury and dissipation and a contempt for the simplicity of his own country; he is fascinated with the privileges of the European aristocrats, and sees with abhorrence the lovely equality which the poor enjoys with the rich in his own country: he contracts a partiality for aristocracy or monarchy; he forms foreign friendships which will never be useful to him, and loses the season of life for forming in his own country those friendships which of all others are the most faithful and permanent: he is led by the strongest of all the human passions into a spirit for female intrigue destructive of his own and others happiness, or a passion for whores destructive of his health, and in both cases learns to consider fidelity to the marriage bed as an ungentlemanly practice and inconsistent with happiness: he recollects the voluptuary dress and arts of the European women and pities and despises the chaste affections and simplicity of those of his own country; he retains thro' life a fond recollection and a hankering after those places which were the scenes of his first pleasures and of his first connections; he returns to his own country, a foreigner, unacquainted with the practices of domestic œconomy necessary to preserve him from ruin; speaking and writing his native tongue as a foreigner, and therefore unqualified to obtain those distinctions which eloquence of the pen and tongue ensures in a free country.... Cast your eye over America: who are the men of most learning, of most eloquence, most beloved by their country and most trusted and promoted by them? They are those who have been educated among them, and whose manners, morals and habits are perfectly homogeneous with those of the country.

But whatever France's faults, Jefferson could console himself on being stationed in Paris rather than London. Early reports of John Adams's experiences in the British capital convinced Jefferson that his dislike of that nation (which he had never visited) was justified. He sympathized with Abigail Adams on her residence among the Britons and offered a facetious explanation for their ungracious behavior.

Paris Sep. 25. 1785.

I receive by Mr. Short a budget of London papers. They teem with every horror of which human nature is capable. Assassinations, suicides, thefts, robberies, and, what is worse than assassination, theft, suicide or robbery, the blackest slanders! Indeed the man must be of rock, who can stand all this; to Mr. Adams it will be but one victory the more. It would have illy suited me. I do not love difficulties. I am fond of quiet, willing to do my duty, but irritable by slander and apt to be forced by it to abandon my post. These are weaknesses from which reason and your counsels will preserve Mr. Adams. I fancy it must be the quantity of animal food eaten by the English which renders their character insusceptible of civilisation. I suspect it is in their kitchens and not in their churches that their reformation must be worked, and that Missionaries of that description from hence would avail more than those who should endeavor to tame them by precepts of religion or philosophy.

William Stephens Smith

Jefferson soon had an unwelcome opportunity to become better acquainted with the British. At the end of February, he received an unexpected visit from William Stephens Smith, John Adams's secretary. Smith brought word that the Portugese minister in London was ready to negotiate a treaty, and "more Important," that Adams had met three times with the ambassador from Tripoli and begged Jefferson to "come here without loss of Time." Jefferson seized the opportunity to discuss his views on the Barbary powers with Adams and arrived in London March 11.

It was Jefferson's only extended visit to England and as a diplomatic mission, it was inconclusive. A commercial treaty was reached with the Portugese envoy, but it was eventually repudiated by the Lisbon government. As for the Tripolitan ambassador, Abdrahamar, he revealed himself as an unabashed extortionist who regaled Adams and Jefferson with a narrative of his country's piratical history and an analysis of the religious justification for enslaving Christian "sinners" encountered on their raids. Jefferson wrote William Carmichael, the chargé d'affaires in Madrid, of the sum needed to exempt American shipping from such treatment.

Paris May 5. 1786.
He asked us thirty thousand guineas for a peace with his court, and as much for Tunis for which he said he could answer. What we were authorized to offer being to this but as a drop to a bucket, our conferences were repeated only for the purpose of obtaining information. If the demands of Algiers and Marocco should be proportioned to this, according to their superior power, it is easy to foresee that the U.S. will not buy a peace with money.

Such ridiculous demands only strengthened Jefferson's determination to resist the time-honored custom of blackmail by the Barbary States. When he returned to Paris, he drew up a plan for a federation with the smaller European maritime powers to act as an international patrol of the Mediterranean. His idea was not adopted at the time, however, and the problem of the Barbary pirates would plague him and the United States for almost twenty years more. The last task Jefferson and Adams undertook together, a final attempt to reach a trade agreement with Britain, was no more successful. The British ministers ignored them, and the bad manners of George III, who turned his back on the diplomats, confirmed Jefferson's contempt for that monarch.

Autobiography, 1821

On my presentation as usual to the King and Queen at their levees, it was impossible for anything to be more ungracious than their notice of Mr. Adams & myself. I saw at once that the ulcerations in the narrow mind of that mulish being left nothing to be expected on the subject of my attendance.

Jefferson's early dislike of Britain as an enemy in wartime hardened into smoldering resentment in time of peace. As he revealed in a letter to Carmichael, Jefferson did not believe that the conflict that had led to the Revolution was really over.

Paris May 5. 1786.
I think the king, ministers, and nation are more bitterly hostile to us at present than at any period of the late war.... Our enemies (for such they are in fact) have for 12. years past followed but one uniform rule, that of doing exactly the contrary of what reason points out. Having early during our contest observed this in the British conduct, I governed myself by it in all prognostications of their measures; and I can say with truth it

never failed me but in the circumstance of their making peace with us.

The only pleasant memories Jefferson carried back to France from Britain were those of English gardens he and Adams toured during his stay. Thomas Whately's *Observations on Modern Gardening* had been Jefferson's botanical bible when he laid out his own gardens at Monticello. In touring some of the famous sites described by Whately, Jefferson was delighted to find that the descriptions he had read so carefully in Virginia were "remarkable for their exactness."

"Notes of a Tour of English Gardens" [April, 1786]
I always walked over the gardens with his book in my hand, examined with attention the particular spots he described, found them so justly characterised by him as to be easily recognised, and saw with wonder, that his fine imagination had never been able to seduce him from the truth. My enquiries were directed chiefly to such practical things as might enable me to estimate the expence of making and maintaining a garden in that style.

In a description of his British visit to John Page, Jefferson could, indeed, find little to commend except those gardens.

Paris May 4. 1786.
The gardening in that country is the article in which it surpasses all the earth. I mean their pleasure gardening. This indeed went far beyond my ideas. The city of London, tho' handsomer than Paris, is not so handsome as Philadelphia. Their architecture is in the most wretched stile I ever saw, not meaning to except America where it is bad, nor even Virginia where it is worse than in any other part of America, which I have seen. The mechanical arts in London are carried to a wonderful perfection.

The best part of his stay was the chance to confirm his ties with the Adamses. Jefferson wrote James Madison of his reassessment of his colleague in London.

Paris Jan. 30. 1787.
You know the opinion I formerly entertained of my friend Mr. Adams. Yourself and the governor [Edmund Randolph] were the first who shook that opinion. I

afterwards saw proofs which convicted him of a degree of vanity, and of a blindness to it, of which no germ had appeared in Congress. A 7-months' intimacy with him here and as many weeks in London have given me opportunities of studying him closely. He is vain, irritable and a bad calculator of the force and probable effect of the motives which govern men. This is all the ill which can possibly be said of him. He is as disinterested as the being which made him: he is profound in his views: and accurate in his judgment except where knowledge of the world is necessary to form a judgment. He is so amiable, that I pronounce you will love him if ever you become acquainted with him.

John Adams, 1788, by Mather Brown

Leaving the Adamses, a haven of American hospitality and affectionate family life, Jefferson must have journeyed to Paris a lonely man. Patsy would soon be of age to marry and leave him, and young Polly still resisted efforts to bring her to France. At forty-three Jefferson had been a widower four and a half years, devoted to the memory of his wife and the education of their daughters. When he returned to Paris, he was vulnerable to emotional attachments as he had never been since Martha's death. Since then he had formed many friendships with women, mainly with the wives of colleagues like Adams and Lafayette and with the stimulating intellectuals of the Paris salons. But there had been no hint of romance in his life. The idleness and dissipation of most of the ladies of the French upper class disgusted Jefferson, and he would hardly have been attracted by one of the glittering creatures he described to Mrs. William Bingham, a beautiful young Philadelphia matron who had visited Paris with her husband.

Country Seats of the United States... BY WILLIAM BIRCH, 1808

Lansdowne, the country home of the William Binghams of Philadelphia

Paris Feb. 7. 1787.

You are then engaged to tell me truly and honestly whether you do not find the tranquil pleasures of America preferable to the empty bustle of Paris. For to what does that bustle tend? At eleven o'clock it is day chez Madame. The curtains are drawn. Propped on bolsters and pillows, and her head scratched into a little order, the bulletins of the sick are read, and the billets of the well. She writes to some of her acquaintance and receives the visits of others. If the morning is not very thronged, she is able to get out and hobble round the cage of the Palais royal: but she must hobble quickly, for the Coeffeur's turn is come; and a tremendous turn it is! Happy, if he does not make her arrive when dinner is half over! The torpitude of digestion a little passed, she flutters half an hour thro' the streets by way of paying visits, and then to the Spectacles. These finished, another half hour is devoted to dodging in and out of the doors of her very sincere friends, and away to supper. After supper cards; and after cards bed, to rise at noon the next day, and to tread, like a mill-horse, the same trodden circle over again. Thus the days of life are consumed, one by one, without an object beyond the present moment....

In America, on the other hand, the society of your husband, the fond cares for the children, the arrangements of the house, the improvements of the grounds fill every moment with a healthy and an useful activity. Every exertion is encouraging, because to present amusement it joins the promise of some future good. The intervals of leisure are filled by the society of real friends, whose affections are not thinned to cob-web by being spread over a thousand objects.

In the summer of 1786, Jefferson met a woman whose accomplishments went beyond those of Parisian socialites—Maria Hadfield Cosway. At twenty-seven, Mrs. Cosway had begun to earn a reputation as a miniaturist, and she shared Jefferson's musical talents. Maria was quite unlike the French aristocrats Jefferson scorned, and she was equally unlike the provincial ladies of Virginia and the serious, intellectual Abigail Adams. An Englishwoman who had spent her girlhood in Italy, Maria Cosway was cosmopolitan and charming—and an incurable flirt. When she visited Paris with her husband Richard, a fashionable painter, they were introduced to Jefferson by the American artist John Trumbull.

It was soon apparent that Jefferson found the blonde, blue-eyed Mrs. Cosway irresistible, and the summer ended with a month of clandestine meetings with Maria. Jefferson was hopelessly infatuated, and Mrs. Cosway encouraged his restrained but flattering advances. Their brief romance ended in October when she and her husband returned to England, and that sad occasion was immortalized by a letter Jefferson composed after bidding her farewell. His "dialogue between my Head and my Heart" is a touching love letter made all the more poignant because the "Head" of the Virginia philosopher and diplomat seems to emerge a victor over the "Heart" of the lonely widower.

Paris Octob. 12. 1786.

[My dear] Madam

Having performed the last sad office of handing you into your carriage at the Pavillon de St. Denis, and seen the wheel get actually into motion, I turned on my heel and walked, more dead than alive, to the opposite door, where my own was awaiting me.... I was carried home. Seated by my fire side, solitary and sad, the following dialogue took place between my Head and my Heart.

HEAD. Well, friend, you seem to be in a pretty trim.

HEART. I am indeed the most wretched of all earthly beings. Overwhelmed with grief, every fibre of my frame distended beyond it's natural powers to bear, I would willingly meet whatever catastrophe should leave me no more to feel or to fear.

HEAD. These are the eternal consequences of your warmth and precipitation. This is one of the scrapes into which you are ever leading us. You confess your follies indeed: but still you hug and cherish them, and no reformation can be hoped, when there is no repentance.

HEART. Oh my friend! This is no moment to upbraid my foibles. I am rent into fragments by the force of my grief! If you have any balm, pour it into my wounds: if none, do not harrow them by new torments. Spare me in this awful moment! At any other I will attend with patience to your admonitions....

[Here the "dialogue" becomes a recollection of Jefferson's brief friendship with the Cosways, from the day they met.]

HEAD. Thou art the most incorrigible of all the beings that ever sinned! I reminded you of the follies of the first day, intending to deduce from thence some useful lessons for you, but instead of listening to these, you kindle at the recollection, you retrace the whole series with a fondness which shews you want nothing but the opportunity to act it over again. I often told you during it's course that you were imprudently engaging your affections under circumstances that must cost you a great deal of pain: that the persons indeed were of the greatest merit, possessing good sense, good humour, honest hearts, honest manners, and eminence in a lovely art: that the lady had moreover qualities and accomplishments, belonging to her sex, which might form a chapter apart for her: such as music, modesty, beauty, and that softness of disposition which

Maria Cosway, engraving after a drawing by Richard Cosway

is the ornament of her sex and charm of ours. But that all these considerations would increase the pang of separation: that their stay here was to be short: that you rack our whole system when you are parted from those you love, complaining that such a separation is worse than death, inasmuch as this ends our sufferings, whereas that only begins them: and that the separation would in this instance be the more severe as you would probably never see them again.

HEART. But they told me they would come back again the next year.

HEAD. But in the mean time see what you suffer: and their return too depends on so many circumstances that if you had a grain of prudence you would not count upon it. Upon the whole it is improbable and therefore you should abandon the idea of ever seeing them again.

HEART. May heaven abandon me if I do! ...

[Next Jefferson fantasized on a visit to America by the two painters: "Where could they find such objects as in America for the exercise of their enchanting art?"]

HEAD. I did not begin this lecture my friend with a view to learn from you what America is doing. Let us return then to our point. I wished to make you sensible how imprudent it is to place your affections, without reserve, on objects you must so soon lose, and whose loss when it comes must cost you such severe pangs. Remember the last night. You knew your friends were to leave Paris to-day. This was enough to throw you into agonies. All night you tossed us from one side of the bed to the other. No sleep, no rest.... This is not a world to live at random in as you do. To avoid these eternal distresses, to which you are for ever exposing us, you must learn to look forward before you take a step which may interest our peace. Everything in this world is matter of calculation. Advance then with caution, the balance in your hand. Put into one scale the pleasures which any object may offer; but put fairly into the other the pains which are to follow, and see which preponderates. The making an acquaintance is not a matter of indifference. When a new one is proposed to you, view it all round. Consider what advan-

Both Maria Cosway and her husband were accomplished painters. Richard drew the charming portrait of Maria (opposite), possibly while they were in Paris. Maria exhibited her painting The Hours *in the Royal Academy, from which the engraving (above) was made by Bartolozzi.*

tages it presents, and to what inconveniencies it may expose you. Do not bite at the bait of pleasure till you know there is no hook beneath it. The art of life is the art of avoiding pain: and he is the best pilot who steers clearest of the rocks and shoals with which it is beset. Pleasure is always before us; but misfortune is at our side: while running after that, this arrests us. The most effectual means of being secure against pain is to retire within ourselves, and to suffice for our own happiness.... Friendship is but another name for an alliance with the follies and the misfortunes of others....

HEART. And what more sublime delight than to mingle tears with one whom the hand of heaven hath smitten! To watch over the bed of sickness, and to beguile it's tedious and it's painful moments! To share our bread with one to whom misfortune has left none! This world abounds indeed with misery: to lighten it's burthen we must divide it with one another.... Let the gloomy Monk, sequestered from the world, seek unsocial pleasures in the bottom of his cell! Let the sublimated philosopher grasp visionary happiness while pursuing phantoms dressed in the garb of truth! Their supreme wisdom is supreme folly: and they mistake for happiness the mere absence of pain. Had they ever felt the solid pleasure of one generous spasm of the heart, they would exchange for it all the frigid speculations of their lives, which you have been vaunting in such elevated terms. Believe me then, my friend, that that is a miserable arithmetic which would estimate friendship at nothing, or at less than nothing. Respect for you has induced me to enter into this discussion, and to hear principles uttered which I detest and abjure. Respect for myself now obliges me to recall you into the proper limits of your office. When nature assigned us the same habitation, she gave us over it a divided empire. To you she allotted the field of science, to me that of morals. When the circle is to be squared, or the orbit of a comet to be traced; when the arch of greatest strength, or the solid of least resistance is to be investigated, take you the problem: it is yours: nature has given me no cognisance of it. In like manner in denying to you the feelings of sympathy, of benevolence, of gratitude, of justice, of love, of friendship, she has excluded you from their controul.... Fill paper as you please with triangles and squares: try how many ways you can hang and combine them together. I shall never envy nor controul your sublime delights. But leave me to decide when and where friendships are to be contracted....

I thought this a favorable proposition whereon to rest the issue of the dialogue. So I put an end to it by calling for my nightcap. Methinks I hear you wish to heaven I had called a little sooner, and so spared you the ennui of such a tedious sermon.... Present me in the most friendly terms to Mr. Cosway, and receive me into your own recollection with a partiality and a warmth, proportioned, not to my own poor merit, but to the sentiments of sincere affection and esteem with which I have the honour to be, my dear Madam, your most obedient and humble servant,

TH: JEFFERSON

Jefferson was left alone in Paris with bittersweet memories of the coquettish Maria and a painful reminder of the romantic interlude: a severely injured right wrist resulting from a mysterious accident on September 18. Jefferson himself never explained the mishap beyond a rather sheepish reply to William Stephens Smith's concerned inquiries: "How the right hand became disabled would be a long story for the left to tell. It was by one of those follies from which good cannot come, but ill may." One theory is that he injured it trying to vault a wall in an attempt to impress Maria. If so, he paid dearly for playing the energetic suitor.

Diagnosed as a dislocation, the injury caused him constant pain in the fall of 1786. The continued swelling and the amount of physical pain indicate that the wrist may actually have been broken and never properly treated. Whatever its cause and precise nature, the injury prevented him from writing, and for an eighteenth-century diplomat in a foreign post, that was a major handicap. William Short could copy many official dispatches and Jefferson tried valiantly to write with his left hand, but his personal correspondence lapsed in the autumn months, and he carefully limited the number and length of official reports.

One topic had to be reported promptly, and proudly, to Secretary Jay: the success of Jefferson's efforts to gain trade concessions from France. Lafayette had guided Jefferson in implementing the proposals given to Vergennes in the fall of 1785. Prominent French business experts, introduced to Jefferson by the Marquis, urged him to propose that the government appoint a committee to consider Franco-American trade. Lafayette undertook this delicate assignment for him, and Calonne, the French

Minister of Finance, approved the proposal and even named Lafayette to the committee. On October 23, Jefferson gave Jay an account of the outcome of the committee's sessions.

Paris Oct. 23. 1786.

...[A] Committee had been established for considering the means of promoting the general commerce with America, and the M. de la Fayette was named of that committee. His influence in obtaining that establishment was valuable, but his labors and his perseverance as a member of it became infinitely more so.... we thought it expedient to bring the general subject of the American commerce before the Committee; and as the members were much unacquainted with the nature and value of our Commercial productions, the Marquis proposed that in a letter to him as a member I should give as particular details of them as I could, as a ground for the committee to proceed on. I did so.... The committee were well disposed, and agreed to report not only the general measures which they thought expedient to be adopted, but the form of the letter to be written by the Minister of finance to me, for the communication of those measures. I have received his letter this morning and have now the honour to inclose it. I accompany it with the one proposed by the committee...: it furnishes a proof of the disposition of the king and his ministers to produce a more intimate intercourse between the two nations. Indeed I must say that, as far as I am able to see, the friendship of the people of this country towards us is cordial and general, and that it is a kind of security for the friendship of ministers who cannot in any country be uninfluenced by the voice of the people. To this we may add that it is their interest as well as ours to multiply the bands of friendship between us.

Houdon's bust of Lafayette

Calonne's letter endorsing the committee's propositions did not solve all of the problems of American trade with France; but it was a triumph for Jefferson and an example of his flexibility as a diplomat and advocate of his country's interests. But even this could not distract him from the continuing, nagging pain of his right arm. His disability increased his interest in an invention he had designed while in England: a portable copying machine that would eliminate much unnecessary writing. He delightedly announced its successful manufacture to Madison and promised to send his friend a duplicate.

Paris Jan. 30. 1787.
Having a great desire to have a portable copying machine, and being satisfied from some experiments that the principle of the large machine might be applied in a small one, I planned one when in England and had it made. It answers perfectly. I have since set a workman to making them here, and they are in such demand that he has his hands full. Being assured that you will be pleased to have one, when you shall have tried it's convenience, I send you one by Colo. [David] Franks. The machine costs 96 livres, the appendages 24. livres, and I send you paper and ink for 12 livres, in all 132 livres. There is a printed paper of directions: but you must expect to make many essays before you succeed perfectly.

In December Jefferson gradually resumed his personal correspondence, using his left hand. That month he learned of Shays' Rebellion, the insurrection in Massachusetts of debtors against creditors. His first reaction was a calm one as shown in these remarks to Ezra Stiles, president of Yale.

Paris Dec. 24. 1786
The commotions which have taken place in America, as far as they are yet known to me, offer nothing threatening. They are a proof that the people have liberty enough, and I would not wish them less than they have. If the happiness of the mass of the people can be secured at the expence of a little tempest now and then, or even of a little blood, it will be a precious purchase.

As Jefferson heard more about those "commotions" in Massachusetts, he took an even more sympathetic position toward the followers of Daniel Shays. He came to see insurrection as an example of the need for expressions of discontent in a free society. This view was expressed to James Madison.

Paris Jan. 30. 1787.
I hold it that a little rebellion now and then is a good thing, and as necessary in the political world as storms in the physical. Unsuccesful rebellions indeed generally establish the incroachments on the rights of the people which have produced them. An observation of this truth should render honest republican governors so mild in their punishment of rebellions, as not to discourage them

too much. It is a medecine necessary for the sound health of government.

Indeed, Shays' Rebellion gave Jefferson an opportunity to articulate a theory of the relationship of public authority to the right of freedom of expression by the governed. He saw less need to punish the insurgents than for America's leaders to draw proper lessons from the incident, as he outlined to Edward Carrington, a Virginia congressman.

Paris Jan. 16. 1787.

The people are the only censors of their governors: and even their errors will tend to keep these to the true principles of their institution. To punish these errors too severely would be to suppress the only safeguard of the public liberty. The way to prevent these irregular interpositions of the people is to give them full information of their affairs thro' the channel of the public papers, and to contrive that those papers should penetrate the whole mass of the people. The basis of our governments being the opinion of the people, the very first object should be to keep that right; and were it left to me to decide whether we should have a government without newspapers, or newspapers without a government, I should not hesitate a moment to prefer the latter.... Cherish therefore the spirit of our people, and keep alive their attention. Do not be too severe upon their errors, but reclaim them by enlightening them. If once they become inattentive to the public affairs, you and I, and Congress, and Assemblies, judges and governors shall all become wolves. It seems to be the law of our general natures, in spite of individual exceptions; and experience declares that man is the only animal which devours his own kind, for I can apply no milder term to the government of Europe, and to the general prey of the rich on the poor.

John Trumbull painted this miniature in London in 1788 for Mrs. Angelica Church; it was a replica of a likeness of Jefferson he had done from life the previous year for the Declaration of Independence.

Even the opportunity to reflect on the nature of revolution could not distract Jefferson from his discomfort. By December, 1786, he had decided to follow his physicians' advice to visit the mineral springs at Aix-en-Provence in the hope the waters might help his wrist heal. Before the accident, he had made preliminary plans to visit southern France to see the famed Canal of Languedoc, and his original itinerary could easily be expanded to include Aix. By February, he had completed arrangements for the trip. His gloomy mood reflected the hardships of the last months. A few days before his departure, he witnessed the opening of the Assembly of Notables, an advisory body convened to prepare some plan to rescue France from economic collapse. Parisians' attitudes toward the Notables prompted Jefferson to write an uncharacteristically dour letter to Abigail Adams.

Paris Feb. 22. 1787.

This occasion, more than any thing I have seen, convinces me that this nation is incapable of any serious effort but under the word of command. The people at large view every object only as it may furnish puns and bon mots; and I pronounce that a good punster would disarm the whole nation were they ever so seriously disposed to revolt. Indeed, Madam, they are gone. When a measure so capable of doing good as the calling of the Notables is treated with so much ridicule, we may conclude the nation desperate, and in charity pray that heaven may send them good kings.

Voyage Pittoresque de la France
BY JEAN BENJAMIN DE LA BORDE, 1780-96

View of the city of Lyon where Jefferson ran into bad weather

Jefferson clearly needed a vacation from Paris and the duties of his office. His carriage left the city on February 28 and he journeyed down the Rhone Valley to Aix. At Lyon he grumbled: "No complaints except against the weather maker, who has pelted me with rain, hail, and snow, almost from the moment of my departure to my arrival here." But his mood improved quickly. He began to fill a notebook with observations on local agriculture, trade patterns, and social conditions, descriptions of forges and bridges, chimneys and pumps. Nearly three weeks after leaving Paris, Jefferson at last saw the Maison Carrée at Nîmes, which he had grown to love secondhand and which had inspired his designs for the Virginia capitol. He told his friend Madame de Tessé of his rapture at actually viewing the ruins of the ancient building that had so long obsessed him.

Nismes. Mar. 20. 1787.

Here I am, Madam, gazing whole hours at the Maison quarrée, like a lover at his mistress. The stocking-weavers and silk spinners around it consider me as an hypochondriac Englishman, about to write with a pistol the last chapter of his history. This is the second time I have been in love since I left Paris. The first was with a Diana at the Chateau de Laye Epinaye in the Beaujolois, a delicious morsel of sculpture, by Michael Angelo Slodtz. This, you will say, was in rule, to fall in love with a fine woman: but, with a house! It is out of all precedent! No, madam, it is not without a precedent in my own history. While at Paris, I was violently smitten with the hotel de Salm, and used to go to the Thuileries almost daily to look at it.

The loueuse des chaises [chair keeper], inattentive to my passion, never had the complaisance to place a chair there; so that, sitting on the parapet, and twisting my neck round to see the object of my admiration, I generally left it with a torticollis. From Lyons to Nismes I have been nourished with the remains of Roman grandeur.

Continuing south to Aix-en-Provence, Jefferson wrote William Short that he had at last escaped the cold winter weather.

Aix en Provence March. 27. 1787.
I am now in the land of corn, wine, oil, and sunshine. What more can man ask of heaven? If I should happen to die at Paris I will beg of you to send me here, and have me exposed to the sun. I am sure it will bring me to life again. It is wonderful to me that every free being who possesses cent ecus de rente, does not remove to the Southward of the Loire. It is true that money will carry to Paris most of the good things of this canton. But it cannot carry thither it's sunshine, nor procure any equivalent for it. This city is one of the cleanest and neatest I have ever seen in any country.

Two days later he added a description of the language spoken in Provence to Short.

Aix Mar. 29. 1787.
I had thought the Provençale only a dialect of the French; on the contrary the French may rather be considered as a dialect of the Provençale. That is to say, the Latin is the original.... it is my Italian which enables me to understand the people here, more than my French. This language, in different shades occupies all the country South of the Loire. Formerly it took precedence of the French under the name of la langue Romans. The ballads of it's Troubadours were the delight of the several courts of Europe, and it is from thence that the novels of the English are called Romances. Every letter is pronounced, the articulation is distinct, no nasal sounds disfigure it, and on the whole it stands close to the Italian and Spanish in point of beauty. I think it a general misfortune that historical circumstances gave a final prevalence to the French instead of the Provençale language.

William Short

Jefferson spent four days trying the baths at Aix. But the treatment of his wrist, the ostensible reason for his visit, did not hold him long. There were better things to do, as he indicated in a letter from Marseilles to Jay: "Having staid at Aix long enough to prove the inefficacy of the waters, I came on to this place for the purpose of informing myself here, as I mean to do at the other seaport towns, of whatever may be interesting to our commerce." His exuberance was apparent in a letter to a friend in Paris, written from the Mediterranean seaport where he remained a week, very much the seasoned traveler.

Marseilles Apr. 5. 1787.
'A traveller, sais I, retired at night to his chamber in an Inn, all his effects contained in a single trunk, all his cares circumscribed by the walls of his apartment, unknown to all, unheeded, and undisturbed, writes, reads, thinks, sleeps, just in the moments when nature and the movements of his body and mind require. Charmed with the tranquillity of his little cell, he finds how few are our real wants, how cheap a thing is happiness, how expensive a one pride. He views with pity the wretched rich, whom the laws of the world have submitted to the cumbrous trappings of rank: he sees him labouring through the journey of life like an ass oppressed under ingots of gold, little of which goes to feed, to clothe, or to cover himself; the rest gobbled up by harpies of various description with which he has surrounded himself....

...I should go on, Madam, detailing to you my dreams and speculations; but that my present situation is most unfriendly to speculation. Four thousand three hundred and fifty market-women (I have counted them one by one) brawling, squabbling, and jabbering Patois, three hundred asses braying and bewailing to each other, and to the world, their cruel oppressions, four files of mule-carts passing in constant succession, with as many bells to every mule as can be hung about him, all this in the street under my window, and the weather too hot to shut it. Judge whether in such a situation it is easy to hang one's ideas together.

From Nice Jefferson wrote to Lafayette, one of the members of the Assembly of Notables then meeting at Versailles, of his "continued rapture" during his travels and urged his young friend to make a similar trip to familiarize himself with his native land and to prepare himself better for political leadership in France.

Nice, April 11, 1787.
I am constantly roving about, to see what I have never seen before and shall never see again. In the great cities, I go to see what travellers think alone worthy of being seen; but I make a job of it, and generally gulp it all down in a day. On the other hand, I am never satiated with rambling through the fields and farms, examining the culture and cultivators, with a degree of curiosity which makes some take me to be a fool, and others to be much wiser than I am.... I have often wished for you. I think you have not made this journey. It is a pleasure you have to come, and an improvement to be added to the many you have already made. It will be a great comfort to you to know, from your own inspection, the condition of all the provinces of your own country, and it will be interesting to them at some future day to be known to you. This is perhaps the only moment of your life in which you can acquire that knolege. And to do it most effectually you must be absolutely incognito, you must ferret the people out of their hovels as I have done, look into their kettles, eat their bread, loll on their beds under pretence of resting yourself, but in fact to find if they are soft. You will feel a sublime pleasure in the course of this investigation, and a sublimer one hereafter when you shall be able to apply your knolege to the softening of their beds, or the throwing a morsel of meat into the kettle of vegetables.

On April 13 Jefferson crossed the Alpes Maritimes into Italy on a mule. His notebook swelled with notes on his dogged research into such things as the secrets of rice culture in the Piedmont, which he hoped to introduce in the American South, and the preparation of Parmesan cheese. On his return to France he made his way to Cette where he continued on the Canal of Languedoc, a link between the Mediterranean and the Atlantic built by Louis XIV in the seventeenth century. It was this canal that had first inspired him to plan the trip and the waterway met all his expectations, he wrote William Short.

On the Canal of Languedoc, approaching Toulouse.
May 21. 1787.
I have passed through the Canal from it's entrance into the mediterranean at Cette to this place, and shall be immediately at Toulouse, in the whole 200 American miles, by water; having employed in examining all it's

Voyage, DE LA BORDE

Jefferson measured the bricks at these ruins of a Roman amphitheater in Bordeaux, which he saw in May.

details nine days, one of which was spent in making a tour of 40 miles on horseback, among the Montagnes noires, to see the manner in which water has been collected to supply the canal; the other eight on the canal itself. I dismounted my carriage from it's wheels, placed it on the deck of a light bark, and was thus towed on the canal instead of the post road. That I might be perfectly master of all the delays necessary, I hired a bark to myself by the day, and have made from 20. to 35 miles a day, according to circumstances, always sleeping ashore. Of all the methods of travelling I have tried this is the pleasantest. I walk the greater part of the way along the banks of the canal, level, and lined with a double row of trees which furnish shade. When fatigued I take seat in my carriage where, as much at ease as if in my study, I read, write, or observe. My carriage being of glass all round, admits a full view of all the varying scenes thro' which I am shifted, olives, figs, mulberries, vines, corn and pasture, villages and farms. I have had some days of superb weather, enjoying two parts of the Indian's wish, cloudless skies and limpid waters....

At Toulouse Jefferson left the canal and made his way on to Paris, still taking notes of vineyards and chateaus and anything else that seemed worthy of description. He arrived in the capital on June 11, rested by his trip and invigorated by the chance to observe new people and places, novel machines, and unfamiliar seaports. The first three years of his mission had been exhilarating. He had built on the foundations of Franklin's embassy with hard work and patience. Despite the limitations placed on his negotiations by the Confederation's lack of tax and commerce powers and a Secretary of Foreign Affairs who did not often share his views, Jefferson had done much to improve trade relations with France. His personal life had been full of friends, intellectual stimulation, and even a romantic affair. Ever the student, Jefferson had come to know France almost as well as his native Virginia. He expected to complete his mission secure in the confidence such knowledge gave him.

Chapter 7

A Rising Race of Republicans

After three years spent studying the French monarchy and devising ways to function with some effectiveness as an envoy of the Continental Congress, Jefferson would spend his last two years in Paris contemplating the disintegration of Bourbon power and the end of the Confederation of states that had sent him abroad. A friend to neither despotism nor inefficient government, Jefferson did not mourn the end of either regime. But he was concerned that the successors to these two discredited systems serve the interests of the French and American peoples.

The political and social changes that colored his last years abroad had already begun while Jefferson toured southern France. On May 25, as he took notes on the vineyards of Bordeaux, delegates met at Philadelphia in a convention called to revise the Articles of Confederation. That same day, Louis XVI dissolved the Assembly of Notables in Paris. Both actions reflected the failure of a political structure: Americans gathered in recognition of the need for a stronger government; the Notables' very existence was a tacit admission by the King that a financial crisis had developed which required him to consult his subjects, even a limited and privileged few, rather than impose his will upon them.

Jefferson was prevented from exerting direct influence on either developing reform movement. His residence in Europe meant that he had to rely on the effect of advice and guidance he had given earlier to friends in America. There was no time to offer immediate encouragement to delegates elected to the Federal Convention, and he could only wait in Paris to learn whether men like Madison and Wythe had been able to implement the changes he and they had advocated so long. Similarly, his position as a foreign diplomat in France meant that he could not properly intervene openly in the country's internal affairs. He was able to counsel friends like Lafayette who led the movement for liberal reforms, but that advice had to be offered discreetly and with no assurance that it would be followed. For a man of Jefferson's temperament, this was often a frustrating predicament. At a time when he would have chosen to take an active role in changing the courses of two nations he loved, he had to content himself with watching, observing, and patiently waiting for a moment when he might be of use.

He had already missed one chance to contribute to events in America. In December, 1786, he had learned that a constitutional convention would be called, but the difficulty of writing with his left hand limited his comments on that event to a brief recommendation to Madison for the separation of governmental powers. Only after his return to Paris in June, 1787, did Jefferson prepare lengthy discussions of specific reforms he thought should be implemented. By then several letters from correspondents had brought details of the election of delegates and of some of the proposals that might be advanced. Madison was chosen as one representative from Virginia and was to become the intellectual leader of the proceedings. Jefferson urged his friend to fight for an independent executive branch, but the advice did not reach Madison until the closing days of the convention.

> Paris June 20. 1787.
> The idea of separating the executive business of the confederacy from Congress, as the judiciary is already in some degree, is just and necessary. I had frequently pressed on the members individually, while in Congress, the doing this by a resolution of Congress for appointing an Executive committee to act during the sessions of Congress, as the Committee of the states was to act during their vacations. But the referring to this Committee all executive business as it should present itself, would require a more persevering self-denial than I supposed Congress to possess. It will be much better to make that separation by a federal act. The negative proposed to be given them on all the acts of the several legislatures is now for the first time suggested to my mind. Primâ facie I do not like it. It fails in an essential character, that the hole and the patch should be commensurate. But this proposes to mend a small hole by covering the whole garment.... Would not an appeal from the state judicatures to a federal court, in all cases where the act of Confederation controuled the question, be as effectual a remedy, and exactly commensurate to the defect.... An appeal to a federal court sets all to rights. It will be said that this court may encroach on the jurisdiction of the state courts. It may. But there will be a power, to wit Congress, to watch and restrain them. But place the same authority in Congress itself, and there will be no power above them to perform the same office.

Jefferson waited several weeks before replying to Edward Carrington who had also favored him with political news during his absence in southern France. It is clear from his reply that Jefferson expected the convention to retain the Articles of Confederation as the basic governmental framework, only adding centralization of the power to regulate commerce. He expounded the theory that the Confederation already had the powers necessary to compel the states to meet national requisitions — that such powers were clearly implied if not explicitly granted by the Articles.

Paris Aug. 4. 1787.

I confess I do not go as far in the reforms thought necessary as some of my correspondents in America; but if the Convention should adopt such propositions I shall suppose them necessary. My general plan would be to make the states one as to every thing connected with foreign nations, and several as to every thing purely domestic. But with all the imperfections of our present government, it is without comparison the best existing or that ever did exist. It's greatest defect is the imperfect manner in which matters of commerce have been provided for. It has been so often said, as to be generally believed, that Congress have no power by the confederation to enforce any thing, e.g. contributions of money. It was not necessary to give them that power expressly; they have it by the law of nature. When two nations make a compact, there results to each a power of compelling the other to execute it. Compulsion was never so easy as in our case, where a single frigate would soon levy on the commerce of any state the deficiency of it's contributions; nor more safe than in the hands of Congress which has always shewn that it would wait, as it ought to do, to the last extremities before it would execute any of it's powers which are disagreeable. — I think it very material to separate in the hands of Congress the Executive and Legislative powers, as the Judiciary already are in some degree. This I hope will be done. The want of it has been the source of more evil than we have ever experienced from any other cause. Nothing is so embarrassing nor so mischievous in a great assembly as the details of execution. The smallest trifle of that kind occupies as long as the most important act of legislation, and takes place of every thing else. Let any man recollect, or look over the files of Congress, he will observe the most important propositions hanging over from week to week and month to month, till the occasions have past them, and the thing

Thomas Rossiter's painting of the Constitutional Convention of 1787

never done. I have ever viewed the executive details as the greatest cause of evil to us, because they in fact place us as if we had no federal head, by diverting the attention of that head from great to small objects; and should this division of power not be recommended by the Convention, it is my opinion Congress should make it itself by establishing an Executive committee.

Jefferson's advocacy of a mere revision of the Articles may have been related to rumors Carrington had relayed that some in America were ready to "go to a monarchy at once." Having witnessed the collapse of France's economy at the hands of an inept king, Jefferson could not conceal his impatience in commenting on such proposals to Benjamin Hawkins, a member of Congress from North Carolina.

Paris Aug. 4. 1787.
And above all things I am astonished at some people's considering a kingly government as a refuge. Advise such to read the fable of the frogs who sollicited Jupiter for a king. If that does not put them to rights, send them to Europe to see something of the trappings of monarchy, and I will undertake that every man shall go back thoroughly cured. If all the evils which can arise among us from the republican form of our government from this day to the day of judgment could be put into a scale against what this country suffers from it's monarchical form in a week, or England in a month, the latter would preponderate....No race of kings has ever presented above one man of common sense in twenty generations.

The best they can do is to leave things to their ministers, and what are their ministers but a Committee, badly chosen? If the king ever meddles it is to do harm.

Jefferson's friends in the convention, bound by an oath of secrecy concerning the proceedings, could not allay his fears by telling him of the debates that summer. There was much to divert his attention from Philadelphia, however, for Paris had broken out in an unprecedented public protest against the monarchy. Jefferson sent a vivid account to John Adams.

> Paris Aug. 30. 1787.
> From the separation of the Notables to the present moment has been perhaps the most interesting interval ever known in this country. The propositions of the Government, approved by the Notables, were precious to the nation and have been in an honest course of execution, some of them being carried into effect, and others preparing. Above all the establishment of the Provincial assemblies... bid fair to be the instrument for circumscribing the power of the crown and raising the people into consideration.... In the mean time all tongues in Paris (and in France as it is said) have been let loose, and never was a license of speaking against the government exercised in London more freely or more universally. Caracatures, placards, bon mots, have been indulged in by all ranks of people, and I know of no well attested instance of a single punishment. For some time mobs of 10; 20; 30,000 people collected daily, surrounded the parliament house, huzzaed the members, even entered the doors and examined into their conduct, took the horses out of the carriages of those who did well, and drew them home. The government thought it prudent to prevent these, drew some regiments into the neighborhood, multiplied the guards, had the streets constantly patrolled by strong parties, suspended privileged places, forbad all clubs, etc. The mobs have ceased; perhaps this may be partly owing to the absence of parliament. The Count d'Artois [the King's brother], sent to hold a bed of justice in the Cour des Aides [court with jurisdiction in matters of tax revenues], was hissed and hooted without reserve by the populace; the carriage of Madame de (I forget the name) in the queen's livery was stopped by the populace under a belief that it was Madame de

A badge worn by the early revolutionaries in France

Polignac's [the royal children's governess] whom they would have insulted, the queen going to the theater at Versailles with Madame de Polignac was received with a general hiss. The king, long in the habit of drowning his cares in wine, plunges deeper and deeper; the queen cries but sins on.

It was November before Jefferson received a copy of the Constitution adopted by the Federal Convention from Adams's secretary, William Stephens Smith. Although it revealed that nothing close to a monarchy had been established, Jefferson was displeased by his first impression of the document, and he did not hesitate to describe his dissatisfaction to Adams.

Paris Nov. 13. 1787.
How do you like our new constitution? I confess there are things in it which stagger all my dispositions to subscribe to what such an assembly has proposed. The house of federal representatives will not be adequate to the management of affairs either foreign or federal. Their President seems a bad edition of a Polish king. He may be reelected from 4. years to 4. years for life. Reason and experience prove to us that a chief magistrate, so continuable, is an officer for life.... Once in office, and possessing the military force of the union, without either the aid or check of a council, he would not be easily dethroned, even if the people could be induced to withdraw their votes from him. I wish that at the end of the 4. years they had made him for ever ineligible a second time. Indeed I think all the good of this new constitution might have been couched in three or four new articles to be added to the good, old, and venerable fabrick, which should have been preserved even as a religious relique.

In a letter the same day to Smith, Jefferson grumbled that the Federal Convention had apparently come to believe the "lies" of the "British ministry" concerning the "anarchy" that the Articles of Confederation had imposed on America. In particular, Jefferson believed that Shays' Rebellion had exerted an influence out of all proportion to its importance. "Our Convention," he wrote, "has been too much impressed by the insurrection of Massachusetts: and in the spur of the moment they are setting up a kite to keep the hen yard in order."

Shays' followers, farmers and veterans, wanted to stop court-ordered foreclosures for debts until the state legislature granted them relief. In their attack on the Springfield arsenal (above), three men were killed by the militia.

Paris Nov. 13. 1787.
God forbid we should ever be 20. years without such a rebellion. The people can not be all, and always, well informed. The part which is wrong will be discontented in proportion to the importance of the facts they misconceive. If they remain quiet under such misconceptions it is a lethargy, the forerunner of death to the public liberty. We have had 13. states independant 11. years. There has been one rebellion. That comes to one rebellion in a century and a half for each state. What country before ever existed a century and half without a rebellion? And what country can preserve it's liberties if their rulers are not warned from time to time that their people preserve the spirit of resistance? Let them take arms. The remedy is to set them right as to facts, pardon and pacify them. What signify a few lives lost in a century or two? The tree of liberty must be refreshed from time to time with the blood of patriots and tyrants. It is it's natural manure.

Jefferson saved his most serious, and lengthy, critique for Madison, who had sent him a copy of the Constitution that arrived in December, along with a letter explaining the background of some of its provisions. Tactfully, Jefferson opened his reply with a list of those provisions he liked.

Paris Dec. 20. 1787.
I like much the general idea of framing a government which should go on of itself peaceably, without needing continual recurrence to the state legislatures. I like the organization of the government into Legislative, Judiciary and Executive. I like the power given the Legislature to levy taxes; and for that reason solely approve of the greater house being chosen by the people directly. For tho' I think a house chosen by them will be very illy qualified to legislate for the Union, for foreign nations &c. yet this evil does not weigh against the good of preserving inviolate the fundamental principle that the people are not to be taxed but by representatives chosen immediately by themselves. I am captivated by the compromise of the opposite claims of the great and little states, of the latter to equal, and the former to proportional influence. I am much pleased too with the substitution of the method of voting by persons, instead of that of

Title page of John Adams's three-volume treatise on government; the first volume was published in London early in 1787 and reached Philadelphia during the Convention.

voting by states: and I like the negative given to the Executive with a third of either house, though I should have liked it better had the Judiciary been associated for that purpose, or invested with a similar and separate power....

[As the author of the Declaration of Independence, with its forthright statement of human rights, Jefferson left little doubt about what he did not like.]

I will now add what I do not like. First the omission of a bill of rights providing clearly and without the aid of sophisms for freedom of religion, freedom of the press, protection against standing armies, restriction against monopolies, the eternal and unremitting force of the habeas corpus laws, and trials by jury in all matters of fact triable by the laws of the land and not by the law of Nations.... Let me add that a bill of rights is what the people are entitled to against every government on earth, general or particular, and what no just government should refuse, or rest on inference. The second feature I dislike, and greatly dislike, is the abandonment in every instance of the necessity of rotation in office, and most particularly in the case of the President. Experience concurs with reason in concluding that the first magistrate will always be re-elected if the constitution permits it. He is then an officer for life.... If once elected, and at a second or third election outvoted by one or two votes, he will pretend false votes, foul play, hold possession of the reins of government, be supported by the states voting for him, especially if they are the central ones lying in a compact body themselves and separating their opponents: and they will be aided by one nation of Europe, while the majority are aided by another. The election of a President of America some years hence will be much more interesting to certain nations of Europe than ever the election of a king of Poland was. Reflect on all the instances in history antient and modern, of elective monarchies, and say if they do not give foundation for my fears, the Roman emperors, the popes, while they were of any importance, the German emperors till they became hereditary in practice, the kings of Poland, the Deys of the Ottoman dependancies. It may be said that if elections are to be attended with these disorders, the seldomer they are renewed the better. But experience shews that the only way to prevent disorder is to render them uninteresting by frequent changes....

[Jefferson admitted that he did "not pretend to decide what would be the best method" of rectifying these flaws, but he urged Madison "not to be discouraged from other trials." He closed his letter with an analysis of his own philosophy.]

I own I am not a friend to a very energetic government. It is always oppressive.... Nor will any degree of power in the hands of government prevent insurrections. France with all it's despotism, and two or three hundred thousand men always in arms has had three insurrections in the three years I have been here in every one of which greater numbers were engaged than in Massachusets and a great deal more blood was spilt. In Turkey, which Montesquieu supposes more despotic, insurrections are the events of every day. In England, where the hand of power is lighter than here, but heavier than with us they happen every half dozen years. Compare again the ferocious depredations of their insurgents with the order, the moderation and the almost self extinguishment of ours.—After all, it is my principle that the will of the Majority should always prevail. If they approve the proposed Convention in all it's parts, I shall concur in it chearfully, in hopes that they will amend it whenever they shall find it work wrong. I think our governments will remain virtuous for many centuries; as long as they are chiefly agricultural; and this will be as long as there shall be vacant lands in any part of America. When they get piled upon one another in large cities, as in Europe, they will become corrupt as in Europe. Above all things I hope the education of the common people will be attended to; convinced that on their good sense we may rely with the most security for the preservation of a due degree of liberty.

Soon after examining the shortcomings of the Constitution, Jefferson was given a sharp reminder of the failings of the old Confederation. Early in 1788 Adams received permission to return home.

Among the many commissions he had held was one to negotiate loans for the United States, principally in the Netherlands. As soon as Adams knew he would be released from his unpleasant duties in London, he notified the bankers in Holland and "referred them to consult with me [Jefferson] in their future difficulties." This was an unpleasant surprise for Jefferson, for America's Treasury commissioners had recently notified the bankers that the United States might have to default on interest payments on old loans because of the unsatisfactory progress of a new loan recently floated in Europe. Willink & Van Staphorst, America's principal bankers in Amsterdam, proposed a plan to meet the crisis and at the same time profit at America's expense. European speculators in America's domestic debt would take up the balance of the new loan if they were allowed to deduct from their payments one year's interest due them on the old obligations. Jefferson probably never seriously believed that this scheme of financial extortion would be approved, but he told the Treasury commissioners: "One thing I could easily determine which was that the proposition was totally out of my province." When Adams visited The Hague in March to announce his departure, Jefferson met him there and subsequently reported to the commissioners the emergency measure he had initiated.

Amsterdam Mar. 29. 1788.

...I set out immediately for that place to get him [Adams] to come on here and join in conferences with the bankers to see what could be done to set the loan in motion again. We came here and our first object was to convince them there was no power on this side the Atlantic to accede to that proposition. At length we prevailed to get them and the brokers to abandon this idea.... It was agreed to push the loan on other grounds. But this appeared not enough. Your letter looked forward to the new government as the only resource for remittance. It was evident that for that to be adopted, it's legislature assembled, system of taxation established, the collection made and remitted, neither this year nor the next would suffice; and that to place the government perfectly at it's ease till this process could be gone through, the years 1789. and 1790. should be provided for as to all our European demands.... this will require another million of florins. The bankers joined us in opinion therefore that as Mr. Adams's powers to borrow had not been revoked, he should execute bonds for another million, which should be kept up till the ratification of Congress could be received. This being done, Mr. Adams was obliged to return to England....I have now waited twelve days since the departure of Mr.

RIJKSMUSEUM, AMSTERDAM

Jefferson stayed at this hotel, The Amsterdam Arms, during his visit.

Adams; and...both bankers and brokers from what they learn...are become well enough satisfied that the month of June will be provided for.

Jefferson was justly proud of his success in meeting this crisis, as he revealed in his *Autobiography.*

Autobiography, 1821

I had the satisfaction to reflect that by this journey, our credit was secured, the new government was placed at ease for two years to come, and that, as well as myself, relieved from the torment of incessant duns, whose just complaints could not be silenced by any means within our power.

At the end of March, Jefferson left Amsterdam and treated himself to a brief tour of a part of Europe with which he was not yet familiar. Instead of returning directly to Paris, he took a roundabout route, traveling up the Rhine and into Germany. His democratic biases were confirmed when he left Holland, with its republican regime, for imperial Germany and noted the "transition from ease and opulence to extreme poverty.... The soil and climate are the same," he remarked pointedly. "The governments alone differ." His notes on this trip showed a characteristic range, from comments on the "sublime" art gallery at Dusseldorf to observations on the hogs—"tall, gaunt, and with heavy lop ears"—that produced "the celebrated ham" of Westphalia. He confessed to William Short that one scene in particular seemed unexpectedly familiar.

Frankfort on the Maine April 9. 1788.

The neighborhood of this place is that which has been to us a second mother country. It is from the palatinate on this part of the Rhine that those swarms of Germans have gone, who, next to the descendants of the English, form the greatest body of our people. I have been continually amused by seeing here the origin of whatever is not English among us. I have fancied myself often in the upper parts of Maryland and Pennsylvania.

At Strasbourg Jefferson crossed the Rhine to continue back through France to Paris. The "awkward figure" of the moldboards on the peasants' plows inspired him to sketch a design for a more efficient plow, and the sight of women working as manual laborers in the French countryside merited an entry in his notes on the journey.

THE FOUNDING FATHERS

In Strasbourg Jefferson stayed at one of the city's oldest hostelries, to the left, on the Ill River.

Gallery of Palais Royal in Paris

Memorandums on a Tour from Paris to Amsterdam, Strasburg and back to Paris [April 19, 1788]

The women here, as in Germany do all sorts of work. While one considers them as useful and rational companions, one cannot forget that they are also objects of our pleasures. Nor can they ever forget it. While employed in dirt and drudgery some tag of a ribbon, some ring or bit of bracelet, earbob or necklace, or something of that kind will shew that the desire of pleasing is never suspended in them. How valuable is that state of society which allots to them internal emploiments only, and external to the men. They are formed by nature for attentions and not for hard labour. A woman never forgets one of the numerous train of little offices which belong to her; a man forgets often.

Jefferson arrived in Paris on the evening of April 23, by now an experienced traveler ready to offer advice to American visitors. In June he sent some hints for traveling abroad to John Rutledge, Jr., the son of a Charleston friend.

[Paris, June 19, 1788]

Buy beforehand the map of the country you are going into. On arriving at a town, the first thing is to buy the plan of the town, and the book noting it's curiosities. Walk round the ramparts when there are any. Go to the top of a steeple to have a view of the town and it's environs.

When you are doubting whether a thing is worth the trouble of going to see, recollect that you will never again be so near it, that you may repent the not having seen it, but can never repent having seen it. But there is an opposite extreme too. That is, the seeing too much. A judicious selection is to be aimed at, taking care that the indolence of the moment have no influence on the decision. Take care particularly not to let the porters of churches, cabinets &c. lead you thro' all the little details in their possession, which will load the memory with trifles, fatigue the attention and waste that and your time.... When one calls in the taverns for the vin du pays they give you what is natural and unadulterated and cheap: when vin etrangere is called for, it only gives a pretext for charging an extravagant price for an unwholsome stuff, very often of their own brewing.

The people you will naturally see the most of will be

tavern keepers, Valets de place, and postillions. These are the hackneyed rascals of every country. Of course they must never be considered when we calculate the national character.

Back in Paris, Jefferson was in a far better humor about the new Constitution. Even before he knew of its progress through the various state ratifying conventions, he confessed to Edward Carrington that its virtues had "gained" on him.

> Paris May 27. 1788.
> I learn with great pleasure the progress of the new Constitution. Indeed I have presumed it would gain on the public mind, as I confess it has on my own. At first, tho I saw that the great mass and groundwork was good, I disliked many appendages. Reflection and discussion have cleared off most of these.

Still, Jefferson had not been won over completely. His objections to unlimited terms for the President had faded, but his insistence on a bill of rights had not. In many states proponents of ratification argued that such provisions should be added as amendments through the process provided in the Constitution; they feared that if a new convention had to be called, the basic structure of the Constitution would be damaged and dangerous delay might result. Jefferson became reconciled to the idea of later amendments, but he demanded that they come as soon as possible. A letter from Madison explained some of the opposition to a bill of rights and contained a reference to the ineffectiveness of "parchment barriers" to tyranny. "In Virginia," Madison reminded his friend, "I have seen the bill of rights violated in every instance where it has been opposed to a popular current." Determined to convince Madison to continue the fight, Jefferson made a vigorous restatement of his views.

> Paris Mar. 15. 1789.
> The [Virginia] Declaration of rights is like all other human blessings alloyed with some inconveniences, and not accomplishing fully it's object. But the good in this instance vastly overweighs the evil. I cannot refrain from making short answers to the objections which your letter states to have been raised. 1. That the rights in question are reserved by the manner in which the federal powers are granted. Answer. A constitutive act may certainly be so formed as to need no declaration of rights. The act itself has the force of a declaration as

Jefferson made this tally in 1791 of the states' votes to ratify ten of twelve amendments (the Bill of Rights) Madison proposed to the First Congress in 1789.

far as it goes: and if it goes to all material points nothing more is wanting. In the draught of a constitution which I had once a thought of proposing in Virginia, and printed afterwards, I endeavored to reach all the great objects of public liberty, and did not mean to add a declaration of rights. Probably the object was imperfectly executed: but the deficiencies would have been supplied by others in the course of discussion. But in a constitutive act which leaves some precious articles unnoticed, and raises implications against others, a declaration of rights becomes necessary by way of supplement. This is the case of our new federal constitution. This instrument forms us into one state as to certain objects, and gives us a legislative and executive body for these objects. It should therefore guard us against their abuses of power within the feild submitted to them. 2. A positive declaration of some essential rights could not be obtained in the requisite latitude. Answer. Half a loaf is better than no bread. If we cannot secure all our rights, let us secure what we can. 3. The limited powers of the federal government and jealousy of the subordinate governments afford a security which exists in no other instance. Answer. The first member of this seems resolvable into the 1st. objection before stated. The jealousy of the subordinate governments is a precious reliance. But observe that those governments are only agents. They must have principles furnished them whereon to found their opposition. The declaration of rights will be the text whereby they will try all the acts of the federal government. In this view it is necessary to the federal government also: as by the same text they may try the opposition of the subordinate governments. 4. Experience proves the inefficacy of a bill of rights. True. But tho it is not absolutely efficacious under all circumstances, it is of great potency always, and rarely inefficacious. A brace the more will often keep up the building which would have fallen with that brace the less. There is a remarkeable difference between the characters of the Inconveniencies which attend a Declaration of rights, and those which attend the want of it. The inconveniences of the Declaration are that it may cramp government in it's useful exertions. But the evil of this is shortlived, moderate, and reparable. The inconveniencies of the want of a Declaration are permanent, afflicting and irreparable: they are in constant progression from bad to worse. The executive in our governments is not the sole, it is scarcely the principal object of my jealousy. The tyranny of the legislatures is the most formidable dread at present, and will be for long years. That of the executive will come in it's turn, but it will be at a remote period. I know there are some among us who would now establish a monarchy. But they are inconsiderable in number and weight of character. The rising race are all republicans. We were educated in royalism: no wonder if some of us retain that idolatry still. Our young people are educated in republicanism. An apostacy from that to royalism is unprecedented and impossible. I am much pleased with the prospect that a declaration of rights will be added: and hope it will be done in that way which will not endanger the whole frame of the government, or any essential part of it.

Book from Jefferson's library on the history and politics of the United States, which he had helped Philip Mazzei prepare in Paris in 1786

Jefferson could be frank with Madison concerning his reservations. In a letter to David Humphreys, an aide to Washington who had written of the general's expected election as the first President, Jefferson offered his official and public position on the new government.

Paris Mar. 18. 1789.
The operations which have taken place in America lately, fill me with pleasure. In the first place they realize the confidence I had that whenever our affairs get obviously wrong, the good sense of the people will interpose and set them to rights. The example of changing a constitution by assembling the wise men of the state, instead of assembling armies, will be worth as much to the world as the former examples we had given them. The constitution too which was the result of our deliberations, is unquestionably the wisest ever yet presented to men, and some of the accomodations of interest which it has adopted are greatly pleasing to me who have before had occasions of seeing how difficult those interests were to accomodate.

David Humphreys

If Jefferson was more sanguine about America's future in the spring of 1788, he was increasingly concerned for France's fate. "On my return from Holland," he recalled, "I found Paris as I had left it, still in high fermentation." The monarchy's efforts to find new sources of revenue met stubborn resistance from the local parlements, which withheld approval for additional borrowing. Delays in implementing reforms suggested by the Notables allowed, in Jefferson's phrase, "a pressure to arise for a fixed constitution, not subject to changes at the will of the king."

Autobiography, 1821

Nor should we wonder at this pressure when we consider the monstrous abuses of power under which this people were ground to powder, when we pass in review the weight of their taxes, and inequality of their distribution; the oppressions of the tythes, of the tailles, the corvées, the gabelles [an impost on salt], the farms & barriers; the shackles on Commerce by Monopolies; on Industry by gilds & corporations; on the freedom of conscience, of thought, and of speech; on the Press by the Censure; and of person by lettres de Cachet. The cruelty of the criminal code generally, the atrocities of the Rack, the venality of judges, and their partialities to the rich; the Monopoly of Military honors by the Noblesse; the enormous expenses of the Queen, the princes & the Court; the prodigalities of pensions; & the riches, luxury, indolence & immorality of the clergy. Surely under such a mass of misrule and oppression, a people might justly press for thoro' reformation, and might even dismount their roughshod riders, & leave them to walk on their own legs.

The Royal Gardens at Versailles were enjoyed only by the well-born.

Finally, Louis XVI responded to public pressure by calling for a session the following May of the Estates General, a legislative body of the nobles, clergy, and common people that had not met since 1614. In September Jefferson wrote Jay that the kingdom seemed tranquil, and he capped his diplomatic duties in November by drafting a paper later printed as *Observations on the Whale-Fishery* that successfully persuaded France to except American whale oil from a general prohibition on its importation. That done, he wrote Jay asking for a brief leave so that he might spend the summer of 1789 in America putting business and family matters in order. As he waited for a reply, Jefferson witnessed the hardships of the French winter of 1788-89, hardships that made the need for reform all the more obvious. He described the conditions to Madame de Bréhan, who was in America with her brother-in-law, France's Minister to the United States.

Paris Mar. 14. 1789

We have had such a winter Madam, as makes me shiver

yet whenever I think of it. All communications almost were cut off. Dinners and suppers were suppressed, and the money laid out in feeding and warming the poor, whose labours were suspended by the rigour of the season. Loaded carriages past the Seine on the ice, and it was covered with thousands of people from morning to night skaiting and sliding. Such sights were never seen before, and they continued two months.

Famine struck France as well. "In cards of invitation to dine in the richest houses," Jefferson remembered, "the guest was notified to bring his own bread." In January Jefferson wrote Dr. Richard Price, an English liberal with republican views, of his optimism with respect to a new political force, the "Patriotic party." If its power were felt in the elections for the Estates General, he thought, France might be saved.

Paris Jan. 8. 1789.

You say you are not sufficiently informed about the nature and circumstances of the present struggle here. Having been on the spot from it's first origin and watched it's movements as an uninterested spectator, with no other bias than a love of mankind I will give you my ideas of it. Tho' celebrated writers of this and other countries had already sketched good principles on the subject of government, yet the American war seems first to have awakened the thinking part of this nation in general from the sleep of despotism in which they were sunk. The officers too, who had been to America, were mostly young men, less shackled by habit and prejudice, and more ready to assent to the dictates of common sense and common right. They came back impressed with these. The press, notwithstanding it's shackles, began to disseminate them: conversation too assumed new freedoms; politics became the theme of all societies, male and female, and a very extensive and zealous party was formed, which may be called the Patriotic party, who sensible of the abusive government under which they lived, longed for occasions of reforming it. This party comprehended all the honesty of the kingdom, sufficiently at it's leisure to think: the men of letters, the easy bourgeois, the young nobility, partly from reflection partly from mode; for those sentiments became a matter of mode, and as such united most of the young women to the party.

Opening session of the Estates General at Versailles, May, 1789

The complicated system of electing members of the Estates went into operation in February. Jefferson advanced some predictions to Jay.

A mob running through the streets of Paris with lighted torches

Paris Jan. 11. 1789.

The moment of crisis will be the meeting of the States; because their first act will be to decide whether they shall vote by persons or by orders. The clergy will leave nothing unattempted to obtain the latter; for they see that the spirit of reformation will not confine itself to the political but will extend to the ecclesiastical establishment also. With respect to the Nobles, the younger members are generally for the people, and the middle aged are daily coming over to the same side: so that by the time the states meet we may hope there will be a majority of that body also in favor of the people, and consequently for voting by persons and not by orders.

In balloting for the Second Estate, the clergy, the results were far better than Jefferson had expected. Older, conservative members of the Catholic hierarchy lost much of their influence to younger, more liberal priests. Jefferson had not received leave to visit America that spring, and he probably did not regret being forced to remain, for he became a daily visitor to the meetings that convened in May. He commented of the opening session at Versailles: "Had it been enlightened with lamps and chandeliers, it would have been almost as brilliant as the opera." But the splendor of the rooms did not conceal the problems facing the Estates General. Nobles and clergy still insisted on voting by order, which would allow them to override the Third Estate or "Commons." At the end of May, the King was called on to arbitrate this dispute; Jefferson advised Lafayette, a member of the nobility who supported the Commons, to exercise moderation. Realistically, Jefferson knew that France was not ready for full, responsible democracy, and he hoped to see the kingdom move slowly but steadily toward a free society. He proposed to Lafayette a charter to be issued by the King and signed by all three estates, but the Third Estate moved too quickly. On June 17 the representatives in the Commons proclaimed themselves the National Assembly and proceeded to consider public affairs without consulting the other two estates. Jefferson did not seem displeased with this abrupt turn when he wrote to Madison the next day.

Paris June 18. 1789.

The Commons have in their chamber almost all the talents of the nation; they are firm and bold, yet moderate. There is indeed among them a number of very hot headed members; but those of most influence are cool, temperate, and sagacious. Every step of this house has been marked with caution and wisdom. The Noblesse on the contrary are absolutely out of their senses. They are so furious they can seldom debate at all.

Shortly thereafter the "talents" of the Commons seemed to triumph. Royal guards barred the National Assembly from its meeting chamber on June 20, but the members promptly found an indoor tennis court for their sessions. Here they subscribed to the Tennis Court Oath which bound the deputies to sit until, in Jefferson's words, "they had settled a constitution for their nation on a solid basis." Within a week the Assembly included a majority of the clergy as well as forty-eight nobles who had cast their lot with the subscribers to the pledge. Public discontent increased, and royal troops began to balk at enforcing the King's decrees. On June 27 Louis XVI was forced to recognize the Assembly's ascendancy, and all nobles and clergymen were ordered to meet jointly with the Commons.

The tempo of revolution continued in July. On the eleventh, Lafayette introduced a draft Declaration of the Rights of Man, a statement Jefferson had assisted him in preparing. On July 14 the Bastille fell to the Paris mob, and with it seemed to fall the last of royal tyranny. Jefferson reported to a fellow diplomat, the Count Diodati, that the way was clear for the establishment of a new regime for the French people.

A 1789 cartoon of Finance Minister Jacques Necker showing Louis XVI how to trick the people of France by hiding a huge deficit from them

à Paris ce 3me. Aout, 1789
The National assembly have now as clean a canvas to work on here as we had in America. Such has been the firmness and wisdom of their proceedings in moments of adversity as well as prosperity, that I have the highest confidence that they will use their power justly. As far as I can collect from conversation with their members, the constitution they will propose will resemble that of England in it's outlines, but not in it's defects. They will certainly leave the king possessed completely of the Executive powers, and particularly of the public force. Their legislature will consist of one order only, and not of two as in England: the representation will be equal and not abominably partial as that of England.... I have so much confidence in the good sense of man, and his qualifications for self-government, that I am never afraid of the issue where reason is left free to exert her force; and I will agree to be stoned as a false prophet if all does not end well in this country. Nor will it end with this country. Here is but the first chapter of European liberty.

But it seemed that Jefferson might well be proved a false prophet. The general outlines of the constitution reported to the Assembly were approved, but the details of the new government divided the patriot party, and Jefferson was given a chance to help solve the crisis. On August 25 Lafayette sent him an urgent note: "I Beg for liberty's sake You will Breack Every Engagement to Give us a dinner to Morrow Wenesday." The pronoun "us" referred to members of the Assembly whom Lafayette hoped "to Coalize as Being the only Means to prevent a total dissolution and civil war." The plea placed Jefferson in an embarrassing position. Although he had given Lafayette encouragement and advice throughout 1789, he had avoided open alliance with the patriots, or with any other French faction. The charter he had submitted to Lafayette in June and his counsel on the Declaration of the Rights of Man had both been offered confidentially. In July, when he was asked to confer with the Assembly's committee on the constitution, Jefferson had declined the invitation to avoid compromising his position as a neutral diplomat. But the crisis of August was so grave that Jefferson disregarded the limits of diplomatic propriety. Thirty years later he recalled the outcome of that decision.

Autobiography, 1821

I assured him of their welcome. When they arrived, they were La Fayette himself, Duport, Barnave, Alexander La Meth, Blacon, Mounier, Maubourg, and Dagout. These were leading patriots, of honest but differing opinions sensible of the necessity of effecting a coaliton by mutual sacrifices, knowing each other, and not afraid therefore to unbosom themselves mutually. This last was a material principle in the selection. With this view the Marquis had invited the conference, and had fixed the time & place inadvertently as to the embarrassment under which it might place me. The cloth being removed and wine set on the table, after the American manner, the Marquis introduced the objects of the conference by summarily reminding them of the state of things in the assembly, the course which the principles of the constitution was taking, and the inevitable result, unless checked by more concord among the Patriots themselves. He observed that altho' he also had his opinion, he was ready to sacrifice it to that of his brethren of the same cause: but that a common opinion must now be formed, or the Aristocracy would carry everything, and that whatever they should now agree on, he, at the head of the National force, would maintain. The discussions began at the hour of four, and were continued till ten o'clock in the evening; during which time I was a

The Comte de Montmorin

silent witness to a coolness and candor of argument unusual in the conflicts of political opinion; to a logical reasoning, and chaste eloquence, disfigured by no gaudy tinsel of rhetoric or declamation, and truly worthy of being placed in parallel with the finest dialogues of antiquity, as handed to us by Xenophon, by Plato and Cicero. The result was an agreement that the king should have a suspensive veto on the laws, that the legislature should be composed of a single body only, & that to be chosen by the people. This Concordate decided the fate of the constitution. The Patriots all rallied to the principles thus settled, carried every question agreeably to them, and reduced the Aristocracy to insignificance and impotence. But duties of exculpation were now incumbent on me. I waited on Count Montmorin the next morning, and explained to him with truth and candor how it happened that my house had been made the scene of conferences of such a character. He told me he already knew every thing which had passed, that, so far from taking umbrage at the use made of my house on that occasion, he earnestly wished I would habitually assist at such conferences, being sure I should be useful in moderating the warmer spirits, and promoting a wholesome and practicable reformation only. I told him I knew too well the duties I owed to the king, to the nation, and to my own country to take any part in councils concerning their internal government, and that I should persevere with care in the character of a neutral and passive spectator, with wishes only and very sincere ones, that those measures might prevail which would be for the greatest good of the nation. I have no doubt indeed that this conference was previously known and approved by this honest minister, who was in confidence and communication with the patriots, and wished for a reasonable reform of the Constitution.

Jefferson may have been more willing to stretch the definition of ministerial protocol because he had learned, three days before the patriots dined at his home, that he had been granted leave to return to the United States. He would at last be able to check up on his affairs in Virginia, and Patsy, almost seventeen, and eleven-year-old Polly would have the "society & care of their friends" as they approached young womanhood. He expected to return to Paris in the spring of 1790 and resume his role as Minister to France and friend to the Revolution, as he indicated to Madison that summer.

> Paris Aug. 28. 1789
>
> I propose to sail from Havre as soon after the 1st. of October as I can get a vessel: and shall consequently leave this place a week earlier than that. As my daughters will be with me... I shall endeavour if possible to obtain passage for Virginia directly. Probably I shall be there by the last of November....I expect to proceed to my own house directly. Staying there two months...and allowing for the time I am on the road, I may expect to be at New York in February, and to embark from thence, or some eastern port.—You ask me if I would accept any appointment on that side the water? You know the circumstances which led me from retirement, step by step and from one nomination to another, up to the present. My object is a return to the same retirement. Whenever therefore I quit the present, it will not be to engage in any other office, and most especially any one which would require a constant residence from home.

Jefferson's plans for a prompt departure were disrupted, however, by illness—probably one of the agonizing headaches he suffered periodically through life. As he recovered in the first week of September, he was visited by Dr. Richard Gem, an English physician who divided his time between London and Paris and between medicine and political theory. Gem was on close terms with many members of France's revolutionary groups and he gave Jefferson a series of propositions based on the premise "that one generation of men in civil society have no right to make acts to bind another...." This premise went to the heart of the dilemma faced by France: the justification for dismantling an old, feudal society whose existence no longer served the needs of the people forced to live within it. Jefferson's remarks on the propositions, contained in the form of a letter to James Madison, constitute one of his most important commentaries on human society and political structure. Modern scholars have concluded that the document, drafted hastily before Jefferson left France in early October, was not really intended as advice to Madison, but was rather Jefferson's last attempt to communicate on-the-spot advice to Lafayette and his fellow reformers through Gem. This interpretation is buttressed not only by the tone of the letter, which was obviously concerned with the realities of French, not American, politics, but also by the fact that it was not even delivered to Madison until early in 1790. Jefferson's answer to the French radicals' dilemma was that "the earth belongs in usufruct to the living."

THOMAS JEFFERSON

Paris September 6. 1789.

The question Whether one generation of men has a right to bind another, seems never to have been started either on this or our side of the water. Yet it is a question of such consequences as not only to merit decision, but place also, among the fundamental principles of every government. The course of reflection in which we are immersed here on the elementary principles of society has presented this question to my mind; and that no such obligation can be so transmitted I think very capable of proof.—I set out on this ground, which I suppose to be self evident, *'that the earth belongs in usufruct to the living'*: that the dead have neither powers nor rights over it. The portion occupied by any individual ceases to be his when himself ceases to be, and reverts to the society.... Then no man can, by *natural right,* oblige the lands he occupied, or the persons who succeed him in that occupation, to the paiment of debts contracted by him. For if he could, he might, during his own life, eat up the usufruct of the lands for several generations to come, and then the lands would belong to the dead, and not to the living, which would be the reverse of our principle....

This principle that the earth belongs to the living, and not to the dead, is of very extensive application and consequences, in every country, and most especially in France. It enters into the resolution of the questions Whether the nation may change the descent of lands holden in tail? Whether they may change the appropriation of lands given antiently to the church, to hospitals, colleges, orders of chivalry, and otherwise in perpetuity? Whether they may abolish the charges and privileges attached on lands, including the whole catalogue ecclesiastical and feudal? It goes to hereditary offices, authorities and jurisdictions; to hereditary orders, distinctions and appellations; to perpetual monopolies in commerce, the arts and sciences; with a long train of et ceteras: and it renders the question of reimbursement a question of generosity and not of right. In all these cases, the legislature of the day could authorize such appropriations and establishments for their own time, but no longer; and the present holders, even where they, or their ancestors, have purchased, are in the case of bonâ fide purchasers of what the seller had no right to convey.

Passport issued to Jefferson by the Commune of Paris and endorsed by Lafayette, the commandant of the Garde Nationale; it permitted the diplomat and his entourage to pass through customs. Jefferson also had one from Louis XVI.

207

Jefferson's desire to use even this last opportunity to guide his French friends was not the whim of a political philosopher who hoped to see his maxims implemented. Instead, it came from his affection for the French and his hope that the Revolution could give political and social justice to the land where he had spent five of the most happy and fulfilling years of his life. In his *Autobiography,* Jefferson closed his recollections of those years with this touching tribute to a people he had come to love only a little less than those he had left behind in Virginia.

Autobiography, 1821

And here I cannot leave this great and good country without expressing my sense of it's preeminence of character among the nations of the earth. A more benevolent people, I have never known, nor a greater warmth and devotedness in their select friendships. Their kindness and accomodation to strangers is unparalleled, and the hospitality of Paris is beyond any thing I had concieved to be practicable in a large city. Their eminence too in science, the communicative dispositions of their scientific men, the politeness of the general manners, the ease and vivacity of their conversation, give a charm to their society to be found no where else. In a comparison of this with other countries we have the proof of primacy, which was given to Themistocles after the battle of Salamis. Every general voted to himself the first reward of valor, and the second to Themistocles. So ask the travelled inhabitant of any nation, In what country on earth would you rather live?— Certainly in my own, where are all my friends, my relations, and the earliest & sweetest affections and recollections of my life. Which would be your second choice? France.

Jefferson sailed from France, his second home, in the early hours of October 8, 1789. He had come five years earlier as an eager, questioning American awed by European culture and pained by the suffering he saw among the subjects of the King at whose court he was to serve. He left behind a nation on the threshold of constitutional government, with the promise of justice and freedom for the people he had come to know so well. As the small packet ship *Anna* moved from the harbor at Le Havre just after midnight, Jefferson may have wondered if, in keeping with his own plans and desires, he would ever see France again.

your draughts will be most negoc[iated]
necessaries for yourself & your me[n]
United States that these draughts
are made payable. I also ask if [any]
nation with which we have interco[urse]
-plies which your necessities may [require]
~~distribution.~~ and our own Consuls in fo[reign]
~~hereby~~ instructed & required to be a[iding]
necessary for procuring your retur[n]
entire satisfaction & confidence to th[e]
Jefferson, President of the United St[ates]
                    for you
general credit, with my own hand.

To
  Cap.t Meriwether Le[wis]

Heroes of the Revolution

Sam and John Adams

By Susan & John Lee

Illustrated by Chuck Mitchell

TALCOTT SCHOOL LIBRARY

CHILDRENS PRESS, CHICAGO

Library of Congress Cataloging in Publication Data

Lee, Susan.
  Sam and John Adams.

  (Heroes of the Revolution)
  SUMMARY: A biography of two cousins, one a leader in the American Revolution, the other the second President of the United States.
  1. Adams, Samuel, 1722-1803—Juvenile literature. 2. Adams, John, Pres. U.S., 1735-1826—Juvenile literature. [1. Adams, Samuel, 1722-1803. 2. Adams, John, Pres. U.S., 1735-1826. 3. Presidents. 4. United States—History—Revolution, 1775-1783—Biography] I. Lee, John, joint author. II. Mitchell, Chuck, illus. III. Title.

E302.6.A2L43   973.3′092′2 [B]   [920]   74-8937
ISBN 0-516-04656-X

Copyright© 1974 by Regensteiner Publishing Enterprises, Inc.
All rights reserved. Published simultaneously in Canada.
Printed in the United States of America.

4 5 6 7 8 9 10 11 12 13 14 15 16 17 18 19 20 21 R 79 78 77 76

Think about the people in your class. Each one is different. Some are short, some tall. Some like reading, and others like math.

It takes all kinds of people to make a class work. Everyone knows who the best students are. Someone is the class leader. Someone else is the funniest. And everyone knows who the class troublemaker is.

History is full of different people, too. These people were not all the same. Some were rich, some poor. Some men were farmers, and some men were traders. Some women made soap for a living, and others sold clothing. History is interesting because people in the past did different things.

This is the story of two very different men. They were cousins, one from the country and one from the city. They lived at the same time, and they went to the same school—Harvard. But each one had a very different life.

973.3 L c.1 Lee		
Sam and John Adams		
AUTHOR / TITLE **ADISTA**		

DATE	BORROWER'S NAME	ROOM NUMBER
2-23-8	Maritza DeJesus	309
3-3-82	Rebecca M	301
5-10-8	Frances Curtin	309

973.3
L
c.1
Lee
Sam and John Adams

TALCOTT SCHOOL LIBRARY

John Adams was the country cousin. He was a famous man. He became the second President of the United States. Today, his name is in our history books.

Sam Adams was John's city cousin. Sam never was rich or famous. He never became President of the United States. Today, when someone hears the name "Adams," they think of John, not Sam.

Sam Adams was a troublemaker. He enjoyed making trouble! His father wanted him to be a minister, but Sam was not interested. Then his father got Sam work in a bank, but Sam did not like adding up numbers.

In 1756, Sam became tax collector for the city of Boston. He did a terrible job. He did not like taking tax money from people. When someone told Sam a hard-luck story, he did not make them pay. The city never had enough money because Sam did not care if the people paid their taxes or not. Sam was even known to say he didn't like money!

One thing Sam hated more than money was the English. In those days, the King of England ruled the land you live in now. There were no states. There were only thirteen colonies along the Atlantic Ocean.

Boston, where Sam lived, was in the colony of Massachusetts. Sam and his wife were English colonists. All the people in the colonies were English. They lived under English law and called England their "mother country."

THE THIRTEEN ORIGINAL STATES
(BASED ON A MAP BY John Mitchell - 1775)

MASS. *

NEW HAMPSHIRE

NEW YORK

MASS. • BOSTON

RHODE ISLAND

CONNECTICUT

PENNSYLVANIA

NEW JERSEY

MARYLAND

DELAWARE

VIRGINIA

NORTH CAROLINA

SOUTH CAROLINA

GEORGIA

ATLANTIC OCEAN

*NOTE: MAINE CLAIMED BY MASSACHUSETTS DURING PRE-REVOLUTIONARY PERIOD.

HORRID MASSACRE!
in King Street Boston,

On Evening of March the Fifth, 1770. When Five of your fellow countrymen, MAVERICK, CALDWELL, ATTUCKS, and CARR.

Lay Wallowing in their Gore! Being basely, and most inhumanly MURDERED!

And SIX others badly WOUNDED! By a Party of the XXIXth Regiment, under the command of Capt. Tho. Preston.

REMEMBER!
That Two of the Murderers Were convicted of MANSLAUGHTER By a Jury, of whom I shall say NOTHING. Branded in the hand! And dismissed. The others were Acquitted. And their Captain PENSIONED!

Also,
BEAR IN REMEMBRANCE That on the 22d Day of February, 1770. The infamous EBENEZER RICHARDSON, informer. And tool to Ministerial hirelings! barbarously.

M...
CHRIS...
Of whom...
On Satur...

A LIST of the Names of those who AUDACIOUSLY continue to act the united sentiments of the body of MERCHANTS thro'out NORTH AMERICA, by importing British Goods contrary to the Agreement.

John Bernard,
(In King Street, almost opposite Vernon's Head).

James McMasters,
(on Treat's Warf).

Patrick McMasters,
(opposite the Sign of the Lamb).

Fiery Samuel Adams made certain that the people were bombarded with leaflets such as these.

*Left, Boston Massacre:
Below, British sympathizer*

12

Sam Adams did not like England. He thought that the colonists could rule themselves without England. He wanted the colonists to be free. He wanted the thirteen colonies to start a new nation.

Sam liked to pick on the English. He liked to talk about the rights of the colonists. He even wrote stories in the newspaper saying that England had no right to tax the colonists. All Sam's friends disliked the English, too.

At first, the English paid no attention to Sam Adams. Wasn't he a failure? He had no job. He wore the same old suit year after year. His house needed repairs. His wife could hardly make ends meet.

In 1765, England gave Sam Adams a chance to make more trouble. They passed a law — the Stamp Act — to raise money. It ordered the colonists to buy stamps. The stamps had to be put on newspapers. They had to be put on wills and deeds. Money from the sale of stamps went to England.

When the news of the Stamp Act got to Boston, Sam Adams saw his chance. He called his friends together, and they decided to make trouble.

Types of stamps issued by the British government in 1765.

On the night of August 14, 1765, people began to meet on the streets of Boston. A huge mob started a bonfire. They tore down the office of the stamp master. They hung a doll on an elm tree. The doll was dressed just like the new stamp master!

Sam Adams was not part of the mob. But everyone knew that Sam Adams told the mob what to do. He told them when to meet and where to go. Soon, the English called Sam Adams the mob master of Boston. They said he looked like the devil. But in 1766, the British took back the Stamp Act.

For the next few years, Sam Adams kept on being a troublemaker. When new tax laws were made, Sam Adams told the colonists not to buy English goods. When tax collectors came to Boston, Sam had people keep the collectors awake with loud drums and Indian war-whoops. When the King of England sent soldiers to Boston, Sam told the colonists to arm themselves.

One snowy day in March of 1770, a mob gathered. They began throwing snowballs at an English soldier. The soldier got mad and hit a little boy with his gun. Then, the mob began to yell, "Kill him! Kill him!"

Soon, more Redcoats came. They were afraid and fired their guns into the mob. They shot Crispus Attucks, a black man, and other colonists.

The next day, a mass meeting was held in Boston. Sam Adams called the killing of the colonists a "massacre." He told the people that the soldiers should leave their city. He got the Governor of Massachusetts to agree. Two weeks later, the Redcoats left town to the happy cheers of Boston colonists.

But the case was not over. The nine soldiers who fired on the mob were still in jail. Would a mob hang them? Would they get a fair trial in Boston? Who would defend them in court?

The man who defended the Redcoats was John Adams, Sam's cousin. John Adams did not like the English, but he believed the soldiers should have a fair trial. When Sam found out his cousin had the case, he was very happy. He knew John hated the English. He was sure the soldiers would be found guilty.

John Adams was born in this frame farmhouse.

John Adams was thirteen years younger than Sam. He was born in 1735, in a country town near Boston. In his free time, John liked to fly kites, swim, shoot marbles, and play ball. John's father wanted his son to be a minister, just as Sam Adams' father had. But when John went to Harvard, he decided not to be a minister. He wanted to be a lawyer.

John got many law cases in his home town. Many people wanted his help. He was a good lawyer.

In 1768, John Adams and his wife moved to Boston. John was busier than ever before. The colonists were always at odds with the English over their rights. In one case, John defended sailors who had been forced into joining the English navy.

On the day after the Redcoats had fired into a Boston mob, John Adams decided to take their case. Like his cousin Sam, he did not like England's rule. He wanted all the soldiers to leave Boston.

But John also believed that the soldiers in jail should get a fair trial. He did not care what his friends said. He was the only lawyer in Boston brave enough to take the case.

John did not think Sam should call the shooting the "Boston Massacre." The mob had tossed snowballs at the soldiers. It called them names. The soldiers shot into the mob to defend themselves from danger.

John worked as hard to defend the soldiers as he did for colonists. He wanted to make sure they got a fair trial. At the end of the trial, the soldiers were found "not guilty."

For the next five years, the people of Boston went on having trouble with the English. They did not like the tax on tea. They did not buy goods made in England.

When English soldiers came to Boston again, the Massachusetts colonists began to practice with their guns. They made bullets and hid them from the British. The colonial soldiers were called Minute Men because they could get ready to fight in a minute's time.

Then, on the early morning of April 19, 1775, English soldiers got in a fight with some Massachusetts Minute Men at Lexington. Shots rang out. Before the day was over, many men on each side were dead.

Sam was nearby when the shooting broke out. "Oh," he said to his friend John Hancock, "what a glorious morning this is." Sam was happy now. He knew this fight would make all the colonists angry.

Sam was right. People in all thirteen colonies were angry about the news of fighting. They decided to have a meeting at Philadelphia in the colony of Pennsylvania. The people in each colony picked men to go to the meeting. The Massachusetts colonists picked Sam Adams, his cousin John, and three other men to go.

The meeting started on May 10, 1775. Many important men were there. Benjamin Franklin came from Pennsylvania, and John Hancock was chosen president of the meeting.

Sam and John Adams did not like the way the meetings went. The men talked and talked. They wrote to King George to try and make up. John did not like sending this letter to the King. Didn't the colonists realize that war had already begun? he asked. Sam was calm on the outside. Better wait, he told his cousin, " 'til the fruit is ripe before we gather it."

John wanted help from the other colonies. Massachusetts could not fight alone. Then he thought of a plan to get the colonies in the south to stand with Massachusetts. On June 15, he spoke to the other men at the meeting. He said that George Washington of Virginia should be chosen head of the colonial army. The men liked John Adams' choice. Everyone voted for George Washington as general of the colonial army.

Not long after, England declared war on the colonists. English ships began to look for American ships at sea. The English paid German soldiers to help their army. In Boston, the English and Americans began to fight again. As the months of 1776 went by, more and more colonists talked about independence from England.

At the meeting in Philadelphia, John Adams and his cousin Sam Adams were leaders of the talks for independence. They worked well together. John made speeches in favor of independence. He was one of five men chosen to write a Declaration of Independence. He told the men to ask France for help. He wanted them to set up an American navy. Day after day, he spoke for freedom from England.

Sam Adams worked hard too. He did not say much at the meetings, but he spent busy evenings. Over a meal or a glass of ale he talked to each man who wasn't sure of independence. Face-to-face, across a table, Sam Adams told these men why independence was so important. He got many men to change their minds.

On July 2, 1776, all the colonies except New York voted for independence. On July 4, 1776, they voted to print the Declaration of Independence written by Thomas Jefferson.

Button Gwinnett
Lyman Hall
Geo Walton
Wm Hooper
Joseph Hewes
John Penn
Edward Rutledge
Thos Heyward Junr
Thomas Lynch Junr
Arthur Middleton

Geo Clymer
Jas Smith
Geo Taylor
James Wilson
Geo Ross
Caesar Rodney
Geo Read
Tho M:Kean

Wm Floyd
Phil Livingston
Frans Lewis
Lewis Morris

John Hancock

Josiah Bartlett
Wm Whipple
Saml Adams
John Adams
Robt Treat Paine
Elbridge Gerry
Step Hopkins
William Ellery
Roger Sherman
Sam Huntington
Wm Williams
Oliver Wolcott
Matthew Thornton

Samuel Chase
Wm Paca
Thos Stone
Charles Carroll of Carrollton
George Wythe
Richard Henry Lee
Th Jefferson
Benja Harrison
Thos Nelson jr
Francis Lightfoot Lee
Carter Braxton

Rich Stockton
Jno Witherspoon
Fras Hopkinson
John Hart
Abra Clark
Rob Morris
Benjamin Rush
Benja Franklin
John Morton

No one was happier than John and Sam Adams. They were among the 56 men who signed the Declaration.

Just as Sam Adams worked all his life for independence, John Adams now worked to build a strong nation. After the colonists won the war for independence, he helped write the peace treaty with England in 1783. Six years later, he was voted the first Vice-President and helped George Washington get the new nation started.

Wooden-domed capitol – looking fro[m] the Anacostia river.

In 1797, John Adams became the second President of the United States. While he was President, John Adams moved from Philadelphia to the nation's new capital. It was named Washington, in honor of the first President.

John Adams moved into a house built just for the President. But the house was not yet done when he got there. John's wife Abigail had to hang the wash up in one of the rooms. John did not have a quiet place to do his work.

The hardest job for President Adams was keeping the new nation out of war with France. The French did not want the United States to be friends with England. They wanted the United States to help them fight a war against England. When the United States did not help, the French got mad. They stopped American ships and stole their goods.

The French did not like John Adams because he would not help them. They said the President was too friendly with England. A lot of Americans who wanted war said the same thing. But this was not the first time people had said John Adams was too friendly with the English.

   President Adams did not care what people said about him. He did not think it would be good for America to go to war. He sent some men to France to make a treaty.

In 1800, France and the United States signed a peace treaty. The danger was over. The new nation stayed out of war because President Adams had the courage to do what he thought was right.

Today, everyone remembers John Adams. He spoke for freedom and signed the Declaration of Independence. He helped Washington get the new nation started. As President, he kept the United States from going to war. When he died on July 4, 1826, it was the 50th birthday of the nation.

John's cousin, Sam Adams, did things differently. He loved freedom more than money or fame. He talked against English taxes. He never tired of telling the colonists about their rights. His fiery leadership helped bring about war between the colonists and the mother country.

The city cousin and the country cousin had different lives. One was called the mob master of Boston. The other became a President. But each in his own way helped bring America into being. Like your class, it takes all kinds of people to make a nation.

About the Authors:

   Susan Dye Lee has been writing professionally since she graduated from college in 1961. Working with the Social Studies Curriculum Center at Northwestern University, she has created course materials in American studies. Ms. Lee has also co-authored a text on Latin America and Canada, written case studies in legal history for the Law in American Society Project, and developed a teacher's guide for tapes that explore women's role in America's past. The writer credits her students for many of her ideas. Currently, she is doing research for her history dissertation on the Women's Christian Temperance Union for Northwestern University. In her free moments, Susan Lee enjoys traveling, playing the piano, and welcoming friends to "Highland Cove," the summer cottage she and her husband, John, share.

   John R. Lee enjoys a prolific career as a writer, teacher, and outdoorsman. After receiving his doctorate in social studies at Stanford, Dr. Lee came to Northwestern University's School of Education, where he advises student teachers and directs graduates in training. A versatile writer, Dr. Lee has co-authored the Scott-Foresman social studies textbooks for primary-age children. In addition, he has worked on the production of 50 films and over 100 filmstrips. His biographical film on Helen Keller received a 1970 Venice Film Festival award. His college text, *Teaching Social Studies in the Elementary School*, has recently been published. Besides pro-football, Dr. Lee's passion is his Wisconsin cottage, where he likes to shingle leaky roofs, split wood, and go sailing.

About the Artist:

   Chuck Mitchell is a Chicago artist who specializes in editorial and book illustration.